Shakespeare and the Late Moral Plays

Shakespeare

and the
Late Moral Plays

Alan C. Dessen

University of Nebraska Press
Lincoln and London

The paper in this book meets the guidelines
for permanence and durability of the
Committee on Production Guidelines for
Book Longevity of the Council on Library Resources.

Library of Congress Cataloging in Publication Data
Dessen, Alan C., 1935–
Shakespeare and the late moral plays.
Bibliography: p.
Includes index
1. Shakespeare, William, 1564–1616—Sources.
2. Moralities, English—History and criticism.
3. English drama—Early modern and Elizabethan,
1500–1600—History and criticism.
4. Shakespeare, William, 1564–1616—Allegory and symbolism.
5. Vice in literature. I. Title.
PR2953.M65D47 1986   822.3'3   85-8625
ISBN 0-8032-1671-8 (alk. paper)

Portions of this book have previously been published in different form:
part of chapter 1 as "The Morall as an Elizabethan Dramatic Kind: An
Exploratory Essay," *Comparative Drama* 5 (1971): 138–59, and portions
of chapter 4 as "The Intemperate Knight and the Politic Prince: Late
Morality Structure in *1 Henry IV*," *Shakespeare Studies* 7 (1974): 147–71.

To Sarah

Contents

Acknowledgments

During its long Journey to Publication, this book has accumulated many debts. Of the many Good Counsel figures I have encountered, let me single out David Bevington, Gerald Graff, and Maurice Charney. For permission to incorporate material originally published in their journals, I wish to thank the editors of *Shakespeare Studies* and *Comparative Drama*. Parts of my argument have been presented at various scholarly gatherings: the MLA convention; the International Medieval Conference at Kalamazoo; and a series on literary allusions sponsored by the Department of English, University of North Carolina (organized by William McQueen). My awareness of the problems and possibilities in the Shakespeare plays treated here has been greatly enhanced by the work of talented theatrical professionals: in particular, Martha Henry, Patrick Stewart, Michael Santo, Pat Patton, Audrey Stanley, and James Edmondson. To Michael I owe the sounds of the trombone as accompaniment to scholarly composition; to Sarah, the joys of word problems. Most of all, Cynthia kept my historicism in touch with the twentieth century, especially the allegorical mysteries of word processing.

Shakespeare and the Late Moral Plays

1

The people make no estimation,
Of Moralls teaching education.
Robert Greene

The Problem and the Evidence

Most students of the drama would agree that the story of "the morality play" has been oft told and well expressed. Thus, a book published in 1983 that links several moral plays to the age of Shakespeare starts not with an elaborate history of the form but with the disclaimer that "excellent comprehensive histories of the morality drama have already been written."[1] With few exceptions, both specialists and general readers are content with the formulations currently available in literary histories and handbooks and, as a result, feel free to forgo any firsthand experience of the raw material. In particular, although several fifteenth-century moral plays have sustained their devotees, few of the many sixteenth-century plays, especially those dating from the reign of Queen Elizabeth, have found their way into student anthologies, college survey courses, or live productions. Rather, behind most treatments of these later plays lie shared assumptions that the development (to many readers, the degeneration) of the moral plays has been accurately mapped, with little need for new voyages of discovery.

This general apathy can quickly turn to hostility, however, when a critic or scholar seeks to link the moral plays to Shakespeare. Even though vestiges of the moral drama do survive in the 1590s and thereafter, our modern preference for the ironic and the subtle over the allegorical and the didactic causes many readers to bridle at the suggestion of any connection between such "primitive" material and Shakespeare's plays, a situation then exacerbated by the heavy-handed treatment of the comedies, histories, and tragedies by many practitioners of this approach. The title of this book may therefore suggest to some readers yet another reductive treatment of Shakespeare's rich characters and images, a scholarly melt-down to some irreducible allegorical core. After all, do we need more ink and paper (or bytes and floppy disks) devoted to Hamlet or Macbeth or Othello as Everyman?

Like Henry V, however, I hope "to mock the expectation of the world"[2] and offer not a reductive but an expansive reading of a group of Shakespeare's plays, to open up rather than close down possibilities. Thus, I find much richness and room for maneuvering in the *and* of my title, for I see in Shakespeare no slavish adherence to any rigid forms or procedures, nor do I read his plays allegorically or view them as theatrical sermons. In addition, my "late moral plays" are not the same titles invoked again and again in most discussions nor are they characterized by a Humanum Genus figure flanked by good and evil angels. Rather, I am concerned with a highly heterogeneous group of plays written, published, and performed during the first half of Queen Elizabeth's reign (the boyhoods of Marlowe and Shakespeare)—in effect, the last wave of the moral dramatic tradition before the advent of Lyly, Kyd, and Marlowe in the mid 1580s. Readers of this book must decide for themselves whether or not this body of drama indeed sheds light on Shakespeare's plays, but these late moral plays certainly *were* there and, as I shall demonstrate, *were* remembered in the 1590s and early 1600s.

Before moving to discussion of specific plays, let me focus upon some problems that bedevil the scholar seeking to establish any such literary-historical links but especially the scholar working with this particular set of materials. A concern with sources, influences, and intellectual contexts has long been a major part

of Shakespeare studies along with other related kinds of scholarship that could be classified as "historical" or contextual. But
recent critics and theorists have challenged the basic assumptions of such "historicism" and have called attention to the inevitable problems that result when the modern reader confronts
the "alterity" or otherness of another age or culture. For some
participants in this ongoing debate, the key question is: Is literary history possible or even desirable? In contrast, other critics
have argued for a "new" historicism or historiography (variously
defined) that would transcend the perceived limitations of the
old. Thus, in an influential essay Hans Robert Jauss argues that
"the method of the history of reception is essential for the understanding of literary works which lie in the distant past," for, in
his terms, "the reconstruction of the horizon of expectations, on
the basis of which a work in the past was created and received,
enables us to find the questions to which the text originally answered and thereby to discover how the reader of that day viewed
and understood the work."[3]

To see some of the facets of this problem, consider a familiar
situation in Shakespeare studies. Thus, a traditional (and still
much practiced) approach to *The Comedy of Errors* or *Titus Andronicus* would be first to read *Menaechmi* or *Thyestes* and then to
discuss Shakespeare's Plautine comedy or Senecan tragedy. Such
an approach, however, although plausible on the surface, masks
various problems. First, any postulation of supposed "Senecan"
elements in *Titus Andronicus* or *The Spanish Tragedy* must take
intò account the fallacy of the unique source, for what if the
same elements are available in Ovid or other equally accessible
authors?[4] Furthermore, can we discuss with any precision the
proposed links between such earlier models and the age of
Shakespeare without some sense of how the Elizabethans understood or "received" Plautus and Seneca (as revealed in commentaries, translations, and alterations made in productions of the
original plays)? Thus, Bruce R. Smith provides suggestive evidence from both Italy and England of various kinds of adaptation, even transformation, of Roman drama to suit sixteenth-
century expectations and assumptions.[5] What if Shakespeare's

"horizon of expectations" for Roman drama was significantly different from ours?

The problem is far more acute with the legacy of the moral plays. Among the works known to have been owned by Ben Jonson are a manuscript of Terence's plays and a printed edition of Aristophanes,[6] so no matter how such plays were "received" or understood they were available to be read (by at least some readers) in the original Latin or Greek and, in many cases, in translation. But some of the moral plays most often cited by modern scholars never found their way into print (e.g., *The Castle of Perseverance*, *Mankind*), while those that were printed or reprinted during the second half of the sixteenth century are, for the most part, little known today and, moreover, do not exhibit the consistency in tone, form, and achievement found in the widely read Roman playwrights. Granted, in most situations we cannot hope to recapture exactly how X would have been understood in the 1590s or early 1600s (so we do not know how Shakespeare would have read or "received" *Rudens* or *Casina* or an anomalous play like *Truculentus*), but we are on especially shaky ground when we try to generalize about Shakespeare's (or anyone else's) understanding of the moral tradition when most formulations about the "morality play" draw upon plays removed in time by about a century, plays (unlike Roman drama) not available to be read, and plays rarely if ever alluded to in Shakespeare's time (e.g., *Everyman*, *The Castle of Perseverance*, *Mankind*).

Such prizing or privileging of the "classic" moral plays from the fifteenth and early sixteenth centuries over their Elizabethan offspring results from several related factors. Most obviously, *The Castle of Perseverance* and *Everyman* by just about any standard are superior as works of dramatic art to *Enough Is as Good as a Feast*, *The Trial of Treasure*, and *All for Money*. Nothing in the later plays matches the scope and majesty of *The Castle* or the tension and climax structure of *Everyman* (an atypical, highly distinctive play that appears to have had no progeny). Regardless of any chronological proximity, scholars understandably gravitate towards the more appealing earlier plays and away from the fourteener couplets and diatribes against materialism found in the 1560s and 1570s. The situation is comparable to that of the golfer who, when asked why he was searching for his ball in a place fifty yards from the spot where it landed, replied: "But there's poison ivy over there."

Since many readers have never even sampled the late moral plays, the roots of the problem go deeper than the issue of individual taste and get entangled (as with the formation of any literary canon) with what Raymond Williams terms "the selective tradition."[7] Thus, when dealing with any historical period, Williams distinguishes among (1) "the lived culture of a particular time and place, only fully accessible to those living in that time and place"; (2) "the recorded culture, of every kind, from art to the most everyday facts"; and (3) "the culture of the selective tradition." The third category turns out to be an almost inevitable result of the second, for, as Williams argues, even the specialist can know only a part of the recorded culture (e.g., how many novels, not to mention other relevant materials, has a specialist in the nineteenth-century British novel actually read?). As a consequence, a "selective process, of a quite drastic kind, is at once evident," a process, in fact, that "begins within the period itself," for "from the whole body of activities, certain things are selected for value and emphasis" while, inevitably, other things are played down or ignored. What results ("the historical record of a particular society") then entails "a rejection of considerable areas of what was once a living culture." As critics of "historicism" delight in pointing out, moreover, a society's view of an earlier culture "will always tend to correspond to its *contemporary* system of interests and values," for, in this "continual selection and interpretation," we inevitably see the past through lenses compacted of our own assumptions and interests. Given the power of such a selective tradition, the modern scholar is vulnerable to the twin pitfalls of what Paul Zumthor terms "naive historicism" and "blind modernism."[8]

In the case of English drama before the age of Shakespeare, David Bevington has called attention to a major force behind the selective tradition, for beneath the surface of the many discussions of this material, from Sidney and Jonson to the present, often lies a distaste for popular theatre that leads "to over-emphasis of classical rediscovery as the main line of development in English Renaissance drama" and therefore "measures literary progress in the sixteenth century only by the degree to which sophisticated learning freed English drama from the fetters of ignorance and bad taste."[9] Bevington's work has helped to make a dent in this assessment, but the selective tradition retains its power, as witnessed by the titles chosen for anthologies and thereby canonized for succeeding generations of students, teachers, scholars, and theatrical professionals.

The problem, moreover, is compounded in this instance by the nature of Williams's "recorded culture"—the extant plays and what is said (or more often not said) about them by contemporary spokesmen. The few comments from figures like Sidney, Gosson, Whetstone, and Puttenham about popular plays between 1560 and 1585 (as opposed to Sidney's tempered praise of *Gorboduc*) are brief and dismissive, as is to be expected from writers who prize the ideals of the classical tradition (e.g., decorum, the unities). Unlike the situation a generation later (when a figure like Heywood could provide an "apology" for popular theatre), no defense or rationale survives on behalf of the Tudor or early Elizabethan dramatists. Granted, as Bevington notes, "one cannot account for these plays by aesthetic laws of unity, correspondence, subordination, and the like," but as he goes on to argue: "if some contemporary had had occasion to speak for the critically inarticulate authors of these plays, and had extracted a pattern or series of patterns from their work, he might have spoken quite differently of repetitive effect, multiplicity, episode, progressive theme" and might have defended "a panoramic, narrative, and sequential view of art rather than a dramatically concise and heightened climax of sudden revelation."[10]

But no such contemporary did speak in behalf of early Elizabethan popular drama. As a result, this body of plays, largely didactic and allegorical and seemingly oblivious to classical form and precedent, has been an obvious victim of the selective tradition and has been in eclipse since the late sixteenth century. Thus, despite the work of scholars like Bevington, few Shakespeareans are aware even of the titles of these plays. Rather, the period just before the great blossoming of English drama is usually represented in anthologies by *Gorboduc*, a "classical" tragedy performed only twice in the early 1560s, and *Cambises*, a "hybrid" tragedy immortalized by Falstaff but, in my opinion, quite unrepresentative of early Elizabethan drama.

Consider one title in eclipse. When treating the decade before Kyd and Marlowe, historians note the importance of 1576–77 as marking the establishment of two permanent public theatres in the London area, a milestone in the development of English drama. But little or no evidence has survived about the effect of such a new home upon plays, players, and procedures (e.g., the growth of the companies, the accumulation of stage properties, and the building of an audience). What *has* survived is Robert Wilson's *The Three Ladies of London*, one of the few plays extant from the early 1580s associated with the new theatres and, significantly, a didactic and allegorical social satire upon materialism similar to (albeit longer and more complex than) the troupe moral plays of the 1560s and 1570s discussed by Bevington. Although little known today, this play was well known enough in its own time to be alluded to by various contemporary writers and to be granted both a sequel (*The Three Lords and Three Ladies of London*) and a rebuttal in a play now lost (*London against the Three Ladies*).[11]

That *The Three Ladies of London* was well known in the 1580s (and remembered by at least one writer in the late 1590s) is a fact that can easily be eclipsed by the power of the selective tradition. Here as elsewhere, today's prevailing tastes (our horizon of expectations) prevail with no difficulty over the extant evidence. But without minimizing the importance of Plautus, Terence, and Seneca (and, to a lesser degree, Aristophanes and Euripides)[12] as models or inspiration, can we safely assume that Wilson's play and its predecessors in the 1560s and 1570s represent a dead end that has no significance whatsoever for the dramatists of the 1580s and 1590s? Some facets of these late moral plays *were* rejected (e.g., the verse forms, once blank verse became the norm), while other features (e.g., overt allegory) left only traces behind, so awareness of the moral drama will not provide an instant key to unlock the deeper meanings of *Doctor Faustus*, *Hamlet*, and *King Lear*. But is it not likely that *some* facets of at least *some* of the plays of the next generation (especially those by dramatists in tune with the popular tradition) will make more sense when viewed in the light of what would have been well known, if a bit old-fashioned, in the 1590s and early 1600s?

The key to such an investigation, then, is not how we or generations before us have read the popular drama before Shakespeare, but rather how these plays were remembered or understood in the late sixteenth century (what Jauss and others refer to as the history or aesthetics of reception). Unfortunately for this argument, the general silence (except for hostile witnesses) often makes it difficult to reconstruct such a formulation. But consider as an analogy the cinematic Western with its many conventions and clichés (white hats versus black hats, rustlers versus lawmen, farmers versus ranchers, the hero's comic companion, the walk-down fight at the climax). Long after the heyday of such a form, the memories or associations linger on, even though the original impetus or naive acceptance may have disappeared, so that later writers or directors can follow, adapt, or even stridently violate the original conventions and expectations. A few generations later, a scholar may have difficulty recapturing the original spirit and sense of "deep structure" that underlies the simple, straightforward Western (and may wonder how any audience could have taken seriously the stilted characters and contrived plots), but that spirit or rationale *was* there and *was* obvious to the original moviegoers (who undoubtedly never took the trouble consciously to formulate their understanding).

One of my basic assumptions, then, is that, like the cinematic Western, the moral plays (which represent the most prevalent form of English drama between midcentury and the 1580s) were likewise known to dramatists and audiences a generation later. Admittedly, to determine how Shakespeare and his contemporaries remembered such plays is no easy matter. Nonetheless, to me it seems self-evident that any argument about the legacy of the moral drama should be based, as far as is possible or practicable, upon Elizabethan evidence, especially the extant plays chronologically adjacent to the age of Shakespeare and the allusions to such plays, rather than upon the plays most often anthologized or most palatable to modern tastes. I do not wish to quarrel with the general propositions advanced about the significance of the Humanum Genus figure for later tragedy, nor am I offering a new monolithic formulation designed to replace the one currently on display in most handbooks. Rather, I am concerned with a variety of dramatic options or theatrical strategies to be found in the late moral plays and therefore available to subsequent dramatists in need of a model to solve a particular problem. That three of the four Shakespeare plays to be discussed at length are histories is no coincidence, for the absence of a precedent in Roman drama (or a body of critical theory) for this genre meant that the dramatist seeking to order his material from Holinshed had no obvious place in the classical or literary tradition to which to turn for such a paradigm.

What I am advancing here, moreover, is not simply yet another claim about influences and sources but rather an argument for the presence of something more basic—an inherited sense of how a certain kind of play could be constructed, comparable to the patterns associated with New Comedy (or the plays built around Humanum Genus). But for complex reasons linked to both sixteenth and twentieth-century assumptions, the options or strategies with which I am concerned have not received the same attention as other, more visible models. In his discussion of similar problems growing out of the modern reaction to Mannerism, John Shearman notes that "contemporary standards" of our age not only "do not give the right guidance to understanding a past age" but, in fact, can be "a positive hindrance." Rather, he argues: "In decoding messages from the other side we get more meaningful results if we use their code rather than ours," for "wherever possible a work of art should be interpreted by throwing it back into the nest of ideas in which it was born."[13] In my view, that "nest of ideas" for the age of Shakespeare includes (among many other things) the late moral plays. Like many Mannerist paintings, however, the particular "code" embedded in these plays often appears alien to the modern sensibility, whether because of their didacticism, their allegory, or their view of the world (again, the analogy to the Western as received a generation later is useful). Nonetheless, such a code did exist and did provide a means to structure human experience for presentation on a stage.

Herein lies the importance for this book of working with both the extant moral plays from the early Elizabethan period and the allusions to such plays in the age of Shakespeare in order to arrive at some approximation of what the moral drama had to offer a later dramatist. *Our* sense of how a play is put together (why B follows A) or our notions of relationship or "character" may at times be askew or limited if based upon a logic of interpretation that cannot accommodate the legacy of the moral plays. Why indeed should we expect Shakespeare to fashion all his scenes, figures, and images to suit our horizon of expectations (or Aristotle's or even Sidney's)? Modern readers and directors often have difficulty with the fifth acts of *Richard III* and *2 Henry IV* and with figures like Richmond and the Lord Chief Justice who are associated with virtue or Virtue and seem (to us) to lack vitality or individuality. But if such figures gain added force from their positioning in their respective plays (e.g., as I shall argue in chapters three and five, from a "deep structure" that assumes a second phase that is to provide a resolution to the "fallen" world of phase one), then our yardstick of "realism" or individuality may be limited, even wrong-headed. Granted, working with the extant plays and the available allusions is no panacea, but awareness of such materials can serve as a useful antidote to the incursions of the selective tradition and "blind modernism."

By this point my reader may be growing dubious about my claims and qualifications (this scholar doth protest too much, methinks), so let me conclude this introductory chapter with a specific example of the gap between modern assumptions and the actual evidence. As some readers will have noted, in my title and throughout this chapter I have been referring to "the moral play," "moral drama," and "the moral tradition," but, for the most part, have sidestepped the most familiar term, "morality play." My reason for what may appear to be an idiosyncratic procedure is quite simple: despite its currency today, "morality play" is *not* a sixteenth-century term. Rather, as Robert Potter has demonstrated, it came into use in the eighteenth century to describe a category of plays necessary for a now discredited theory about the development of English drama.[14] Granted, *moralité* was used to describe a form of drama across the channel (and occurs in various French–English dictionaries), but the obvious English equivalent is rarely if ever applied to contemporary drama during the sixteenth century. Nor are the other terms familiar today readily at hand. For example, although both the title page and prologue describe *Everyman* as a "moral play," such linking of the adjective "moral" to dramatic kinds is also hard to find.[15] Rather, the works *we* might term "morality plays" are described on title pages or other documents as comedies, interludes, or histories, often with such modifiers as "godly" or "pithy." But "moral," as applied to a literary work "that deals with or treats of the ruling of conduct; that has the teaching of morality as its motive; that conveys a moral" (OED, 3b), is rarely linked to dramatic kinds during the heyday of "the morality play."

In contrast, one comparable term *is* to be found late in the period. For example, the Revels Accounts record performances of "A Morall of the marriage of Mind and Measure" (1578) and "A Comedy or Morall devised on A game of the Cards" (1582);[16] in 1582, Stephen Gosson admits having written "a Morall, Praise at parting";[17] and in 1584 George Whetstone refers to "Stage-plays (unproperly called, Tragedies, Comedies, and Moralls)."[18] A decade later, two popular writers use the term when looking back at the earlier drama. Thus, in Robert Greene's *Groatsworth of Wit* (1592) the Player tells Roberto that he was once "a country Author, passing at a Morall, for 'twas I that penned the Morall of man's wit, the Dialogue of Dives, and for seven years' space was absolute Interpreter to the puppets. But now my Almanac is out of date: *The people make no estimation, / Of Moralls teaching education.*"[19] Similarly, in 1592–93 Thomas Nashe refers to "the old Vice in the Moralls" and "the old Morall,"[20] while as late as 1606 Thomas Dekker alludes to "the old Moralls at *Maningtree*."[21] One of the last extant plays to fit our notion of "morality play," *The Three Lords and Three Ladies of London* (1589), is described both in the Stationers' Register and on its title page as a "pleasant and Stately Morall." And in 1639 R. Willis describes *The Cradle of Security*, a lost play from the 1560s or 1570s, as one of the "harmless moralls of former times."[22]

This group of allusions poses no particular problem for the historian. The first set from 1578–84 indicates that a "morall" corresponds to what we would term a late moral play (or "morality play"), even though among the extant plays only *The Three Lords* (a belated example) is described as such. The allusions from the 1590s and later would then appear to confirm such a definition. Certainly, *The Cradle of Security* as described by Willis appears to have been a typical late moral play; *The Three Lords*, although exhibiting some new features (e.g., three witty pages reminiscent of Lyly's plays) retains the basic components of the earlier *The Three Ladies of London* (e.g., the four knaves or vices, the allegorical ladies, hapless Simplicity); Greene's backward look at "the Morall of man's wit" or "Moralls teaching education" and Nashe's references to "the old Vice" and "the old Morall" are what a modern reader would expect from more sophisticated writers describing the dramatic fare of a previous generation. The term "morall," the historian can then argue, was a relatively late arrival used to describe the "morality play" in its declining years. The adjective "old" as used twice by Nashe would therefore be clinching evidence that the morall or "morality play" was a dead issue by the 1590s and would support F. P. Wilson's judgment, based upon Greene's couplet, that by 1592 "the people had no liking for 'Morrals' of any kind. Their day with 'the people' was over."[23]

But a third reference from Nashe does not associate the morall with the past, for in 1596 he counters Gabriel Harvey's threat of a tragedy with: "Comedy upon Comedy he shall have, a Morall, a History, a Tragedy, or what he will."[24] Even more suggestive, the Stationers' Register records the entry on May 27, 1600, of "A morall of Cloth breeches and velvet hose, As it is acted by my lord Chamberlain's servants." This lost morall, presumably based upon Greene's *A Quip for an Upstart Courtier or a Quaint Dispute Between Velvet Breeches and Cloth Breeches* (1592), was the property of the leading dramatic company in England and was considered important enough to warrant a conditional entry in the Register. Whether a "morality play" in our sense or a social satire modeled on Greene or both, this particular *morall* was apparently part of the repertoire performed by Shakespeare and his colleagues as late as 1600 (along with *As You Like It, Henry V, Julius Caesar, Twelfth Night,* and *Hamlet*).

Nor does Nashe's list or the entry of *Cloth Breeches and Velvet Hose* represent the end of the available evidence. On the contrary, I have been able to find more allusions to the *morall after* 1600 than before. For example, although earlier lists of dramatic kinds usually did not include the *morall* (Whetstone's and Nashe's are the exceptions), later lists often do. Thus, in the Induction to Marston's *What You Will* (1601), Doricus asks if the play is "*Comedy, Tragedy, Pastoral, Morall, Nocturnal,* or *History?*" (p. 233) In Webster's Induction to *The Malcontent* as revised for the King's Men (printed 1604), Condell describes the work as "neither satire nor moral, but the mean passage of a history" (ll. 52–53). In *The Gull's Hornbook* (1609) Dekker tells his gull to call attention to himself by sitting on the stage; then, to disgrace the dramatist, "in the middle of his play, be it pastoral or comedy, morall or tragedy, you rise with a screwed and discontented face from your stool to be gone."[25] In his commendatory poem affixed to Heywood's *Apology for Actors* (1612), John Taylor describes the drama as "a true transparent Crystal mirror" that can show the audience its own vices "either in Tragedy, or Comedy, / In Morall, Pastoral, or History," while in Part III of the apology Heywood himself argues that "there is neither Tragedy, History, Comedy, Morall, or Pastoral, from which an infinite use cannot be gathered."[26] Similar lists also turn up in legal documents, for although earlier dramatic licenses (e.g., for Leicester's, Sussex's, or Strange's Men) did not cite the *morall,* the analogous documents during the reigns of Kings James and Charles regularly refer to "Comedies tragedies histories Enterludes Moralls Pastorals Stageplays and such like."[27]

In addition to Marston, Webster, Dekker, and Heywood,

Middleton too makes repeated references to the morall in his non-dramatic prose satire, *The Black Book* (1604). [28] Although most dictionaries of the period provide only the expected definitions of *moral* or *morality*, a notable exception is Randle Cotgrave's *A Dictionarie of the French and English Tongues* (1611), [29] which translates *Moraliser* as: "To moralize, to expound morally, to give a moral sense unto; also, to act a Morall, or Enterlude of manners"; and *Moralité* as: "Morality; a moral sense, or subject; also, a Morall, an Enterlude or Play of manners" (with "manners" understood, presumably, as a rendition of the Latin *mores*). Heywood too provides a definition, for in his *Apology for Actors* he argues that the goal of a morall "is to persuade men to humanity and good life, to instruct them in civility and good manners, showing them the fruits of honesty, and the end of villainy" (F3v). Unfortunately, this forthright statement is of relatively little value for solving the puzzle of the seventeenth-century morall, because, in his effort to justify each dramatic kind, Heywood describes all five in much the same terms, so that his comments on the morall are not markedly different from those on tragedy or especially those on comedy ("in which is taught, what in our lives and manners is to be followed, what to be avoided"—F1v). Moreover, the only other extant play (besides *The Three Lords and Three Ladies of London*) to which the term is attached is *Two Wise Men and All The Rest Fools*, a seven-act curiosity published in 1619 that is more a series of discourses than a play.

That a host of knowledgeable theatrical professionals allude to the morall as a familiar dramatic kind in the early seventeenth century may be puzzling, even startling, but such allusions *are* there. Admittedly, despite two extant examples and two definitions the historian today is still very much in the dark as to exactly what kind of play Marston, Webster, Dekker, Heywood, and Middleton had in mind or what kind of play the King's Men and the other Jacobean dramatic companies were licensed to perform. My own conjecture is that by this point the morall was no longer associated with overt allegory or Humanum Genus or the Vice but had evolved into moralized comedy or social satire with a strong didactic emphasis at the close, as in *A Knack to Know a Knave*, *Your Five Gallants*, *The Phoenix*, *How a Man May Choose a Good Wife from a Bad*, *The Fair Maid of Bristow*, and *The Royal King and Loyal Subject*. [30] My purpose in introducing these allusions, however, is not to defend such a conjecture but rather to confront the reader nurtured on the traditional formulation about the decline of "the morality play" with this anomaly. The questions then follow: When reconstructing our history of Elizabethan drama, what constitutes evidence? On what basis are we to establish the horizon of expectations about the moral drama in the age of Shakespeare? Are we to place our trust in the selective tradition, as epitomized in our anthologies and literary handbooks, or are we to turn to the comments and conceptions of the figures who were there—in this instance, figures responsible for many of the major plays of the period?

The moral of my case study is that we do not know as much as we often think we know about drama and theatre in the age of Shakespeare. Rather, we should bear in mind the comments of Arthur W. Schlesinger, Jr., about his participation in the Kennedy administration: "In retrospect, I shudder a little when I think how confidently I have analyzed decisions in the ages of Jackson and Roosevelt, traced influences, assigned motives, evaluated roles, allocated responsibilities, and, in short, transformed a dishevelled and murky evolution into a tidy and ordered transaction." Schlesinger concludes: "The sad fact is that, in many cases, the basic evidence for the historian's reconstruction of the really hard cases does not exist—and the evidence that does exist is often incomplete, misleading or erroneous." [31] Shakespeare neatly summed up the habit of mind behind this scholarly desire for the "tidy and ordered transaction" when he had Olivia tell Cesario: "I would you were as I would have you be" (III.i.139). Thus, I suspect that the allusions to the morall in the seventeenth century have had little impact upon the formulations set forth in our literary handbooks not because these allusions are difficult to find but because they do not mesh well with the conclusions many theatre historians would prefer to draw.

In dealing with the dramatic legacy inherited by Shakespeare and his contemporaries, how then are we to avoid the perplexity of an Olivia or the fate of a Malvolio who found it easy to "crush" the evidence presented him in order to gain his desired result? To focus solely upon anomalies like the morall would only prove perverse in the long run, for the handbook formulations about the development of Elizabethan drama, although sometimes too tidy and ordered in Schlesinger's terms, have lasted for so long because they do fit much of the evidence. Yet there are advantages in focusing upon the anomalies, the exceptions that test the general rules. Close attention to what is available in the late moral plays can provide some fresh and potentially fruitful models or paradigms that, in turn, can be brought to bear upon familiar texts, including several plays that have posed continuing problems for modern interpreters. Herein lies the justification for this book.

2

The Public Vice and the
Two Phased Moral Play

Although provocative for the dramatic historian, the seventeenth-century allusions to the morall do not offer any major
new insights to the interpreter of Shakespeare's plays. After all,
we have no evidence that Shakespeare conceived of any of his
own plays as a morall (an anomaly like *Timon of Athens* might be
a distant possibility), nor is the didactic emphasis characteristic
of many Elizabethan and Jacobean moralized comedies and tragedies a feature of his plays. What then of the options or models
found in the late moral plays and therefore available to the next
generation of dramatists? As with the morall, are any clues available in allusions from Shakespeare's contemporaries?

To provide a definitive answer to the latter question would require reading all the material in print and in manuscript between
roughly 1580 and 1620, a task I have not performed. For over
twenty years, however, I have been collecting such allusions and
have searched at length in the most fruitful areas (e.g., epigrams,
satires, the Marprelate controversy). From such materials, certain categories do emerge, most of them consistent with features
of the extant moral plays. Significant too are some of the silences,
particularly the absence of allusions to Mankind or Everyman or

Humanum Genus, the figure many modern scholars identify with "the morality play." As demonstrated by plays such as *Doctor Faustus* and *Othello*, that paradigm was still available (and, as I have argued elsewhere, could be used for one scene rather than an entire play),[1] but with the exception of an occasional reference to the stock figure of Lusty Juventus or to the Wit plays (as in the play-within-the-play of *Sir Thomas More*), I have found in the age of Shakespeare little or no specific mention of that moral play hero who dominates our scholarship and conception of the form.

Rather, as would be expected by anyone who has read the extant plays of the 1560s and 1570s, a high percentage of the allusions recall the dominant figure of the late moral tradition, the Vice. For example, many writers allude to the Vice's status as jester, fool, or buffoon. In fact, several compilers of early dictionaries include such associations in their definitions. For example, Randle Cotgrave translates the French *mime* as "a vice, fool, jester, scoffer" and *sot* as "a fool, or vice in a play";[2] John Florio translates the Italian *mimo* as "a jester, a vice in a play";[3] John Minsheu translates the Spanish *mómo* or *mómio* as "a Vice or jester in a play."[4] In his translation of Pliny, Philemon Holland expands the Latin *mima* into "a common vice in a play" and, a sentence later, describes "such another vice that played the fool and made sport between whiles in enterludes."[5] In his *Art of English Poesy* (1589), George Puttenham sees rhyme misused by "buffoons or vices in plays,"[6] while one of the Marprelate tracts describes a figure "as merry as a vice on a stage."[7]

Other authors, however, find more serious implications in this merry, jesting Vice. In his *Anatomy of Abuses* (1583) Philip Stubbes draws upon the familiar association when he asks: "who will call him a wise man, that playeth the part of a fool and a vice?" but in the previous paragraph Stubbes had noted sarcastically that good examples *are* to be found in the theatre: "if you will learn to play the vice, to swear, tear, and blaspheme both Heaven and Earth."[8] Similarly, Gabriel Harvey can equate "jesters and vices" yet elsewhere attack Robert Greene as "the second Toy of London; the Stale of Paul's, the Ape of Euphues, the Vice of the Stage, the mocker of the simple world."[9] Jonson's

The Devil Is an Ass provides a backward look at the Vice from the perspective of the "modern" world of 1616 sophisticated in evil and deception. Thus, Iniquity the Vice comments as he carries off Pug the inept devil: "The *Devil* was wont to carry away the evil; / But, now, the Evil out-carries the *Devil*" (V. vi. 76–77), a deliberate inversion that twice equates the Vice not with "fool" or "jester" but with "the Evil." For Stubbes, Harvey, and Jonson, that same scoffing or jesting figure could be linked to a different tone, a different set of implications—a mocking of the world, a blasphemy of heaven and earth, Evil.

In more specific terms, the attribute of the Vice most often cited in the age of Shakespeare is his dagger of lath. In 1583, William Rainolds argues that Bishop Jewel's position "would better become some merry fellow making sport upon a stage, with a furred hood and a wooden dagger." [10] A few years later, the author of *Martin's Month's Mind* (1589) anticipates the time when his opponents "shall put off their fool's coat, and leave snapping of their wooden dagger, and betake themselves to a soberer kind of reasoning, (which will be very hard for such vices to do)." [11] The interlude contained within *Sir Thomas More* includes a Vice (Inclination), a stage direction that reads "*flourishing his dagger*," and a line: "my dagger about your coxcombs shall walk" (ll. 1068–70). In 1603, Samuel Harsnet refers repeatedly to the nimble Vice who belabors the Devil with his wooden dagger [12] (a passage often cited in scholarly glosses), while *The Owl's Almanac* (1618) describes "Madame *Vice*, or old *Iniquity*, with a lath dagger painted, according to the fashion of an old *Vice* in a Comedy." [13] In Jonson's *The Devil Is an Ass*, Satan describes the situation fifty years earlier "when every great man had his *Vice* stand by him, / In his long coat, shaking his wooden dagger" (I. i. 84–85); again, in Jonson's *The Staple of News* (1626), Tattle states that she would "not give a rush for a *Vice*, that has not a wooden dagger to snap at everybody he meets" (Second Intermean, ll. 11–13). Similarly, in the final scene of Chapman's *The Widow's Tears* (1605) observers commenting on the foolish Governor first ask: "O desert, where wert thou when this wooden dagger was gilded over with the title of Governor?" and then add:

"Nay, the Vice must snap his Authority at all he meets; how shall't else be known what part he plays?" (V.v.164–66, 218–19). In *Twelfth Night* Feste refers to "the old Vice" and his "dagger of lath" (IV.ii.121–23), and Falstaff alludes to the dagger of lath (*1 Henry IV*, II.iv.129) and the "Vice's dagger" (*2 Henry IV*, III.ii.297).

If allusions (as opposed to modern formulations) are to be our guide, the Elizabethans also remembered vividly one other feature of the late moral drama, the Vice's exit to Hell at the end of his career upon the Devils' back. This action is to be found in only one extant play, Fulwell's *Like Will to Like* (1568), where according to the stage direction the Vice (Nichol Newfangle) "*rideth away on the Devil's back*" (p. 357). In two earlier plays, a vicious protagonist rather than the Vice exits in this fashion. Thus, in W. Wager's *The Longer Thou Livest* (1559) the foolish Moros asks to be carried away by the Devil and is obliged by Confusion, the figure of retribution ("I will carry thee to the devil indeed; / The world shall be well rid of a fool"—ll. 1853–56). In the same author's *Enough Is as Good as a Feast* (1560), Satan praises the Vice, addresses the worldly and avaricious members of the audience, and then bears off the fallen protagonist, Worldly Man, on his back (s.d. to l. 1471). In a lost play, *The Cradle of Security*, the prince (who represents the sinners of the world) "was carried away by wicked spirits."[14]

Apparently, this bit of stage business then remained familiar to a generation of playgoers and dramatists. For example, in 1592 Thomas Nashe attacks the usurer who "shall ride to Hell on the devil's back (as it is in the old Morall)."[15] In 1603, Harsnet describes "the old Church-plays, when the nimble Vice would skip up nimbly like a Jack an Apes into the devil's neck, and ride the devil a course, and belabor him with his wooden dagger, till he made him roar."[16] Several plays from the age of Shakespeare incorporate some version of this exit. In *A Knack to Know a Knave* (1592), the Bailiff of Hexham (the father of the four knaves) is carried off at his death by a devil ("*Enter Devil, and carry him away*"—l. 373). In Robert Greene's *Friar Bacon and Friar Bungay* (1589), the clownish Miles meets a devil, expresses interest in visiting Hell, puts on spurs, and announces: "Oh Lord here's even a goodly marvel, when a man rides to hell on the Devil's back." The stage direction reads: "*exeunt roaring*" (ll. 2072–73). In Lodge and Greene's *A Looking Glass for London and England* (1590), a figure tries to frighten Adam the clown by masquerading as a devil; among his threats are: "Come get up on my back, that I may carry thee" (ll. 1716–17). Sir Oliver Owlet's Men, the bumbling theatrical troupe in *Histriomastix* (1599), present a fragment of a moral interlude that begins with the stage direction: "*Enter a roaring Devil with the Vice on his back, Iniquity in one hand; and Juventus in the other*" (C4r).

Of particular interest are the comments on this notable exit by Ben Jonson. As late as 1626 Jonson has one of his foolish choric figures in *The Staple of News* praise the Devil who "would carry away the Vice on his back, quick to Hell, in every Play where he came, and reform abuses" (First Intermean, ll. 64–66). In 1618 Jonson told William Drummond that "according to Comedia Vetus, in England the devil was brought in either with one Vice or other, the Play done the devil carried away the Vice."[17] Jonson's comment to Drummond about the moral drama provides his explanation of the ironic transformation of this exit in *The Devil Is an Ass* where the Vice (Iniquity) carries off the inept devil (Pug) and calls attention to the inversion in the couplet cited earlier ("The *Devil* was wont to carry away the evil; / But, now, the Evil out-carries the *Devil*"). Here one of the major dramatists of the period has, with some fanfare, invoked the link between the jesting Vice and the Devil and has made that link an essential part of his satiric strategy.

What then can we learn from these allusions to the late moral plays found in the age of Shakespeare? First, the reader who expects considerable mention of Everyman or Humanum Genus will be disappointed. In contrast, the wealth of allusions to the Vice[18] (no surprise to anyone acquainted with the extant plays) supports Bernard Spivack's proposition "that whereas the older moralities were about man, the later ones are about the Vice." According to Spivack, "it is now the Vice whose role bounds the scope of the play, as Mankind degenerates, in a dramatic sense,

into a series of incidental figures upon whom he repeats his performance and multiplies the display of his cunning," so that the
moral drama is no longer "a chronicle of human life" but "becomes a succession of his activities."[19] Although Spivack's formulation about the shape and emphasis of such plays is too narrow, he does not exaggerate the pivotal role played by the Vice.

Still, to recognize the prominence or visibility of the Vice in
both the extant plays and the subsequent allusions is not necessarily to grasp how later dramatists would have understood (or
"received") this figure and then adapted him to their own uses.
Thus, except for glosses on three or four passages in Shakespeare's
plays, few scholars have treated the dagger of lath as a significant
image, while the Vice's exit on the Devil's back is rarely considered an essential feature of the moral drama or an action worthy
of note. The association of the Vice with buffoon, fool, or jester
does fit well with various scholarly analyses that call attention to
that figure's role in "morality variety shows,"[20] but the link to the
Devil in the famous exit and Jonson's equation of the Vice with
"the Evil" introduce another set of associations usually omitted
from such discussions. Admittedly, the late moral play Devil is
often a comic, blustering figure who sets the Vice in motion and
is mocked in the process. Nonetheless, the association between
the two figures (with the consequent linking of the Vice to sin,
Hell, and damnation) is prominent both in the extant plays and
the memories of the next generation. Thus, the entertainment
function of the Vice-comedian is to be found in the late moral
drama and is remembered, but the diabolic associations (as well
as the implications for the Vice's victims and society) give that
humor a distinct edge. As Robert C. Jones argues, the Vice provides a "dangerous sport" both for his on-stage victims and for
the spectator, who is encouraged to "move from engagement in
the entertainment of the vices to judgment that places that sort
of entertainment in perspective."[21]

With these allusions in mind, let me turn to a series of moral
plays that span roughly thirty years, with my focus less upon the
comic energy of the Vice (admittedly, an essential feature) than
upon other less discussed elements: the dagger of lath; other

weapons; the Vice's fate; and, perhaps most important, the general shape of the play. My survey will be selective, not comprehensive, for my goal is not to rewrite the history of this dramatic kind. Rather, I wish to isolate for subsequent use some common features and a sense of "deep structure" shared by a number of plays and consistent with the allusions cited earlier. Although different dramatists with different goals (or sermons) may push the same conventions in different directions, nonetheless some common denominators can be noted that can help us better to understand plays of the next generation.

Let me start with a transitional play that lacks a Vice, *Wealth and Health* (1554). Here we can see what Bernard Spivack terms the "fission" of the Humanum Genus hero,[22] for the dramatist provides not a central protagonist named Respublica or Albion Knight but rather three figures, Wealth, Health, and Liberty, whose fortunes enact the recent history of England. These three figures are corrupted, moreover, not by a single Vice but by two figures, Ill Will and Shrewd Wit (who, to the Marian author, epitomize Protestant private judgment), and ultimately are restored to health by Remedy (proper authority). With no single figure to represent England, the role of the vices has undergone some changes, for Ill Will and Shrewd Wit epitomize not forces within three "human" heroes but forces active in the kingdom as a whole that have led to the decline of England's wealth, health, and liberty. Here, as in plays of the next decade that also exhibit the failings of society at large, the Vice or vices have a public dimension that transcends the temptation of any single Mankind figure (although that Vice may still generate one or more such corruptions). In addition, even in an early play like *Wealth and Health* the dramatist has set up a circumscribed sphere of influence for his vices who can go so far but no farther. Thus, Remedy announces that, despite the tribulations of the three protagonists, we should "be all of good cheer," for even though the vices may "reign a while, wrongfully and unjust / Yet truth will appear and their misdeeds blame." Eventually, he argues, regardless of their apparent power, "craft will out and deceit will have a fall" (ll. 931–37). The power of these vices (and later the Vice) is temporary, for the short term only, a formulation that lasts throughout the period and indeed becomes basic to the dramatic career of the Vice.

Although limited as a play or work of art, *Wealth and Health* nonetheless provides a useful example of the problem facing various mid century dramatists who, whatever their political or religious stances, wanted to display on-stage a sinful world or a society corrupted by a particular force and then provide their answer (hence Remedy). Whatever his origins, the emergence of the Vice as the central figure in the interludes of the 1560s and 1570s represents a practical theatrical answer to this problem, an answer that apparently satisfied a wide range of dramatists and audiences. The spectator was therefore regularly confronted with a lively, often very funny figure who sets up a special bond with his audience and then acts out with wit, energy, and comic violence the power of some corrupting force upon society (e.g., Covetousness, Revenge, Newfangledness, Infidelity, Inclination) only to be defeated or transcended in the play's final movement. At some point almost every Vice wields his dagger with comic bravado against foes or even allies, but ultimately he is thwarted, in some cases by an opposing figure wielding a more powerful weapon (e.g., a sword of Justice). Although only one extant play presents a Vice actually carried off on the Devil's back, most Vices are disposed of in some decisive fashion, with a high percentage arrested (after a considerable struggle) and then hanged. Quite a few plays, then, exhibit a consistent pattern: a jesting Vice, who embodies a force that threatens society as a whole, brandishes his dagger of lath and has his moments of fun and dominance (often while one or more victims are led into sin) only to be arrested or eclipsed in a second climactic movement that brings him, his weapon, and what he has come to represent under control. As in the various allusions, the Vice can be both jester and threat, for his is a "dangerous sport" that initially entertains us but, in the long run, has ominous implications.

Consider some examples of how the Vice can function in such a two phased movement. Early in *King Darius* (1565) the three vices (including the Vice Iniquity) gang up upon and berate one virtue, with the Vice threatening Equity with violence and at several points invoking his dagger (e.g., "I will rap my dagger about thy pate"—p. 54). Equity, however, disdains "such vain gauds" and "deriding mocks" ("if He be on my side, I care not for you all"), and draws strength instead from an alternative weapon ("you neither know Him nor His rightful rod"—pp. 56–57). In contrast, when outnumbered by virtues in his final scene, the Vice keeps trying to exit ("Farewell again I say, / I must go my way") but is prevented, along with much emphasis upon "a vengeance for thee prepared," "Hell fire is thine," and God's "just rod" (pp. 76–78). Then, at the climax of this action: *"Here somebody must cast fire to Iniquity,"* with Constancy adding: "For thy wickedness thou shalt have this." As he *"goeth out,"* the Vice's exit line is: "Nay, I go to the devil, I fear," suggesting some link to the departure on the Devil's back, while the virtues praise God who "hath plucked him away" and "with His rod, / Which is upright, / Hath this man destroyed" (pp. 78–79). The same figure that had dominated the earlier scenes here is contained, punished, and disposed of in some highly theatrical fashion involving fire, with the virtues calling attention to an alternative force associated with the rod of God's justice. The Vice and his fellow vices, it should be noted, never meet King Darius or any other Mankind figure but rather are linked by the virtues to the general state of the kingdom and, at times (see pp. 48, 53), through the pronoun *you*, to the audience as well.

In contrast, in an earlier play, *Nice Wanton* (1550), another Iniquity (here never specifically designated as the Vice) does tempt and corrupt two figures, Dalilah and Ismael. In the climactic trial scene, when the convicted Ismael implicates Iniquity as his accomplice, the allegorical figure threatens: "He that layeth hand on me in this place: / Shall have my brawling iron laid on his face." The stage direction reads: *"They take him in a halter and he fighteth"* (B4r). Although no dagger is mentioned here (or earlier when Iniquity struck Dalilah), the same figure that had dominated the two protagonists in the first phase of the action is now literally and figuratively arrested, so that his threats no longer carry any force. Similarly, Inclination in *The Trial of Trea-*

sure (1567) can be bridled early in the play by Just and Sapience, but, confident that his victim, Lust, will release him, the Vice assures us: "though that I be bridled a while, / The colt will at length the courser beguile" (p. 280). At the climax of the play, however, Just leads in a struggling, complaining Inclination "*in his bridle shackled*" (p. 297) and even tightens the reins. Although the Vice promises to "rebel, yea, and rebel again" (p. 299), he is led off to prison under control, an exit juxtaposed with the display of the fates of Lust and Treasure (turned to dust and rust) and the awarding of the crown of Felicity to Just. The continuing threat posed by man's "beastly inclination" is both placed in a larger salvific framework and linked to a recurring bridle-snaffle-shackle image that provides a theatrically visible answer to the Vice's energy and threat.

Consider as well how the Vice and the two phased action can be incorporated into three well known stories. First, in Thomas Garter's *Virtuous and Godly Susanna* (1569) the Vice Ill Report is instrumental in getting the two judges to condemn the heroine; later, after Daniel appears as judge, the Vice helps to lead the two false judges to execution while continuing to serve as chief comedian (e.g., dropping a stone on someone's foot, putting on a judge's gown). But with the appearance of his opposite, True Report, the Vice's wit and comic energy no longer work for him (e.g., he fails to convince anyone that he is really Will, not Ill, Report and that his opponent is Hugh, not True). Rather, as is typical of these plays, the formerly successful comic violence and disruption now are brought under control: "*Here they struggle together, the Gaoler casts the Rope about Ill Report's neck*" (ll. 1367–68). Then, instead of going directly to Hell, the Vice is taken off to be hanged, and the Devil enters to forecast Ill Report's fate in Hell owing to his failure to destroy Susanna. Again, the same figure that had controlled the action (and entertained the audience) throughout much of the play is judged, arrested, and taken off for hanging in a final phase characterized by an ideal judge, Daniel, and the Vice's symbolic opposite, True Report.

The same pattern is to be found in John Pickering's *Horestes* (1567) where the Vice Revenge not only persuades Horestes to kill the murderers of his father but also acts out his power in scenes with two country bumpkins and two soldiers. As one scholar has pointed out, this Vice symbolizes "an evil which is demonstrated not only in the main line of action, but also in subordinate scenes of broad comedy which echo the play's major theme."[23] But after his string of successes, Revenge's last appearance is as a beggar "*with a staff and a bottle or dish and wallet*" (l. 1233), a "sudden mutation" that he attributes to the arrival of Amity who "is unto me revenge most contrary. / And we twain together, could not abide" (ll. 1254, 1258–59). The banishment of the Vice, who is "driven without comfort, away from their gate" (l. 1266), is followed by the crowning of Horestes by Truth and Duty and a sermon by Truth on the lasting quality of "a kingdom kept in Amity, and void of dissension" as opposed to the land afflicted with "dissension and strife" defined as "the path to decay" (ll. 1371–77). Again, the Vice that had dominated the action is transformed into a beggar, denied his original power, and replaced by his allegorical opposites who provide the audience with the answer or remedy to his threat.

Similarly, the Vice Haphazard in *Apius and Virginia* (1564) epitomizes not only a weakness to which Apius is susceptible but also an amoral attitude (roughly defined as "take a chance—perhaps you may get what you want") that pervades the world of the play (e.g., in episodes involving Apius's servants or in Haphazard's soliloquy that catalogues his influence over various parts of society—ll. 386–407). But after Apius has been condemned by Justice and Reward, the Vice spells out his distinctive rationale one last time in a long speech (ll. 1081–1115) in which he decides to ask for his reward, reasoning: "the worst that can hap is but a no" (l. 1106). But the same "haphazard" approach that earlier had worked for Apius and the servants now yields the "reward" of a rope, so although the Vice tries "*to go forth,*" he is forced to "stay a while" (ll. 1142–43) and eventually is led off by Virginius to be hanged. The final speeches of Fame, Memory, Justice, and Reward then stress how Virginia's death "shall ever reign / Within the mouth and mind of man, from age to age again" (ll. 1194–95) as opposed to the short term power of

Haphazard that has been transcended in this final movement of the play.

The presence of both the Vice and various allegorical alternatives in a world also populated by figures like Susanna, Horestes, and Apius may jar the sensibilities of modern readers who view such a combination as evidence of the primitive nature of English drama before "the triumph of realism" in the age of Shakespeare. Yet despite their limitations, these renditions of famous stories show how early Elizabethan dramatists were able to use the Vice both as an entertainer *and* as an allegorical index to the central issues of the play. Equally revealing, the final phase of each rendition is clearly linked to the fate of the Vice, so that the diminution or arrest of this formerly dominant figure is brought about by allegorical opposites (True Report; Amity, Truth, and Duty; Reward and Justice) who then epitomize the new situation at the end in a manner analogous to the climaxes of *Wealth and Health, King Darius*, and *The Trial of Treasure*. The Vice and the two phased movement were thus available as a formula that could be adapted to various ends, including the presentation of well known stories not necessarily associated with the moral play.

The components of this dramatic formula vary widely from play to play. For example, the fate of the Vice (or of a human protagonist) can be played off against the reward offered a figure who has chosen the path of virtue. As already noted, the appearance of Revenge as a beggar is followed immediately by the crowning of Horestes; in *The Trial of Treasure*, the bridling of the Vice and the fate of Lust are juxtaposed with the presentation of a crown to Just; and in *Like Will to Like*, the corruption and fall of three pairs of human figures are contrasted to the perseverance of Virtuous Living who gains a sword and a crown. This last play may have offered the spectator a two phased progression built around a recurring property, a chair. Thus, early in the play (p. 321) the Vice sits in such a chair as a judge to ponder whether Tom Tosspot or Ralph Roister deserves the promised patrimony (beggary); moments later (p. 330), the chair is used by Hance, the drunken Fleming. In contrast, the chair becomes a seat for

Virtuous Living (p. 342), who receives not a misleading promise from the Vice but a sword and a crown from Honor and God's Promises. Then, despite his threat to "stick you both with this woodknife" (p. 350), the Vice is beaten by Ralph Roister and Tom Tosspot and left "*on the ground groaning*," at which point Severity the judge enters, bearing a sword (p. 351), to pass judgment on Cuthbert Cutpurse and Pierce Pickpurse, presumably while sitting in the chair. In this play the halters and the sword of Justice are used on these two thieves, not on the Vice. Nonetheless, the Vice's dagger fails him late in the action against figures he formerly had controlled and, moreover, is juxtaposed with alternative weapons: the sword awarded Virtuous Living and the sword carried by Severity. In addition, especially if Severity delivers his judgment from the chair, a succession of seated figures (including the Vice exiting on the Devil's back) underscores the phases of the action.

The most revealing example of this formula is to be found in George Wapull's *The Tide Tarrieth No Man* (1576). Throughout the first two-thirds of this play Courage the Vice controls the action, dominating both his lieutenants and a wide range of victims through threats and cunning while entertaining the audience. At several points the dramatist calls for stage violence (once "*to prolong the time*" while an actor is off-stage making a difficult costume change—l. 1214.s.d.); at one such moment Wapull specifically directs: "*Out quickly with his dagger*" (l. 200.s.d.). In contrast to the obvious (and highly theatrical) power of the Vice, the audience witnesses the plight of Christianity, a figure who should be wearing the well known Pauline armor but, owing to the wicked nature of the world, is instead "deformed" in appearance. As the elaborate stage direction tells us (at l. 1439): "*Christianity must enter with a sword, with a title of Policy, but on the other side of the title, must be written God's Word, also a shield, whereon must be written Riches, but on the other side of the shield must be Faith.*" At one point, Faithful Few turns the titles so that Faith and God's Word take their proper place, but moments later Christianity is forced to resume the burden of Riches and Policy because of the continuing depravity of Greediness and the Vice.

Both the plight of Christianity and the success of the Vice (who acts out his influence over a landlord, a courtier, a usurer, and a young married couple) demonstrate what is wrong with the world presented in the first phase of this action. In the final scene, however, at the urging of Faithful Few, the Vice is arrested by Correction in the presence of Authority, a figure who bears "this sword of God's power" (l. 1837). In typical fashion, Courage resists ("*he draweth his dagger and fighteth*"—l. 1821.s.d.), seeking to reassert the power displayed throughout much of the play, but here the same dagger that earlier had dominated the action fails to protect its wielder when juxtaposed with the sword of God's authority and the correction that accompanies it. Then, once the Vice has been taken off under arrest, Faithful Few can restore Christianity's sword of Truth and shield of Faith to their pristine state, the culminating action of the play. The formula implicit in other moral plays is here spelled out and fully realized in terms of two sets of weapons, two contrasting powers, and two phases of the action that, taken together, present one moral thesis.

The significance of the Vice's arrest is enhanced by an earlier analogous scene. According to the information presented on the title page, in the middle of this play the actor playing the Vice must exit to reappear moments later as the poor but honest Debtor who refuses to bribe the Sergeant and therefore is led off to prison (while wealthy figures like Greediness and No Good Neighborhood bend the law). Despite its obvious point about the corrupt world, this brief scene may seem gratuitous to the modern reader—at least until that reader links it to the final movement when Courage tries to flee from Faithful Few and Authority (who carries a sword and is addressed in judicial terms) only to be grasped by Correction who is told: "thine office do, / Take here this caitiff unto the jail" (ll. 1813–14). Clearly, in function (if not in costume as well), Correction is a positive or heavenly version of that corrupt sergeant who led off the impoverished debtor (with the latter role performed by the same actor now portraying the Vice—his only such double in the play). As with the deformed versus restored Christianity, the spectator is

offered two stages in a process that structures the entire play—
the movement from the domination of the Vice and his worldly
interpretation of the proverbial title (*carpe diem*) to the emergence of Faithful Few and Christianity with their heavenly version of the same proverb (see lines 43–49). The importance of
the role played here by Authority and Correction, moreover, is
reinforced by the description of the lost *The Cradle of Security*
which also climaxed with the appearance of two old men, "the
one in blue with a Sergeant at Arms, his mace on his shoulder,
the other in red with a drawn sword in his hand"—figures identified as "the end of the world, and the last judgment."

The Tide Tarrieth No Man deserves special attention for several
reasons, including the fact that Wapull develops the possibilities
in dagger and sword further than any other moral dramatist. But
I cite this play too because of the suggestive allusion that turns
up a decade later in *Martin's Month's Mind* (1589) where one section of the tract provides Martin's supposed final words to his
sons: "The wooden dagger may not be worn at the back, where
St. Paul's sword, hangs by the side: neither can he well find fault
with the *corner* cap; that weareth the furred night cap on his
head, as I did. These gambols (my sons) are implements for the
Stage, and beseem Jesters, and Players, but are not fit for *Church
plotters, nor commonwealth casters*, such as we are." The marginal
note reads: "Martin's wardrobe, a wooden dagger and furred
night cap."[24] This complex allusion may stand at several removes
from the practice of the late moral drama. Nonetheless, I find it
highly suggestive that a religious controversialist in the late
1580s would choose as contrasting images the Vice's dagger and
St. Paul's sword of faith, the same opposing images invoked by
Wapull in his play from the mid 1570s, the same opposition of
dagger and higher weapon employed or implied by other moral
dramatists as well. Again, we are presented with what appears to
be a well known opposition between two weapons that epitomize
two alternatives that in turn signal two phases or movements of
a play.

Further evidence late in the period for such a two phased
movement is provided by Robert Wilson's *The Cobbler's Prophecy*

(1590), a curious blend of moral play, social satire, and mythology. Much of the play is dominated by Contempt (never specifically named the Vice or given a dagger), an allegorical figure who stands for "envy and dissension among the several estates and for the resultant turmoil and injustice in the realm."[25] Contempt's successes during the first movement include, on the level of the gods, the corruption of Venus (who is pregnant and diseased) and the degradation of Mars and the Muses, and, in the kingdom of Boeotia, the corruption of various "estates" figures (e.g., a courtier, a country gentlemen). Although this allegorical prime mover is never arrested or punished, the curing of the kingdom is made possible when, in a climactic scene, the duke, his daughter, the priest, and the scholar transcend their individual failings and burn the cabin of Contempt. With less severe limits on the number of actors, Wilson's play can provide scenes and effects more complex than were possible in the moral drama of the previous generation, but the same basic pattern is at work in which a diseased Boeotia-England is cured in a climactic action that transcends the allegorical force epitomized in one previously dominant figure.

From this selective sampling of four decades of moral drama emerges no single paradigm to replace the well known Humanum Genus figure of the fifteenth and early sixteenth century. Still, the Vice does stand out as a prominent figure in almost every popular play of the 1560s and 1570s (and left his mark upon Matthew Merrygreek in *Ralph Roister Doister* and Diccon in *Gammer Gurton's Needle*). But for the reader not vitally interested in the development of drama just before the age of Shakespeare, what can be learned from the function or functions of this highly visible figure? In particular, in what way are the Vice, his accoutrements, and his place in a larger pattern relevant to the dramatists of the next generation who rarely resorted to overt allegory but were equally concerned with the health of the kingdom and the working out of various social and providential forces?

To some degree, the partial answers to such questions assumed or advanced by scholars have obscured the full range of possibilities. Thus, several knowledgeable historians of the period have argued that the Vice was or quickly became a figure with a distinctive appeal of his own and therefore, in effect, independent of his play. For example, in his gloss on Jonson's comment to Drummond about the theatrical convention invoked in *The Devil Is an Ass*, C. H. Herford cites the passage noted earlier from Puttenham (that equates "vice" and "buffoon") to prove that "Jonson is wrong, historically, about the Vice." Herford grants that the Vice was the opponent of goodness in the early interludes, but argues that "in Jonson's day the original significance was lost, and the Vice had sunk to the level of a clown."[26] Similarly, in his study of the origins of the Vice, F. H. Mares argues that even when the Vice "appeared as an agent of evil in a morality play, he always maintained a degree of freedom from the allegorical framework"; in the next generation, moreover, "the recollections of his activities have little suggestion of moral significance about them."[27] According to this argument, the Vice (like some of Shakespeare's characters today) took on a life of his own untrammeled by his original environment.

A somewhat different argument draws not upon the Vice's skill as an entertainer or clown but rather upon his expertise as a tempter of Mankind. Thus, scholars regularly cite the Vice, like the stage Machiavel, as a major prototype for the many villain-seducers who populate Elizabethan tragedies and histories. Prince Hal reinforces such a link when he describes Falstaff as "that reverend vice, that grey iniquity, that father ruffian, that vanity in years" and "that villainous abominable misleader of youth, Falstaff, that old white-bearded Satan" (*1 Henry IV*, II.iv. 431– 32, 439–40). Although the tempting of Mankind is not a central concern of the late moral plays, various Vices do spend some or occasionally much of their on-stage time as corrupters or misleaders of representative figures (as in *Nice Wanton*), with some of the most fully realized Vices having several such scenes (e.g, Nichol Newfangle, Courage).

But to be satisfied solely with the Vice-as-clown or the Vice-as-tempter is to settle for part truths that may obscure other options available to the age of Shakespeare. Admittedly, both the extant plays and the later allusions link the Vice to the jester or buffoon, but, as noted earlier, at least some allusions support a grimmer view of both his role and his humor. According to Bernard Spivack, "farce alone is only the dramatic glitter of his role, not its homiletic substance," for "his double nature and the double nature of the moral play make it impossible to resolve him into a buffoon merely, as much as we may be tempted to get rid of the problem by so resolving him." By quoting a representative sampling of the execrations and epithets addressed to the Vice within various plays, Spivack demonstrates how "this darker picture is endlessly confirmed by the moralities themselves."[28]

Similarly, the Vice can be a tempter or, as in *The Tide Tarrieth No Man*, an encourager of weak or sinful figures. Yet some Vices have no such temptation scenes (e.g., Iniquity in *King Darius*) or spend only a fraction of their on-stage time in such activities or are seen in action with figures already depraved who therefore need no inducement. Rather, given the allegorical nomenclature and the larger goals of many moral dramatists, the Vice often embodies a quality, force, idea, or sin pervasive in the "world" of the play, something that is to be acted out in a variety of ways, one of which may be the corruption of individual figures (assuming such corruption has not already taken place). By focusing upon temptation and fall, the modern interpreter may therefore be imposing a later model or set of assumptions upon the Vice, one that satisfies our sense of psychological process but fails to take into account his full function or potential, especially his public role wherein a dramatist uses a Vice to single out what is wrong with an entire society. Again, as with the translation of the Vice into a mere clown or buffoon, the interpreter often metamorphoses this distinctive figure into terms more amenable to the twentieth century, which finds the process of temptation more accessible than the allegory of the health of a kingdom.

A similar problem with selective interpretation is to be found in modern reactions to the second phase of the moral plays. For many readers today the final orderings (the heart of the theatrical sermons) seem obligatory or imposed, especially in contrast to the vitality of the Vice in phase one, so that the triumphant authority figures who set forth the dramatist's "message" appear dull and wooden, a product of what T. S. Eliot calls the "conventional moralizing of the epoch."[29] The modern critic who does take the trouble to read these plays therefore prefers the antics of the Vice to the homilies of the virtues (just as some readers of *Paradise Lost* prize Satan over Adam or God). As a result, the endings of the moral plays are seen as heavyhanded and merely obligatory, a charge leveled as well against the fifth acts of *Richard III* and *2 Henry IV*.

But is there any basis for the assumption that the endings of these moral plays lacked force or integrity for their original audiences? For one witness to the contrary, consider the testimony of Ralph Willis who describes the final moments of *The Cradle of Security* where two old men, representing the end of the world and the last judgment, "struck a fearful blow upon the Cradle" so that everyone vanished except for the corrupted prince who represented the wicked of the world. According to Willis writing some sixty or seventy years later: "This sight took such impression in me, that when I came towards man's estate, it was as fresh in my memory, as if I had seen it newly acted." Certainly, not all theatrical sermons had such an effect upon their spectators (although the allusions to the Vice's exit on the Devil's back suggest that other features of the moral climaxes were also remembered vividly). But when dealing with an age in which preachers drew enormous audiences, can we, largely on the basis of a modern aversion to the didactic, casually dismiss the original logic of these moral plays, especially if that logic may help us to understand more fully some facets of the drama in the age of Shakespeare? In a related context, Rosemond Tuve notes that "where we brush off the didacticism or the figurative reading of tales and stress their interest as straight recording or anecdotal narrative, the didacticism was . . . just as interesting, to a Renaissance reader of old books." Rather, she calls attention to "the lameness of some of the story sections, those portions we have been taught to think were the focus of literary interest and the author's real concern," and the obvious significance attached to the moralizations, the parts we have been taught were "tacked on to satisfy public, church, the stuffy bourgeois—anyone, in short, but the composing author."[30] Similarly, to relish the Vice but reject his fate is to allow our tastes to obscure a paradigm that would have been meaningful, if a bit old-fashioned, to Shakespeare and his contemporaries.

In conclusion, the Vice *is* a jester and entertainer; he *can* function as a tempter. Yet both these roles can be means to various dramatic ends, some of which may be missed if the modern reader concentrates solely upon entertainment and temptation. In particular, the Vice can epitomize what is wrong with an entire society rather than with a single Mankind figure, and, especially when opposed by allegorical personae who eventually control and supersede him, he can function effectively within a larger structure of which he is the most visible single part but a part nonetheless, not an independent entity. The Vice's fate can therefore serve as a major signal for the audience, especially if at first we enjoy his antics (like those of Richard III or Volpone). Our growing awareness of the implications of his actions, both for his victims and for himself, should call attention to the "dangerous sport" linked to the superficial glitter and appeal of vice, just as the nature of his opponents and the weapons they wield should instruct us about the larger issues of the play. The comic energy and dominance of the Vice are central to these plays but are also short-lived, with built-in limitations that tell us something important about the dramatic world in which he dwells. Regardless of any modern distaste for the virtues and moralized endings, the key to many late moral plays lies in the final phase in which the Vice is arrested and usually hanged by his allegorical opposites. Whatever the individual dramatist's point of view or diagnosis, this combination of a public Vice and a two phased action provides a workable formula to realize in the theatre both a diseased kingdom and a remedy.

The general paradigm developed in this chapter does not fit every late moral play, but, unlike the Humanum Genus pattern, it does recur in a high percentage of the plays extant between the 1550s and the 1580s. This dramatic formula was therefore available to the next generation, whether as an option to be adapted or, more subtly, as a "deep structure" taken for granted as one way of organizing the elements of a play (analogous to New Comedy). Given the limited nature of the evidence (especially the paucity of stage directions), I find it difficult to determine how widespread were images or techniques like the combination of the dagger of lath and the answering sword of Justice, but clearly the theatrical appeal of the Vice could be put to work in behalf of dramatic goals that push beyond entertainment alone to encompass the treatment and resolution of issues important to the dramatist. That the dagger of lath and the exit to Hell are remembered well in the next generation is then a tribute to both the energy of the dominant Vice in phase one and the importance of his fate in phase two when his dagger fails him and only Hell or hanging lies ahead. Jonson's equation of the Vice with Evil and Hell suggests to me not that he was mistaken about the earlier drama but rather that he knew its personae and strategies well enough to make shrewd use of them for his own satiric purposes.

To conceive of the Vice solely as an independent comedian or a tempter of Everyman is, then, to screen out options in the late moral drama that may help us to understand more fully Shakespeare's techniques for setting up his own version of a diseased kingdom. The chapters that follow will therefore concentrate upon four plays (*Richard III, 1* and *2 Henry IV*, and *All's Well That Ends Well*), three of which contain specific allusions to the Vice and all of which have been linked by scholars to the moral drama (with particular emphasis upon the Vice-like characteristics of Richard III, Falstaff, and Parolles). My continuing question will be: what advantages are to be gained by viewing these plays, especially their versions of phase two, in the light of the moral play options developed in this chapter?

3

My dagger, little cousin? With all my heart.
Richard III, III.i.111

Two Phased Structure in *Richard III*

Most postulations about Shakespeare's debt to the moral plays result not from firm evidence but from the critic or historian's perception of comparable figures or patterns (as with the often suggested link between the Humanum Genus figure and Othello). In contrast, to link Richard III and the Falstaff of *1 Henry IV* to the Vice is to follow Shakespeare's own cues as set up by specific lines within the two plays. Such passages, however, represent only a point of departure, for the modern interpreter still must confront the meaning and function of these allusions. Granted, most scholars find few difficulties here. Thus, the author of one often cited essay states that the "obvious allusions to the stock figures of the old religious and moral plays" scattered throughout Shakespearean drama "require little glossing for the person who knows anything at all about the early English drama,"[1] a position implicitly reaffirmed by the remarkably consistent annotations of these passages in modern editions. But, as demonstrated in the previous chapter, our sense of the Vice and the late moral play often does not correspond to the horizon of expectations shared by Shakespeare and his audience. What then is the result when a fuller understanding of the public Vice and the two phased action is brought to bear upon the specific allusions and the larger problems found in *Richard III* and *1 Henry IV*? Consider first III.i of *Richard III* where Richard is onstage with Prince Edward, the son of Edward IV soon to be murdered in the Tower. After a brief but impressive comment from the young prince, Richard says, aside: "So wise so young, they say, do never live long." When Prince Edward asks: "What say you, uncle?" Richard responds: "I say, without characters fame lives long," but then adds, for the audience: "Thus, like the formal Vice, Iniquity, / I moralize two meanings in one word" (III.i.79–83). G. Blakemore Evans's gloss in the Pelican edition (p. 572) typifies modern annotations of this passage. First, "formal Vice Iniquity" is explained as "the conventional Vice figure called Iniquity (the Vice in sixteenth-century morality plays symbolized in one character all the vices)," while "moralize two meanings in one word" is glossed as "play on a double meaning (as the Vice did) in a single phrase (i.e. *live long*, l. 79)." Editors and historians rightly point to the Vice's habitual use of just this technique: one meaning or quip for his victim, another true one, aside.[2]

Richard, then, is pointedly calling our attention to his use of a form of verbal trickery associated with the best known theatrical figure of the previous generation. The interpreter therefore can treat this allusion as no more than a kind of shorthand appropriate for the 1590s, Shakespeare's way of summing up deftly what Richard is doing at this one moment in a fashion meaningful for the original audience but obscure today (and hence often cut from modern productions). Scholars conversant with the late moral plays, however, often go a step further and find broader implications in this overt link between Richard and such an earlier prototype, with an emphasis upon the genealogy of Shakespeare's figure (an approach commonly taken to Falstaff as well). For example, Wolfgang Clemen recalls the Vice's expertise "at twisting the meaning of words and at the art of double entendre" as well as his ability to intersperse "his diabolical tricks with coarse jests and wordplay designed to entertain the audience" and suggests that "Richard's gift for verbal irony may well have stemmed from this source." Clemen also suggests that Richard may have "inherited from the allegorical *Vice*" that "triumphant glee with which he applauds his own skill at disguise and deception and his ability to cause trouble" along with his tendency to invite applause for his success at dissembling.[3] Similarly, Sidney Thomas links Richard (and Marlowe's Barabas) to the Vice Dissimulation, arguing that Shakespeare has taken over and "deepened" the old tradition "and created a figure of real human significance."[4] Anthony Hammond provides a lengthy list of Richard's Vice-like characteristics that includes "strange appearance, use of asides, discussion of plans with the audience, disguise, long avoidance, but ultimate suffering of punishment, moral commentary, . . . , self-explanation in soliloquy, satirical functions which include an attack on women, and various signs of depravity such as boasting and conceit, enjoyment of power, immoral sexuality."[5]

The best-known treatment of Richard as Vice is provided by Bernard Spivack. Building upon the massive documentation earlier in his book, Spivack observes that Richard uses the term "formal" in his allusion "to explain that, although he appears something different from the conventional and obvious Vice of the popular stage, he is imitating the method of that role." Spivack then links that method to specific speeches and devices. For example, the famous speech in 3 *Henry VI* on setting "the murderous Machiavel to school" (III.ii.124–95) "is neither more nor less than another version of the *moral pedigree* of the Vice, although we notice a naturalistic modification." Focusing largely upon the first two acts of *Richard III*, Spivack argues that "no 'formal Vice' weeps more fluently than Richard"; "none enjoys a happier intimacy with the audience"; and "by none is the art of deceit so lavishly cultivated, so merrily held up for exhibition." Nowhere is Richard "more brilliantly the Vice," he notes, than in "his ability to make others quarrel" (e.g., I.iii, II.i) or in his other "divisive achievements" with a wide range of figures. Spivack climaxes his analysis with a discussion of Richard's successful wooing of Lady Anne which he describes as "homiletic bravura in the dimension of display."[6]

Although illuminating for the dramatic historian, such discussions of Richard as Vice often seem reductive to the reader or spectator and at times appear to call into question Shakespeare's artistry or control. Indeed, Spivack goes so far as to argue that "the historical figure who ruled England dissolves into the theatrical figure who ruled the English stage" (p. 395), for, in his view, "we shall look in vain" in Richard for "character" or "motivation" in our terms. Rather, "for as long as the archaic role grips him" (presumably, for Spivack, the first half of the play) "he is compelled by its homiletic principle to display himself as the type of villainy, his regal ambitions lapsing into such obscurity that we remember them only by an effort" (pp. 403–4). Rather than invoking the terms of psychological realism characteristic of modern criticism, Spivack instead refers to "the unnaturalistic dimension of his role," "the repetitive and gratuitous deceit surviving out of the old Christian metaphor," and "the homiletic transparency of a personification in the morality drama" (pp. 406, 404). Here, in effect, Richard *is* a Vice.

Few of the many admirers of both title figure and play have accepted Spivack's conclusions. Rather, most critics acknowledge the Vice, along with the Senecan tyrant[7] and the stage Machiavel, as one of Richard's theatrical ancestors, but nevertheless consider the specific allusion (along with one other earlier passage)[8] of limited value in any analysis of Shakespeare's major themes and images. After all, given the reductive trap lurking ahead, what is to be gained by pursuing the link between Richard and the Vice? But remember the associations with this distinctive figure developed in the previous chapter, in particular the dagger of lath found regularly in the extant plays and often linked to the Vice by later writers, including Shakespeare himself. Thus, moments after Richard's allusion to "the formal Vice Iniquity," his other young nephew, Richard of York, asks: "I pray you, uncle, give me this dagger," to which Richard responds: "My dagger, little cousin? With all my heart."[9] In the bantering that follows, the two Richards playfully discuss the dagger and "the sword to it," with Gloucester concluding: "What, would you have my weapon, little lord?" (III.i.110–22) Moments after Richard compares himself to the Vice, Shakespeare places considerable emphasis upon his dagger, two passages that have no apparent connection for the modern reader but do fit together for a spectator in the early 1590s.

Since references to Richard's dagger do not appear elsewhere in the quarto or Folio, we have no way of knowing whether this distinctive weapon or the potential link to the Vice recurs out-side this scene (and distanced from the allusion to "the formal Vice Iniquity"). Shakespeare could easily have had the original actor (presumably Richard Burbage) use such a weapon at key moments, snapping it at potential victims in the fashion remem-bered by Jonson and Chapman, but no such signals survive in our texts. Of potential significance is the crucial stage business early in the play when Richard "*lays his breast open*," gives his sword to Lady Anne, admits his crimes against Henry VI and Prince Edward, and offers her the opportunity to kill him (I.ii. 173–96). At least twice before the climactic fight with Richmond, Richard's weapons are highly visible, with his sword in I.ii, even though in the hands of Anne, displaying his particular power, and the dagger of III.i an ominous prelude to the murder of the two young princes.

Even though evidence within the text is lacking, several ref-erences outside the play indicate some association between Richard and his dagger. Thus, Holinshed twice singles out this weapon. According to one passage, when Richard "went abroad, his eyes whirled about, his body privily fenced, his hand ever upon his dagger, his countenance and manner like one always ready to strike again." Elsewhere, Holinshed describes Richard as "ever unquiet," biting and chewing his lower lip: "beside that, the dagger which he wore, he would (when he studied) with his hand pluck up and down in the sheath to the midst, never draw-ing it fully out."[10] Such behavior is recalled in *The True Tragedy of Richard III* (1591) where the page describes Richard when alone: "if he hear one stir he riseth up, / And claps his hand upon his dagger straight, / Ready to stab him, what so e'er he be" (ll. 1778–80). Even more suggestive is Samuel Rowlands's de-scription in 1600 of gallants who "like *Richard* the usurper, swag-ger, / That had his hand continual on his dagger."[11] If Rowlands is indeed referring to Shakespeare's Richard III, the allusion suggests a repeated and very noticeable bit of stage business derived from Holinshed but also consistent with the link between Richard and the Vice. Even if the modern reader accepts this hypothetical dagger play as buttressing the link between Richard III and the Vice, the basic interpretative question remains: what is the point of such an allusion or connection? In the most limited sense, Richard's invocation of this prototype in III.i may only be a shared joke with the audience, a glancing allusion to provide a momentary comparison meaningful in the early 1590s but dispensable today. To go a step further, the allusion to "the formal Vice Iniquity" may be Shakespeare's way of signaling one facet of Richard's theatrical ancestry and therefore underscoring his skill at deception and intrigue, his distinctive humor, his manipulation of language, and his evil or threat to society. But, given the material presented in the previous chapter, need we stop here? If indeed Shakespeare is presenting to his audience in the 1590s a Richard who is Vice-like or clearly analogous to the Vice (a link established both by verbal allusions and by theatrical signals like the dagger), what are the implications for the play as a whole? In particular, if the paradigm of the public Vice and the two phased play is part of our horizon of expectations, how are we to react to both Richard III and *Richard III*?

With or without reference to the moral drama, many critics have described Richard (like the public Vice) as an epitome of what is wrong with England. For example, Hammond argues that "the Vice formed in Shakespeare's mind the natural theatrical mode of expressing inordinate evil, evil which springs from a context of decayed public morality, evil which has no satisfactory rational explanation" (p. 101). This "decayed public morality" has also been much in evidence throughout the three parts of *Henry VI*, so that, in Edward I. Berry's terms, the Vice "provides a natural symbol of the inhuman and anarchic residue of the dissension those plays portray," for this allegorical figure "demands little adjustment to become an embodiment of the accumulated perversions of civil war." Richard's chilling line "I am myself alone" (3 *Henry VI*, V.vi.83), as Berry notes, "merely translates into 'human' form a state of being which for the allegorical Vice is a necessary metaphysical condition." "In naturalizing the Vice-figure," according to Berry, "Shakespeare has adapted the allegorical alienation of the role to the moral and social alienation of the times he depicts: the Vice becomes an embodiment of the final stage of a long historical process."[12]

At the end of this process in this the last play of the tetralogy, Richard then acts out in extreme form what lies behind the many betrayals and moral compromises associated with figures like Clarence, Hastings, Buckingham, the various murderers, and even Lady Anne, not to mention lesser figures like the Mayor, the Cardinal, and other clergymen (a group Wilbur Sanders terms the play's "moral casualties").[13] A series of choric comments (e.g., in II.iii, III.vi, IV.i, and IV.iv) further link the health of the kingdom to Richard (a link perceived by readers and spectators without recourse to the Vice). As noted by A. P. Rossiter, Richard like the Vice becomes "the generator of roars of laughter at wickednesses (whether of deed or word) which the audience would immediately condemn in real life." For Rossiter, "a good third of the play is a kind of grisly *comedy*; in which we meet the fools to be taken in on Richard's terms, see them with his mind, and rejoice with him in their stultification." In this view of the play, Richard "inhabits a world where everyone deserves everything he can do to them; and in his murderous practical joking he is *inclusively* the comic exposer of the mental shortcomings (the intellectual and moral deformities) of this world of beings depraved and besotted."[14] Richard entertains us, exposes others, and epitomizes his world.

To posit a general analogy between Richard and the Vice (with or without the dagger) is by now commonplace; to suggest a link to the public Vice who epitomizes what is wrong with the kingdom is merely to put in slightly different terms a familiar reading of this play. But what of the larger two phased movement also associated with the Vice and the late moral plays? As Rossiter and other critics have noted, the facets of Richard that have continued to fascinate readers and spectators for centuries are exhibited primarily in the first three acts only to change or evaporate in IV.ii with Richard's accession to the throne and his thrust against the two princes in the Tower. "On the face of it," in Rossiter's terms, Richard may be "the demon-Prince, the caco-demon born of hell, the misshapen toad," yet "through his prow-ess as actor and his embodiment of the comic Vice and impish-to-fiendish humour, he offers the false as more attractive than the true (the actor's function), and the ugly and evil as admirable and amusing (the clown's game of value-reversals)."[15] By Act IV, however, if not sooner, "the ugly and evil" have ceased to be "ad-mirable and amusing." Rather, we are faced with the kind of "dangerous sport" provided by the previous generation's Vice-comedian that for much of the play entertains us (at the expense of various victims) until the full implications of our laughter and detachment become clear.[16] Like the Vice, Richard engages us with his demonic energy, his intelligence, and his obvious supe-riority to those around him, but, also like the Vice, that domi-nance is short-lived and doomed, especially when his Vice-like energy and amorality collide with a worthy opponent, a symbolic opposite who introduces a frame of reference or alternative set of values that cannot be mocked away, ignored, or subverted.

Many readers, however, especially those who prize the Vice-like wooer of Lady Anne and manipulator of Clarence, Hastings, the Greys, and the Mayor, are uncomfortable with Shakespeare's final movement. Although the terms in which such discomfort is expressed vary widely, many would agree with Michael Neill's as-sessment that the "weakness" of the play's conclusion lies "not in the dramaturgy of Richard's moral collapse but in the dramatist's moralization of his fall, in his refusal to confront the real issues which the play raises."[17] The most forceful argument for such a failure on Shakespeare's part is provided by Wilbur Sanders who starts his provocative chapter by quoting from Richmond's speech that ends the play (V.v.15–41), a speech he associates with "an election speaker, addressing an audience cleared of hecklers and packed with supporters, as he scores easy points against the abominated and unrepresented opponent and paints a rosy future for right-thinking men." "If this is the deeply felt centre of the play and the fount of its profoundest discoveries," argues Sanders, "then the play offers only a profound platitude, and most of the rest is either botched or totally irrelevant." Sanders, however, does find "plenty of life in *Richard III* still," but "to cherish that life" he suggests "that certain amputations must be performed—starting, I suggest with this speech." According to his argument, "the kind of human/critical awareness which Shakespeare has set in motion in the course of the play makes short work of the platitude with which he tries to wind it up," for "he has created an audience which is now too wary of simplifications to be fobbed off with this one." Throughout his subsequent analysis, Sanders then finds in the final movement only "a wooden rectitude" or "something willed and rhetorical" or "a stratum of moral platitude" (in his terms, "the heart beats elsewhere"), so that in his final paragraph he laments Shakespeare's introduction of "the idea of Providence, which, disconcertingly allied with a naive chauvinism, leaves the closing minutes of the play sadly contracted to the stature of Tudor propaganda."[18]

Neill and Sanders speak for many readers uncomfortable with the final phase of *Richard III*, especially Richard's decline at the expense of Richmond (a discomfort, as suggested by Sanders, often reflected in heavy cuts by directors in Act V). No "historical" explanation or justification will fully counter such a reaction (just as no scholarly argument will offset the modern reader's preference for the Vice over the virtues who control the final phase of the late moral plays). But can a twentieth-century formulation of "the real issues" or a modern distaste for "wooden rectitude" or "moral platitude" fully account for the strategy Shakespeare has chosen not with us but with his audience of the early 1590s in mind? Like Rossiter, I too am dubious about writing off *Richard III* as "early work," "an evasive, criticism-dodging term" (p.4) that masks a refusal to accept what the play has to offer us. Rather, I prefer to work with the assumption that here, early in his career, Shakespeare is providing his version of a dramatic paradigm obscure today but well known to his intended audience and is therefore taking for granted a horizon of expectations that assumes, even demands, that a Vice-like figure be confronted, exposed, arrested, and punished once his dramatic career has been played out. What if, in the minds of the original artist and spectators, both the Vice-like villain-hero and his symbolic opposite (to whom most of the supposedly tacked-on platitudes are given) were both constituent parts of one available paradigm or dramatic strategy? How would such an alternative model drawn from the late moral plays affect our sense of the shape of *Richard III?*

One immediate result is a rationale or logic behind Richmond's role and presence. Admittedly, Shakespeare does not introduce into his history play an allegorical emissary from God wielding a sword of Justice, but he does provide for Richard's ultimate antagonist and symbolic opposite images and associations that follow the pattern found in the late moral plays. Thus, in his major speeches Richmond calls upon God, "whose captain I account myself," to put "thy bruising irons of wrath" in his soldier's hands "that they may crush down with a heavy fall / The usurping helmets of our adversaries" and to "make us thy ministers of chastisement" (V.iii.109–14). Later, in his oration to his army, Richmond is given such lines as: "God and our good cause fight upon our side; . . . For what is he they follow? . . . One that hath ever been God's enemy. / Then if you fight against God's enemy, / God will in justice ward you as his soldiers; . . . Then in the name of God and all these rights, / Advance your standards, draw your willing swords" (ll. 241–65). To critics like Sanders, such speeches may smack of the "wooden rectitude" or moral platitudes of a suspect modern speaker, but in the early 1590s, even putting aside Tudor propaganda, Richmond's presence (as defined and developed here) would have fulfilled the climactic part of a familiar pattern or paradigm in terms amenable to the historical world and images of this play.

Richmond's role as an alternative, moreover, is not limited solely to Act V, for even discounting the brief prophetic moment with Henry VI (*3 Henry VI*, IV.vi.65–76), Shakespeare has carefully prepared us for his appearance. Significantly, we first hear of Richmond just after Richard's high water mark as deceiver and manipulator (his duping of the Mayor and citizens in

III. vii) and just before our first view of him as king. In the midst of the gloom and despair of IV. i, Dorset is told by his mother: "if thou wilt outstrip death, go cross the seas, / And live with Richmond, from the reach of hell" (ll. 41–42), an injunction repeated by the Duchess of York ("go thou to Richmond, and good fortune guide thee!"—l. 91). "This slaughterhouse" (l. 43) in Richard's England is therefore contrasted to the alternative space where Richmond dwells. Again, in the next scene, where Richard disdains Buckingham and seeks out murderers for the two princes, he receives the news that "Dorset is fled to Richmond" (IV. ii. 84), news that so preoccupies him that he twice gives injunctions to Stanley about Richmond's mother (ll. 86, 91–92), recalls Henry VI's prophecy "that Richmond shall be king" (ll. 94–97), worries away at that prophecy (ll. 99–100), focuses again on Richmond's name (l. 102), and ends by recalling a disturbing moment when he was startled because of another prophecy that he "should not live long after I saw Richmond" (l. 106). Similarly, in the next scene Richard seems to be in control when he gets news of the princes' deaths, outlines his disposition of rival claimants to the throne, and reveals that he is to be Richmond's rival for the hand of young Elizabeth ("to her go I, a jolly thriving wooer"— IV. iii. 43), but the scene ends with news of Buckingham's revolt and the Bishop of Ely's flight to Richmond, news that elicits from Richard: "Ely with Richmond troubles me more near / Than Buckingham and his rash-levied strength" (ll. 49–50).

At the end of the long IV. iv, Richmond then ceases to be a removed symbolic alternative and becomes instead a direct threat to Richard. Immediately after the usurper's apparently successful wooing of Queen Elizabeth, Ratcliffe arrives with news of "a puissant navy" riding "on the western coast" with Richmond as admiral, so that "to our shores / Throng many doubtful hollow-hearted friends, / Unarmed, and unresolved to beat them back" (IV. iv. 433–39). At this point, moreover, Richard clearly begins to lose control, as evidenced by his sending both Catesby and Ratcliffe off without first giving them their messages. When Stanley arrives with news that "Richmond is on the seas" (l. 462) and that "stirred up by Dorset, Buckingham, and Morton, / He makes for England, here to claim the crown" (ll. 467–68), Richard explodes: "Is the chair empty? is the sword unswayed? / Is the king dead? the empire unpossessed?" (ll. 469–70) The remainder of the scene brings news both good and bad for Richard, much of it revolving around Richmond, news that climaxes with the announcement of a landing "with a mighty power" at Milford (l. 533). The brief scene that follows (often cut in production) adds an important coda, for not only do we hear of more figures "of great name and worth" resorting to Richmond (IV.v.16) and of Stanley's true allegiances, but Stanley also reveals that Queen Elizabeth "hath heartily consented" that Richmond, not Richard, "should espouse Elizabeth her daughter" (ll. 7–8), a revelation that gives new resonance to Richard's "relenting fool, and shallow, changing woman!" delivered at her exit in the previous scene (l. 431). As a result, "princely Richmond" (IV.v.9), who finally does appear in V.ii with a new set of companions (Oxford, Blunt, Herbert) and much reference to "God's name" (ll. 14, 22), conscience (l. 17), and "perpetual peace" (l. 15), has already won a battle (for the hand of young Elizabeth) Richard had deemed crucial (and thought he had won).

Richard's failure to win (and keep) either the consent of Queen Elizabeth or the hand of young Elizabeth (as opposed to his equally difficult yet successful wooing of Lady Anne in I.ii) is but one of several revealing instances wherein the energy, rhetoric, and intelligence that had won him victory after victory in the first three acts now fail him in the final phase of the action. The reasons for such a change may be complex, but one obvious key is the presence, starting in IV.i, of an alternative figure around whom figures like Dorset, Ely, and eventually Stanley (not to mention the "many doubtful hollow-hearted friends") can rally (in contrast to the two helpless boys in the Tower). In this final movement of the play, Richard no longer displays his special Vice-like relationship with the audience or characteristic demonic humor (so scholars linking Richard to the Vice often skip over the last two acts). Nonetheless, if the critic or scholar has in mind a paradigm that includes the arrest and punishment of the Vice, the latter phase of Richard's career is as much a part of the traditional pattern as the much admired first phase. In-deed, the more closely one looks at this play in terms of such a two phased movement, the more evident becomes Shakespeare's carefully wrought dramatic strategy that involves far more than Richmond as a heavy-handed spokesman for wooden rectitude or Tudor propaganda.

Indeed, if the modern reader has in mind not merely the single figure of the Vice but rather the general two phased move-ment of the late moral play, many details and events fall into place, for Richard's decline clearly is linked to the failure of spe-cific tactics and even of specific properties that earlier had served him well. Most obviously, the same arguments that had suc-ceeded with Lady Anne either fail or do not hold for very long with Queen Elizabeth (in a scene in which Richard is forced to go far beyond his original brief and hazard his future fortunes in his "myself myself confound" speech—IV.iv.397–405). Simi-larly, the divisive tactics that had eliminated a series of rivals, enemies, and roadblocks (Clarence, the Greys, Hastings, the two princes, Buckingham) no longer work against Richmond and what he stands for in Act V. Like Revenge faced with Amity, Ill Report faced with True Report, or Courage faced with Au-thority and Correction, the Richard who had seemed unstop-pable is now stymied, even flustered, when forced to confront his symbolic opposite.

Consider some specific moments and images. To justify to the Mayor and to the world the rapid execution of Hastings, Richard and Buckingham enter "*in rotten armor, marvellous ill-favored*" (III.v.o.s.d.). This outlandish costume then has a significant effect upon the subsequent scene, for the more bizarre the ap-pearance of these two figures, the more of a sardonic twist is given to their scarcely believable claims about Hastings and to the intimidated Mayor's acceptance of "all your just proceedings in this cause" (l. 66). But this ungainly armor, mockingly thrust on against nonexistent enemies in Act III, reappears in Act V as the armor that does not or cannot protect Richard (who appears "*in arms*"—V.iii.o.s.d.) against Richmond (and, as in *Macbeth*, much can be done in production with the arming before the battle of one or both of these figures). Like many other images in this play, the rotten armor has an immediate and distinctive impact upon the tone and meaning of III.v (where Richard appears to be in total control, able to dare other figures not to believe him) but takes on a far different meaning when the opponent is not the Mayor (or the two helpless princes or Hastings or Clarence) but the untainted Richmond, God's captain, who fills the moral and political vacuum in which Richard has thrived. As with Haphazard in *Apius and Virginia*, the same strategy that had worked consistently for Richard earlier in the play only leads to disaster when he must confront his version of Reward.

Relevant too is the role played by visible figures of religion, for among the many lesser figures Richard manipulates or intimidates are several clergymen who, thanks to their distinctive costumes, stand out for the viewer's eye. First, in III.i Buckingham (obviously speaking for Richard) persuades the Cardinal that "you break no privilege nor charter" by removing young Richard of York from sanctuary; the Cardinal joins the list of "moral casualties" when he responds: "My lord, you shall overrule my mind for once" (III.i.54, 57). Next, Richard's sending off the Bishop of Ely for strawberries (III.iv.31–34, 46–47) provides a small but highly visible example of his ability to move around or control a figure of religion. Most revealing is the appearance of "*Richard aloft, between two Bishops*" (III.vii.94.s.d.), glossed by Buckingham as "two props of virtue for a Christian prince, / To stay him from the fall of vanity," along with "a book of prayer in his hand—/ True ornaments to know a holy man" (ll. 96–99). Here and throughout this scene, Richard's pose of piety ("O, do not swear, my lord of Buckingham"—l. 220) clearly is based upon his shrewd sense of which façade best will suit his purpose—here to win the support of the Mayor and citizens. For the Machiavel aspiring to be king, the cloak of religion is a useful tool, a politic ploy with no substance, just as conscience can be written off as merely "a word that cowards use, / Devised at first to keep the strong in awe" (V.iii.310–11).

But Richmond's presence in Act V (like the presence of the virtues opposed to the Vice) provides a new standard by which to measure such choices or strategems. Few readers will miss the obvious heavenly associations Shakespeare attaches to this untainted figure, but much easier to miss (and not picked up in any production I have seen) is the potentially significant contribution of Sir Christopher Urswick in IV.v. Even when this moment *is* included in a modern production, this one-scene figure often is telescoped together with someone else (so in the 1978 production at the Oregon Shakespearean Festival Urswick became Oxford), but important here is the fact that, as noted by Hammond (p. 302), Urswick was "a priest, chaplain to the Countess of Richmond." Not only does this brief scene reveal Richard's failure with Queen Elizabeth and the rising tide of support for Richmond, but, in contrast to those figures so easily manipulated in Act III, one of the two speakers is a clergyman, a preview of the religious imagery to be associated with Richmond and an epitome of that larger framework Richard (like the Vice) must confront. If Urswick (who is not mentioned again) is then included among "*the Lords*" (V.iii.223.s.d.) or the "*others*" (V.ii.0.s.d.) who attend Richmond, the presence of at least one figure of religion would serve as the counterweight to the cardinal and bishops of Act III.

Similarly, many other images, small and large, link the two phases of the play. For example, the sun that "disdains to shine" on Richard before the battle (V.iii.279) recalls earlier moments in his heyday (as in his mocking self-praise after wooing Anne: "Shine out, fair sun, till I have bought a glass, / That I may see my shadow as I pass"—I.ii. 262–63). The appearance of eleven ghosts calls to mind the price in human lives Richard was glad to pay to gain and keep the crown, but his "coward conscience" speech (V.iii.178–207) reveals that the price is even higher than he had bargained for, while, in the context of phase two, his final order for an execution (of young George Stanley—l. 345) is never carried out. In Acts III and IV Lord Stanley had been too weak to oppose Richard, most notably in his silent exit along with the others when Richard delivers his sentence on Hastings and then announces: "The rest that love me, rise and follow me" (III.iv.79). But in the final phase, given a worthy alternative in

Richmond, the wavering Stanley can make his pivotal decision at the risk of his son's life and emerge as the figure who presents the crown to Henry VII.

As in the moral plays, the absence of informative stage directions prevents us from seeing how specifically Shakespeare chose to set up such links or contrasts. Particularly unhelpful is the Folio stage direction for the climactic fight: "*Alarum, Enter Richard and Richmond; they fight; Richard is slain*" (V.v.o.s.d.). Consider some of the possibilities left open by "*they fight.*" For example, in at least two recent productions (Stratford Festival Canada 1977, Oregon Shakespearean Festival 1978) the blow that killed Richard echoed unmistakably the thrust he asked for but did not receive from Lady Anne in I.ii, an echo that underscores the difference between his Vice-like control of phase one and his loss of control to an alternative force in the final movement. If Richard is killed with his own weapon (an often used conclusion to modern stage fights), his fate would confirm Buckingham's assertion of the power of "that high All-seer" who forces "the swords of wicked men / To turn their own points in their masters' bosoms" (V.i.20–24). To emphasize Richmond's role as God's captain, his blows (delivered with a distinctive weapon analogous to the sword of Justice) could fall with more than human force, or, conversely, the staging could emphasize not Richmond's strength but Richard's weakness or surprising ineptness when faced with his symbolic opposite. Especially for the original audience, a Richard armed only with a dagger compelled to fight a sword-bearing opponent would evoke the familiar (and expected) climax to the career of such a Vice-like figure. I am *not* suggesting an exit to Hell on the Devil's back, but since no indication is provided for the disposition of Richard's body, some kind of distinctive removal could reinforce such a pattern (e.g., a descent of the body through a trap-door into stage "hell"). Whether or not Richard's weapon is beaten down, broken, or otherwise diminished, the final moments epitomize the failure of a figure and force that had been dominant.

I introduce such conjectures about staging not to exhibit my ingenuity but to suggest how easily (and emphatically) a production of *Richard III*, then or now, could develop a two phased pattern comparable to that found in the moral drama. Given the horizon of expectations in the 1590s (that included, among many other things, the late moral plays), to view Richard solely as a modern "character" or even as a Vice-like intriguer whose activities cease to be of interest somewhere in Act IV is to screen out meaningful parts of the larger design. Rather, the obvious allusion in III.i and the possible links to the Vice's dagger should serve as a signal to lead the informed spectator to a fuller understanding of the entire play, especially Act V and the role played by Richmond. Disdain for the moralization of Richard's fall and Richmond's wooden rectitude may suit the modern palate, but on what basis, after all, are we to determine "the real issues" or the true shape of this early but nonetheless well crafted and fully realized Shakespeare play?

In conclusion, let me emphasize that I am not claiming that Richard's allusion to the Vice is a Rosetta Stone with which a modern reader can decipher a language otherwise untranslatable. Nonetheless, many associations shared by Shakespeare, his fellow actors, and his original spectators *have* been lost. Many of these losses will never be recovered; indeed, often the modern reader will not even be conscious that something has been lost. But historical scholarship can retrieve at least some of these contextual materials—in this instance, shared associations drawn from the legacy bequeathed by the late moral plays. As skeptics delight in pointing out, such a scholarly approach to allusions and other contextual problems has, upon occasion, produced a parade of learning that overwhelms the text (an academic version of Hamlet's thinking too precisely on the event). Yet as W. W. Greg observes: "Every item of historical evidence performs a two-fold function: positively it enlarges the basis we have to build on, and enables us to extend the structure of valid inference; negatively it is often of even greater service in limiting the field of admissible conjecture."[19] To apply the findings presented in chapter two to *Richard III* is to build upon Shakespeare's own allusions so to extend our understanding of the figures, images, and larger structure found in one of his best known plays.

4

Nor can one England brook a double reign
Of Harry Percy and the Prince of Wales
1 Henry IV, V.iv.65–66

Dual Protagonists in *1 Henry IV*

As with *Richard III* (or *Othello* or *Macbeth*), to posit a link between *1 Henry IV* and the moral plays is to tread familiar ground. Indeed, for the first such suggestion the literary historian can cite no less of an expert than Prince Hal himself who describes Falstaff as "that reverend vice, that grey iniquity, that father ruffian, that vanity in years" (II.iv.431–32). Using Hal's analysis as their cue, scholars have offered a detailed account of Falstaff's dramatic bloodlines that often includes considerable reference to the Vice and the allegorical tradition. The reader with a genealogical bent can therefore choose among such formidable figures as Gluttony, Riot, Sloth, and Vanity (alone or in various combinations) for the honored spot at the top of the fat knight's family tree.[1]

With such allegorical possibilities already at hand, it is an easy leap to seeing Prince Hal, the Vice's companion, as a Humanum Genus figure, an Every Prince with a psychomachia conflict.[2] Thus, in one of the classic studies of its kind, John Dover Wilson argues that *Henry IV* is "Shakespeare's great morality play." The plays and tales involving the Prodigal Son, according to Wilson, invariably contain "the same three principal characters: the tempter, the younker, and the father with property to bequeath and counsel to give," so he argues that Shakespeare has presented Hal as younker, Falstaff as tempter, and Henry IV as the father figure whose property to be bestowed is the kingdom itself. Such a formulation neatly ties together many strands of the two plays and is basic to Wilson's thesis "that the reign of this marvellous Lord of Misrule must have an end, that Falstaff must be rejected by the Prodigal Prince, when the time for reformation came."[3]

Although this approach to the two plays has won many adherents, Wilson himself admitted that his account of Shakespeare's dramatic plan did not include many "alluring stretches" and several significant figures, most notably Hotspur (p. 15). Admittedly, many readers have viewed these two plays primarily in terms of Falstaff and Prince Hal, but these two figures do not dominate the dramatic time of *1 Henry IV*. If one eliminates the overplot scenes (e.g., I.i, parts of Act V) and other expository moments (e.g., II.i, IV.iv), the prince and his circle are allocated I.ii, II.ii (the robbery), II.iv (the famous tavern scene), III.ii (Hal's interview with his father), III.iii (the second tavern scene), IV.ii (Falstaff and his ragged army), V.i (Hal's challenge), the battle scenes, and the concluding V.v. But the rebels are allotted equal time: in the long latter part of I.iii (the plot), in II.iii (Hotspur with the letter, then with his wife), in III.i (with Glendower and Mortimer), in the pre-battle scenes (IV.i, IV.iii), and in V.ii where Hotspur receives the king's supposed message. To describe Hal as Every Prince and *1 Henry IV* as analogous to *Mankind* or *Lusty Juventus* or *Wit and Science* is therefore to simplify and distort Shakespeare's carefully wrought structure, to let a preconceived notion of "the morality play" take precedence over the evidence.

To note such limitations is not necessarily to deny Wilson's basic insights or the potential links between *1 Henry IV* and the late moral plays. After all, in a variety of ways (especially in the famous tavern scene) Falstaff *is* associated with the Vice. But, as noted in chapter one, Wilson's proposition about "Shakespeare's great morality play," like many similar arguments, is based upon a limited and at times misleading conception of the form as received in the age of Shakespeare, a narrowed horizon of expectations that then can constrict the view of the modern interpreter. In particular, the axiomatic equation of "morality play" (again, *not* a sixteenth-century term) with the Humanum Genus figure can stand between us and the actual models or paradigms available in the late moral plays. Conversely, to confront the potential in such plays is to open up various possibilities (in *1 Henry IV* and elsewhere) that otherwise many remain obscure.

Consider the basis for the formulation about "the morality play" assumed by Wilson and most scholars. For roughly a century (between the 1420s and the 1530s) the extant moral plays clearly do share many features, so that a protagonist named Humanum Genus, Mankind, Everyman, or Wit is at the center of such plays as *The Castle of Perseverance, Mankind, Everyman, Nature, The Interlude of the Four Elements, Magnificence, The Interlude of Youth, The World and the Child*, and *Wit and Science*. That Mankind figure and the accompanying dramatic formula (involving virtues, vices, temptation, and repentance) then does persist, with some adjustments, into at least a few plays of the early Elizabethan period: Wager's *The Longer Thou Livest* and *Enough Is as Good as a Feast*; a few "hybrid" tragedies like *Cambises* and *Horestes*; and, perhaps, such lost plays as *The Cradle of Security* and *The Play of Plays and Pastimes*. Most of the later plays, however, bear little resemblance to *The Castle of Perseverance* or *Everyman*, so that *All for Money, Like Will to Like*, and *The Tide Tarrieth No Man* (to cite three representative examples) clearly lack the "morality play" gene and therefore are treated by many scholars as degenerate offspring of the original healthy stock. Thus, Willard Farnham describes the earlier plays as "mainly intent upon grasping human nature in some form of abstraction standing for mankind as a whole," but then notes that the protagonist of the sixteenth century plays "tends to lose the abstract quality of *Humanum Genus*." Farnham therefore concludes that "the morality in Elizabeth's reign is obviously drawing near the end of its service as a literary form. With few exceptions it shows distinct loss of ability to attain unification in a central character, and it shows a related tendency to rambling diffuseness."[4]

To test this hypothesis, let me introduce some relevant facts. First, a look at one scholarly guide[5] reveals forty to forty-five titles of extant or lost moral plays between 1400 and 1558 but, in contrast, 50 titles between 1559 and 1590. Admittedly, such a numerical yardstick, especially when based largely upon titles rather than extant texts, is arbitrary and potentially misleading, but such figures do make it difficult to envisage "the morality play," however defined, withering away during the second half of the sixteenth century or "obviously drawing near the end of its service as a literary form" (especially if one also factors in the evidence about the morall from 1578 through the seventeenth century). What we know about extant and lost plays, moreover, suggests a supple, all-purpose dramatic kind that could be presented at court or in the provinces, could be adapted to many different ends, and could take many shapes. Thus, although many of these plays are associated with small touring troupes, during this period several lost plays were performed before the queen, while an extant play, *Liberality and Prodigality*, was performed before her as late as 1601.[6] As to theme or emphasis, in addition to their traditional homiletic concerns the dramatists were able to use this form for religious controversy, social satire, and even a defense of the players and the stage against Puritan attack (*The Play of Plays and Pastimes*).[7] As to dramatic form, the extant plays provide a wide variety of options, ranging from the public Vice and two phased action described in chapter two to the anomalous *All for Money* with its thematically linked episodes but no consecutive plot.

Such observations, however, do not answer Farnham's charge that the late moral plays fail "to attain unification in a central character." But why should they? On what basis has a Humanum Genus figure been made the essential criterion for "the morality play"? Rather, as Madeleine Doran reminds us, "multiplicity is one of the first things that strikes us as characteristic of sixteenth century literary art," for the major authors "saw beauty in multiplicity of detail" and looked at the world in terms of "abundant variousness."[8] Similarly, as David Bevington notes, classical precept may have stressed "aesthetic laws of unity, correspondence, subordination, and the like," but Elizabethan practice placed a premium upon "repetitive effect, multiplicity, episode, progressive theme."[9] If Everyman, Wit, or Youth is no longer the protagonist of the late moral play, can the historian ignore what may be a development rather than a degeneration of an earlier model or paradigm? Not to consider such a possibility is to bow to the selective tradition and to impose neoclassic or modern expectations upon a lively Elizabethan dramatic form that has been accurately described as "the dominant mode of popular dramatic expression for about a century."[10]

In chapter two I dealt with one alternative to "unification in a central character" found in the late moral plays (the public Vice and the two phased action). Let me turn now to another related paradigm. First, consider the avowed purpose of Ulpian Fulwell's *Like Will to Like* (1568): to demonstrate "not only what punishment followeth those that will rather follow licentious living, than to esteem and follow good counsel: and what great benefits and commodities they receive that apply them unto virtuous living and good exercises" (p. 304). To achieve this homiletic goal, however, Fulwell does not resort to a Humanum Genus figure and a psychomachia conflict but offers instead a Vice (Nichol Newfangle) who manipulates and corrupts six vicious figures who, taken together, provide "an inventory of social evil: vile language, rioting, heavy drinking, thievery, and beggary."[11] The alternative way of life is posited dramatically through Virtuous Living who stands in firm opposition to Tom Tosspot, Cuthbert Cutpurse, and the other fallen figures. Similarly, in *The Tide Tarrieth No Man* (1576) George Wapull presents his moral thesis by means of a Vice and his many victims (a grasping landlord, a greedy usurer, an aspiring courtier, an extravagant young married couple) and supplies an alternative in Faithful Few, who perseveres and ultimately rescues Christianity. To preach their dramatic sermons, both dramatists have set up an emphatic contrast between a series of degenerate figures drawn from contemporary society (all vulnerable to the Vice and what he stands for) and their virtuous, godly counterparts who are given less dramatic time but nonetheless are expected to carry a good deal of moral freight. The absence of a Humanum Genus figure as the dramatic focus does *not* necessarily indicate the absence of form or structure. Rather, Fulwell and Wapull *do* employ an appropriate theatrical strategy, albeit one not prized by scholars like Farnham. A related strategy can be seen in an earlier play, W. Wager's *Enough Is as Good as a Feast* (1560), which provides not a wide range of degenerate figures but rather two protagonists, one virtuous and one vicious. The long opening scene presents the confrontation between Worldly Man and Heavenly Man in which the former is converted, so that when he next appears he is accompanied by and satisfied with Enough. But the Vice (Covetous) and his henchmen win Worldly Man away from Enough and lead him into various abuses of his earthly possessions. As a result, at the height of his prosperity Worldly Man denies his debts and obligations, ignores the Prophet's message of impending doom, is struck down by God's Plague, and finally is carried off by Satan, who encourages all worldly men in the audience to follow the same path. Although Wager devotes much of his dramatic time to this vicious figure, Heavenly Man does play a major role in the opening scene and makes a brief but significant appearance (ll. 949–69) after the Vice's successful temptation of his counterpart. Then, in the final scene Heavenly Man, Enough, and Contentation provide a lengthy analysis of Worldly Man's career and praise the life devoted to heavenly treasure and satisfied with enough, with Heavenly Man rewarded with Rest rather than with God's Plague and damnation. Although dramatic time may not be equally distributed, the dramatist's thesis is conveyed primarily through the contrast between these two protagonists who act out alternative ways of life. In addition, Covetous, who places much emphasis upon his cap, gown, and chain, and Enough, who is plainly dressed, are set off against each other, both in costume and as choices open to the protagonists. In short, Wager contrasts two ways of life by means of two allegorical protagonists, each with a set of companions who epitomize the choices made.

The most fully developed example of this dramatic strategy is to be found in *The Trial of Treasure* (1567). In his opening scene the anonymous playwright provides a confrontation between Lust and Just that starts with recriminations and culminates in a wrestling match in which Lust appears "*to have the better at the first*" (p. 266) but eventually is cast down and driven off the stage. Allegorically, we have been shown "the conflict of the just, / Which all good men ought to use and frequent," for every man should strive against his version of Lust: "And though, at the first, he seem sturdy to be, / The Lord will convince him for you in the end" (pp. 266–67). Through this verbal and physical confrontation, the dramatist has begun his play with a working definition of the two ways of life basic to his thesis, and called attention to the short term strength of Lust and the ultimate victory of Just thanks to "the might of his spirit that dwelleth in me." The way of Lust is further defined in the second scene when this already corrupted figure accepts as his servants the Vice Inclination and his allegorical henchmen. Throughout these scenes, moreover, the author provides continual signposts to point us towards the contrast at the basis of his strategy (e.g.: "Thus see you how men, that are led by their lust, / Dissent from the virtuous, goodly and just"—p. 275).

In the third and fourth scenes the dramatist sets up the first of two simple yet revealing visual analogues. First, Just and Sapience discuss "treasures here gotten" which are "of a vanishing kind" as opposed to "treasures of the mind" that "do continually remain." With Sapience as his guide, Just then bridles the Vice, a highly visible stage action that demonstrates how "every man, that will be called Just," should "bridle and subdue his beastly inclination, / That he in the end may obtain perfect trust, / The messenger of God to give sight to salvation" (p. 279). Moments later, however, Lust reverses this process and unbridles the Vice (who has promised to lead him to Lady Treasure). In obvious homiletic terms, the bridling of Inclination allows man to "obtain perfect trust," while the unbridling is associated with the hope for a treasure that (in spite of the Vice's assurances) obviously will not "continually remain." In an economical and the-

atrically effective fashion, this back-to-back bridling and unbridling has further developed the contrast between these two ways
of life.

In subsequent scenes the playwright produces a similar effect
by bringing on-stage, again in back-to-back actions, the only two
female figures in the play along with their attendant satisfac-
tions. First, Just appears with Trust, "a *woman plainly apparelled*,"
and Contentation to provide a lengthy analysis of "true trust"
and "celestial treasure" (pp. 283–85). This heavenly alternative
is countered by Lust's appearance accompanied by Treasure, "*a
woman finely appareled*" (p. 288), and by Pleasure, who "will be
always with Treasure in sight" (p. 291). Clearly, Lady Treasure is
analogous to Lady Trust and Pleasure is analogous to Contentation (a relationship that could easily be heightened by means of
costume or blocking). To drive home the allegorical thesis, the
Vice tells Lust how well off he is compared to those who choose
"the life of the just," for "they be compelled to possess contentation, / Having no treasure but trust of salvation" (p. 290).
Again, as with the bridling-unbridling, the dramatist offers us a
highly visible contrast between two ways of life, this time by
means of analogous figures and comparable situations.

The play's conclusion comes as no surprise. Lust ignores God's
Visitation (who takes away Pleasure) and persists in his foolish
trust in Treasure until he is taken off by Time, who returns with a
similitude of dust and rust to signal the ends of Lust and Treasure.
In contrast, Just bridles the Vice a second time, receives a crown
from Trust, and earns Consolation. Although the dramatist's
message is no different from that found in *Enough* or other similar
works of the period, what *is* distinctive here is the tightly knit
dramatic structure built around dual protagonists, each representing a way of life, each accompanied by analogous companions (Lady Trust and Lady Treasure, Contentation and Pleasure,
even God's Visitation and Consolation). At the center of the
play lies a series of episodes that spell out the basic contrasts in
consecutive scenes by means of the bridling and unbridling of the
Vice or the introduction of visually analogous figures who epitomize the key choices. Here then is a moral play from Queen

Elizabeth's reign with a carefully wrought dramatic strategy well suited to its homiletic goals, a strategy that may be an offshoot of the Humanum Genus model but nonetheless a branch with some significant variations and therefore some distinct advantages over the original stock. If the reader can isolate structure and technique from content, here is a paradigm from the late moral plays with a decided potential for comparing two attitudes or characters or ways of life, a paradigm that could prove fruitful for a dramatist concerned with issues other than the fall of Worldly Man or Lust. "Unification in a central character" is decidedly *not* the sole means by which the late moral dramatist could achieve his goals.

What then are the implications of this paradigm for the age of Shakespeare? Consider in particular the recurring formal problems faced by the authors of the many history plays found at the end of the century. Thus, Irving Ribner has argued that "the morality drama contained elements admirably suited to the dramatic presentation of history in such a way that the didactic ends of Tudor historiography might be served." Most important, according to Ribner, was the "sense of form" available in the moral drama "by which the elements of history could be related to one another and made to constitute a meaningful whole." Ribner's next sentence then reveals the "sense of form" he has in mind: "The stock morality device of *Humanum Genus* torn between good and evil angels, for instance, could easily be translated into terms of a king torn between good and evil counselors, as we have so clearly illustrated in *Woodstock* and *Richard II*." For Ribner, then, "the dramatic pattern of the morality play," by which he means "the stock morality device of *Humanum Genus* torn between good and evil angels," was incorporated into the Elizabethan history play "where it is perhaps most perfectly and strikingly evidenced in *Henry IV*."[12]

Although Ribner's formulation (like Wilson's) can be fruitful (e.g., for *Woodstock*), it does not make allowances for any "dramatic pattern" other than that associated with the Humanum Genus figure and therefore precludes any later developments in the moral drama that might in turn have yielded other paradigms

for an Elizabethan dramatist writing a history play. But, as I have
also argued in chapter two, such dramatic evolution *is* to be
found during the second half of the sixteenth century, even
though the relevant plays are little known today (despite the
work of Bevington and T. W. Craik).[13] Admittedly, I know of no
evidence that *The Trial of Treasure* served as a direct source for
later plays, but, given the small number of plays that have survived from this period,[14] the presence in even one or two of dual
protagonists and analogous companions suggests that such a dramatic strategy was one recognized means to achieve the homiletic goals announced by Fulwell. Again, as with the morall versus "the morality play," the question arises: where in the moral
drama should the historian look for "a sense of form by which the
elements of history could be related to one another and made to
constitute a meaningful whole"? In the best known plays canonized by the selective tradition? Or in the plays printed and presumably performed during the boyhoods of Marlowe and Shakespeare? To me it seems obvious that any fair account of the legacy
of the moral drama must deal with the horizon of expectations of
the age of Shakespeare rather than that fostered by our anthologies and handbooks.

Even when plays like *The Trial of Treasure* are taken into account, however, many problems remain in assessing that legacy.
Thus, despite any evidence adduced from the late moral drama,
the modern reader cannot assume that every set of contrasting
characters found in a history play or comedy has roots in the
moral plays. Common sense, rhetorical tradition, or even the
source materials used by the dramatist could lead to such a choice.
For example, *Clyomon and Clamydes*, a knightly romance with
two heroes, has little in common with *The Trial of Treasure*,
while plays like *Old Fortunatus*, *The Dutch Courtesan*, and *Eastward Ho* are at best distant cousins. Rather, any descendants of
the type of play best represented by *The Trial of Treasure* will exhibit not only dual protagonists (admittedly, only a general link)
but also symbolic companions, parallel groupings, and analogous
situations in consecutive scenes. The essential criterion is the
entire dramatic strategy, not merely the presence of two contrasting heroes.

Several early historical plays have at least some affinity with this dramatic model. Peele's *The Battle of Alcazar* (1589), for example, is structured around the two claimants to the throne, Abdelmelec and Muly Muhamet, each of whom has analogous companions and significantly divergent attitudes towards Heaven and Fortune. The central concerns of the play—the virtues of a rightful title and the attendant perils of ambition and usurpation—are presented largely through the continuing dramatic contrast between two protagonists who embody opposed ways of life. Similarly, Lodge's *The Wounds of Civil War* (1588) depicts the struggle between Marius and Scilla, each with a sharply defined point of view. Through various parallel actions and through the alternating scenes of Act III, Lodge develops his distinction between Fortune's conqueror and Fortune's fool.

Consider in particular the way in which the anonymous author of *The Life and Death of Jack Straw* (1591) has structured his play around his titular figure and Richard II. For example, the alternation of scenes between the two protagonists or their supporters is consistent and is basic to the fabric of the play. Both Jack Straw and the king, moreover, embody opposing attitudes on major questions (e.g., personal gain versus the good of the kingdom); each has something to learn about himself and his role if he is to realize his goals and not be manipulated by others. Also of interest are the companions of the two protagonists. Parson Ball, the prime spokesman for rebellion, is the rebel equivalent first for the Archbishop, a contrasting figure of religion at the side of Richard II, and later for the Lord Mayor, who in his exhortation to his soldiers echoes Ball's words to the rebels (see ll. 862–65, 970–74). At the climax of the play, the rebel captain, who has placed his trust in false companions, is destroyed, while the king, who wisely has placed his trust in Newton and the Lord Mayor, is victorious and can therefore announce to the rebels that he "will be your Captain and your friend" (l. 963). Such a strategy linked to dual protagonists and related techniques provides interesting evidence of how the emerging history play could find an appropriate dramatic pattern in the late moral plays without recourse to a central Humanum Genus figure.[15]

To turn from *The Trial of Treasure* and *Jack Straw* to *1 Henry*

IV, however, is to move from dramatic possibilities to artistic re-alization. The reader not lead astray by the Humanum Genus will-o'-the-wisp can readily see how an expanded horizon of ex-pectations about the moral drama, one that can encompass dual protagonists and analogous companions, sheds revealing light upon Shakespeare's dramatic strategy. As C. L. Barber observes: "We are invited, by the King's unfavorable comparison in the opening scene, to see the Prince in relation to Hotspur,"[16] for here Henry IV orchestrates the public assumptions of the play—that Hotspur is "so blest a son," "amongst a grove the very straightest plant," "sweet fortune's minion and her pride," while "riot and dishonor stain the brow / Of my young Harry" (I.i.80–86). Clearly, two public value judgments have been made in this opening scene, judgments that award Hal lower if not failing grades when judged by Hotspur's standard.

In the next two scenes, however, Shakespeare calls into ques-tion these initial judgments upon the two young men, one of whose ages has been drastically changed in defiance of history to enhance the parallel.[17] First, we are shown how Hal has been spending his time. The prince's opening speech signals his shrewd awareness of Falstaff's way of life in which "to demand the time of the day" is superfluous (I.ii.11); Sir John's assertion that "I must give over this life" (ll. 89–90) is then immediately tested ("where shall we take a purse to-morrow, Jack?") and exposed as a pretense. This prince obviously is *not* the traditional moral pro-tagonist (Youth, Wit, Lusty Juventus) led astray by Riot and Dis-honor, for Riot (if one accepts that equation with Falstaff) is not in control but rather is tolerated and enjoyed. The much dis-cussed soliloquy that ends the scene reinforces our impression of Hal's self-awareness. The prince sets up a revealing analogy, cit-ing "the base contagious clouds" that "seem to strangle" the sun but, in reality, are only permitted "to smother up his beauty from the world" until that moment that he (sun-son) may "please again to be himself." Although Hal is aware of how "this loose behavior" appears to the world and to his father, he argues that "when" (not "if") he throws it off, such a "reformation" will "show more goodly and attract more eyes / Than that which hath no foil to set it off." Such self-conscious control over his present and future image to the world should prevent the audience from underestimating this politic figure, a mistake made by his father, his companions, and his antagonists. In sharp contrast to Hal's control of himself and his surroundings, despite his apparent immersion in vice, we next see Hotspur's lack of such control and awareness, despite his impressive credentials. Thus, after the angry departure of the king, Shakespeare sets up the analogous pattern basic to his strategy in this play. In the latter part of I.ii, two figures had been on-stage (a youth and an old man) when a third figure arrived with a plot (the Gadshill robbery). Here in I.iii, the audience sees before them Hotspur and Northumberland, rather than Hal and Falstaff, with Worcester, rather than Poins, entering with the plot, against the king's crown rather than the king's money (or crowns). Each of the plots, moreover, is centered around the respective young man whose participation is essential for the ultimate effect (to expose Falstaff, to gain the necessary support for the rebellion).

As in *The Trial of Treasure*, moreover, such parallel staging calls attention to a contrast basic to the play. In the earlier scene the prince had displayed his control of himself, his situation, and the old man who accompanied him; indeed, the plot was directed *at* Falstaff. But Hotspur displays no such control over his plot or his old men. Rather, this second young protagonist is rash, hot-tempered, and lacking in any subtlety or craft, as shown in his anger at the king's dismissal of Mortimer's cause, his enthusiasm for danger that can lead to Honor, and his excitement over the "noble plot." The two old men therefore must wait for the subsiding of this tantrum that ties "thine ear to no tongue but thine own" (l. 237). But the staging of the scene can make clear that Hotspur's outbursts are in reality under the control of the two old men who are subtly manipulating this tempestuous figure. Thus, during Hotspur's first tirade, Worcester and Northumberland redirect and reinforce the young knight's anger by blandly conversing about Richard II's proclamation that Mortimer was to be "the next of blood" (l. 146). A warrior rather than a politician, Hotspur then has a sudden insight into the king's motives, an insight that the audience has seen implanted by figures seeking to use him. Although he had earlier mocked the courtly popinjay, this young knight fails to recognize the more insidious danger to be found at court, the manipulation that can undermine the selfhood and self-control of the individual.

As the scene progresses, the ringing speeches on that Honor that must be worn "without corrival" (l. 207) sound suspect in a context in which Hotspur is reacting to stimuli supplied by companions with questionable motives (particularly Worcester, an old man who has been singled out for criticism by both the king and Westmorcland). Meanwhile, the many verbal echoes of the previous scene (e.g., time, debt, "redeem"), the parallel staging, and Hotspur's mocking of "that same sword-and-buckler Prince of Wales" who could be "poisoned with a pot of ale" (ll. 229, 232) remind us of Hal as the alternative young man. Although figures within the world of the play undoubtedly would accept Hotspur's public image, the audience has heard Hal's soliloquy and witnessed his superiority to *his* old man. The heroically minded reader or spectator may find Hotspur's initial stance more appealing than the prince's calculated biding of his time, but Shakespeare is testing such heroic assumptions by placing Hotspur's statements and gestures in a murky political context in which a naive warrior may lose his battle before it is fought. By displaying the alternative path followed by this second young man, Shakespeare is underscoring what Hal is *not* and further defining those qualities (not always the most appealing or idealistic ones) necessary for the effective ruler. As in *The Trial of Treasure*, the dramatist is using alternating scenes, analogous companions, and parallel staging to distinguish between his dual protagonists—here a politic prince and an intemperate knight.

In Acts II and III Shakespeare further develops this dramatic strategy. First, Hotspur acts out his inability to accept any truths that do not mesh with his heroic code when he finds only cowardice in a letter that, in fact, offers a perceptive critique of the intended rebellion ("the purpose you undertake is dangerous, the friends you have named uncertain, the time itself unsorted, and your whole plot too light for the counterpoise of so great an opposition"—II.iii, 10–13). Such immersion in a self-contained world places him at the opposite extreme from Prince Hal who could rightly state: "I know you all" (I.ii.183). Hal's speech to Poins at the outset of the next scene serves as his equivalent to Hotspur's reaction to the cautious letter. In contrast to the fiery knight's contempt, the prince announces that he has "sounded the very bass-string of humility" with the drawers and "all the good lads in Eastcheap" (ll. 5–6, 13–14) and, in the process, has learned their language ("good boy," "dyeing scarlet," "hem!" and "play it off") and won their hearts. Hal concludes: "I tell thee, Ned, thou hast lost much honor that thou wert not with me in this action" (ll. 18–19), a use of "honor" and "action" that Hotspur certainly would not understand. In contrast to Hotspur's self-induced deafness, Hal again has shown his ability to play a part (a truant, a robber in a buckram suit, a drinking companion) and learn languages other than his own to achieve his goals. An actor need only brandish a piece of paper (with the new words Hal has learned or Francis's pennyworth of sugar) to heighten the parallel to Hotspur and his letter.

The contrast between the two young men is further developed through the practical joke played upon Francis the drawer. Here Hal's offer of money and his testing of Francis's bond to the vintner is played off against first Poins's and then Hal's use of the drawer's name as a stimulus to elicit a mechanistic response (verbally—"Anon, sir"; physically—a movement towards the speaker), a response that eventually causes the prince to conclude: "That ever this fellow should have fewer words than a parrot, and yet the son of a woman!" (ll. 94–95). The stage action presents the image of Francis as a puppet jerked by two competing strings until "*they both call him. The Drawer stands amazed, not knowing which way to go*" (l. 76.s.d.). Although Poins is left in the dark about the point behind this joke (ll. 86–88), the spectator sees that Prince Hal is firmly in control and, indeed, serves as a puppetmaster who can manipulate Francis's actions because of his knowledge of what makes the puppet work. Of those on stage in Act II, only the prince fully grasps the essential nature of his companions and is therefore able to use that knowledge to

manipulate others, to be a controller rather than one of the controlled. In contrast, Francis, by being so easily manipulated, calls
into question his credentials as a "son of a woman" and serves as
a comment upon Hotspur's subjection to the promptings of the
two old men in I.iii. In particular, the young knight's heroic code
may be his loftier equivalent to Francis's "Anon, sir," his version
of a predictable response that can be anticipated and hence manipulated. To heighten this parallel, a director need only have
Francis's scurrying about the stage echo Hotspur's frenetic movements in II.iii [18] or have the drawer, between Hal and Poins, correspond to the young knight caught between Worcester and
Northumberland in I.iii.

The exuberant baiting of Falstaff then provides more evidence
of Hal's superiority. Falstaff's "coward on instinct" may be a bril-
liant comic improvisation, but it certainly does not deceive the
prince, who twits his old man (ll. 266–77), successfully cross-
examines Bardolph when Falstaff is off-stage, and toys with "instinct" (ll. 338, 354). The old man's claim—"I knew ye as well
as he that made ye" (ll. 253–54)—only emphasizes again how
no one in the play truly "knows" Hal, whether because of a
vizard and buckram suit or a supposed stain of Riot and Dishonor
on his brow, while the prince is the sole figure, here or elsewhere, who can claim with any force: "I know you all" (echoed
ironically by Falstaff's "I know not what you call all"—l. 175).
Even granted the enormous disparity between Francis and Falstaff
as comic butts, Hal plays the same role of controller, puppetmaster, and stage manager in both instances. In contrast to
Hotspur in the previous scene, the prince displays his ability to
listen to, observe, and learn from those around him, whether the
lads of Eastcheap, Francis, Bardolph, or Falstaff.

The first part of the famous play extempore that follows shows
us Falstaff in the role he would like to be playing—father figure
and controller for his young man. The stage image of Falstaff
above, with his chair, dagger, and cushion, and Hal below, as
subject and son, acts out the conception of truant prince held by
Henry IV, Hotspur, and England as a whole. Here, in addition,
is a visual summary of the potential trap awaiting both of the

youthful protagonists, a trap associated with subjection to an old man. But in the second act of this interlude the prince reverses the roles and plays father figure and controller to his old man, a reversal for which there is no equivalent in Hotspur's dramatic career. Significantly, Hal, unlike Hotspur (or Youth or Wit), is not deceived or misled by his old man. Rather, Shakespeare makes it clear that the prince's summary comment ("I do, I will") is based upon an accurate assessment of his companions (emphasized again through the papers from Falstaff's pockets), complete control of himself (in evidence since I. ii), and total awareness of the debt that remains to be paid, the role that must be assumed, and the world that eventually must be banished. Hal's four revealing words are in themselves enough to explain his ultimate victory over Hotspur if only in the vision that allows him to see the future in the present (as in his soliloquy) and steer his own independent course through uncharted political and moral waters.

In keeping with Shakespeare's dramatic strategy, this major display of Hal's abilities is followed by the most revealing display of Hotspur's limitations. The first half of III. i presents Hotspur's baiting of Glendower, first through his scoffing at the magician's claims to supernatural powers, then through his proposal to change the course of the Trent, and finally through his mocking of poetry and the Welsh language. All these nonhistorical incidents invented by Shakespeare[19] heighten Hotspur's blunt, headstrong nature that cannot make allowances for the idiosyncrasies of others, even his own allies. In the previous scene, Hal had learned the language of the lads of Eastcheap, controlled Francis, Bardolph, Falstaff, and even the Sheriff, and shown his understanding of both his present surroundings and his future role ("I will"). In contrast, Hotspur does not truly grasp his own role in this rebellion or the tenuous bonds that tie his allies to him ("the purpose you undertake is dangerous, the friends you have named uncertain . . .") and therefore allows personal pique to triumph over politic control.

With Glendower off-stage, both Mortimer and Worcester chide Hotspur for his willful, impolitic behavior. First, Mortimer notes that, unlike the young man, the Welshman has been exercising considerable restraint, for "that man is not alive / Might so have tempted him as you have done / Without the taste of danger and reproof" (ll. 171–73). Worcester adds an important political context:

> In faith, my lord, you are too willful-blame,
> And since your coming hither have done enough
> To put him quite besides his patience.
> You must needs learn, lord, to amend this fault.
> Though sometimes it show greatness, courage, blood—
> And that's the dearest grace it renders you—
> Yet oftentimes it doth present harsh rage,
> Defect of manners, want of government,
> Pride, haughtiness, opinion, and disdain;
> The least of which haunting a nobleman
> Loseth men's hearts, and leaves behind a stain
> Upon the beauty of all parts besides,
> Beguiling them of commendation.   (ll. 175–87)

Even though Hotspur's "greatness, courage, blood" on the battle-field remain beyond question, this shrewd politician argues that heroic virtues out of control can become politic vices that lose men's hearts. While Hal is moving to erase the stain of Riot and Dishonor supposedly on his brow, Hotspur stands accused of staining the beauty of "all parts besides" through his "willful-blame" behavior.

The latter part of this scene provides a symbolic gloss on Hotspur's inadequacies by means of the obvious language barrier between Mortimer and his wife. Here again Shakespeare calls our attention to the recurring problem of communication, for Mortimer's literal inability to understand Welsh corresponds to Hotspur's less obvious but far more significant inability to fathom Glendower's language, superstitions, and habits of mind (his Welshness). Unlike Hal, who mastered the language of East-cheap, both Mortimer and Hotspur are symbolically isolated from their surroundings and from those companions of whom they have most need. When the much maligned Glendower does call for ethereal musicians who "hang in the air a thousand leagues from hence" (l. 223), "*the music plays*" (l. 227.s.d.), a supernatural response that enhances the magician's claims and counters the gibes of the incredulous Hotspur (ll. 54–55). Taken as a whole, this scene displays at length Hotspur's failings in the political rather than the chivalric arena. As in his rejection of the letter in II.iii, this irascible yet charming young knight is totally committed to his personal heroic code and to his no-nonsense attitudes towards superstition, poetry, oaths, and language, to the extent that he can set up a barrier between himself and a figure like Glendower who may be essential to his cause. Like Francis, Hotspur too can fall short of his potential as "son of a woman" because of such semiautomatic responses based upon hair-trigger reflexes and simple assumptions about the world around him. Although to the world at large it is Hotspur with his military credentials who appears better prepared for the confrontation ahead, to the audience it is Hal who has been schooled (or has schooled himself) into an awareness of what is demanded of him and how he must rise to those demands—through language, control, and vision, not through scoffs, self-isolation, and subjection to others. In consecutive scenes both young men bait their companions (another parallel that could be heightened by analogous blocking), but Hal's handling of Francis and Falstaff proves his control and superiority while Hotspur's mishandling of Glendower only stresses his inadequacy.

Shakespeare takes this pattern of alternating scenes one step farther, for the confrontation in III.i between a young man and an old man who is a potential ally is followed by Hal's confrontation with another highly significant old man who has already been antagonized by his apparently dissolute life. Like Worcester, Henry IV is much concerned with the political repercussions of his young man's image, here the supposed "inordinate and low desires" that have made the prince "almost an alien to the hearts / Of all the court and princes of my blood" (III.ii.12, 34–35). According to this master politician, Hal (like Richard II) "hast lost thy princely privilege / With vile participation" (ll. 86–87). But in spite of his shrewdness, the king's critique of his son cannot be accepted by an audience that has seen repeated demonstrations of Hal's control of himself and others. Similarly, that audience by now should look askance at Henry IV's comparison between Hotspur (a "Mars in swathling clothes" who has gained "never-dying honor"—ll. 112, 106) and his son ("my nearest and dearest enemy"—l. 123). The king's long disquisition on political image-making that can "pluck allegiance from men's hearts" (l. 52) does not take into account evidence the audience has seen and heard—for example, how the prince has won the right "when I am king of England" to "command all the good lads in Eastcheap" (II.iv.13–14). Unlike the audience, Henry IV has not heard Hal's first soliloquy nor his "I do, I will."

Whether here or in I.i, the king's judgments upon Hotspur and Hal have been based upon the concept of Honor as understood by "all the world" (l. 93), an Honor that can be affected "by smiling pickthanks and base newsmongers" (l. 25). In the pivotal moment of this scene when the prince defends his past and makes his promises for the future (ll. 129–59), Hal uses this concept as a common language between himself and his father, the common language missing for Hotspur and Glendower or for Mortimer and his wife. Thus, the prince, referring to the supposed stain of Dishonor upon his brow, promises to "redeem" all past offenses so that, "in the closing of some glorious day," he "will wear a garment all of blood, / And stain my favors in a bloody mask, / Which, washed away, shall scour my shame with it." In a revealing passage, Hal then invokes the Honor that is little more than a commodity. In this view, Hotspur becomes the prince's "factor," engaged "to engross up glorious deeds on my behalf," an agent under contract who eventually will be called "to so strict account / That he shall render every glory up" or else Hal "will tear the reckoning from his heart." Just as the prince had understood and thereby controlled both Francis and Falstaff, so here he can grasp and use the assumptions of his father to cancel out his apparent truancy and rejoin the public world of the play. In contrast to Hotspur's linguistic deficiency with Glendower, Hal has mastered the public language of "glorious deeds," "glorious day," "glory," "honor," and "honor and renown."

Whether or not he truly is an orthodox adherent to such a chivalric code, the prince can use such terms to win over the most
significant old man in the play. The series of alternating moments that started as early as I.ii here reaches a climax when
Hotspur's political lapses of III.i are countered by Hal's politic
victory.

Since the paths chosen by the two protagonists have now
been displayed, Shakespeare can concentrate upon the implications of their choices without the same emphatic alternation of
scenes. First, Hotspur must face the reality he so far has failed to
admit. The first rebuff, the news of Northumberland's illness,
does not daunt him, because he can argue that his father's absence "lends a lustre and more great opinion, / A larger dare to
our great enterprise, / Than if the earl were here" (IV.i.77–79).
As in III.i, Worcester provides the politic view (e.g, that "it will
be thought" by outsiders "that wisdom, loyalty, and mere dislike / Of our proceedings kept the earl from hence"), but Hotspur is concerned not with politics and men's hearts but with his
heroic code, "a larger dare," Honor waiting to be plucked from
the pale-faced moon. Similarly, when Hotspur's snide question
about "the nimble-footed madcap Prince of Wales" (l. 95) elicits
Vernon's glowing description of the new Hal (ll. 97–110), the
fiery knight impatiently cuts off the description ("this praise doth
nourish agues"—l. 112), again showing his unwillingness to hear
unwelcome truths.

The final news, that Glendower "cannot draw his power this
fourteen days" (l. 126), provides the most telling indictment of
Hotspur's impolitic course of action. Admittedly, Shakespeare is
by no means explicit, but surely the elaborate Welsh-baiting of
III.i is designed to offer some explanation for Glendower's failure
to appear at Shrewsbury. Mocking the advice of the letter of
II.iii, ignoring Worcester's politic vision here and in III.i, and
failing to see the strings controlling him, this angry young knight
is acting out the blindness and impetuosity that distinguish him
from the alternative young man who does succeed in the same
hostile, debilitating world. Falstaff's antiheroic comments in the
next scene, especially his description of his "pitiful rascals" as

"food for powder" (IV.ii.61–64), then spell out the ugly reality behind the chivalric rhetoric confidently set forth by Hotspur, another captain leading his men to their deaths. Significantly, it is Hal who cross-examines the false captain in IV.ii and demonstrates his superiority to such suspect captaincy in any form.

Hotspur's delegation of his authority to Worcester and Vernon leads to his absence from the meeting between the rebels and the king, an absence that signals his isolation from the realities of the play. This confrontation between the two shrewd old men,[20] Henry IV and Worcester, is followed by the public emergence as a chivalric hero of another young man who can grant his counterpart full honors as "active-valiant," "valiant-young," "daring," and "bold" (V.i.85–92) yet nonetheless assert himself and his promise for the future, creating for himself a new image that Hotspur is unable to recognize or accept. Hal's proposal "to save the blood on either side" by trying "fortune with him in a single fight" (ll. 99–100) is his alternative to Hotspur's "die all, die merrily" (IV.i.134) or Falstaff's "food for powder," for the prince, who realizes that "in both your armies there is many a soul / Shall pay full dearly for this encounter, / If once they join in trial" (ll. 83–85), can posit the value in the human life to be lost. Hal's rising to the occasion is more than an admission of having "a truant been to chivalry" (l. 94); rather, it involves an insight and depth of understanding rarely found in this factional, short-sighted world.

Despite several ringing speeches and a moving call to arms, Hotspur has no equivalent opportunity to rise to the occasion, because his old man never reveals to him "the liberal and kind offer of the king" (V.ii.2). Since the suspicious Worcester lacks faith in Henry IV's guarantees (at least for those without Hotspur's "excuse of youth and heat of blood"—l. 17), this young man is never made aware of the options available to him. The hot-headed warrior, who has continually rebelled against his uncle's politic advice (how to handle Glendower, when to fight), has had no combat experience in dealing with such a deception—unlike Hal, who saw through his old man's lies in II.iv. Similarly, Hotspur cannot accept the image of the new Prince

Hal provided by Vernon (ll. 51–68) but only scoffs at this report ("Cousin, I think thou art enamorèd / Upon his follies"—ll. 69–70). Although Hal could give his opponent full honors in his challenge, Hotspur is unable or unwilling to accept an eye-witness report and cannot move beyond the world's limited view of the prince. Within a brief dramatic moment, Hotspur has displayed his inability to evaluate accurately both a supposed friend and a known foe, a lapse in understanding that has much to do with his coming downfall.

The young knight's subsequent call to arms, like his speeches on Honor in I.iii, provides a highly theatrical rendition of his chivalric appeal, but the full dramatic meaning of this speech involves more than what this heroic figure thinks he is saying. The heart of his statement (ll. 81–88) is based upon a warrior's view of the relationship between time and heroic action. If "the time of life is short," the hero should strive not "to spend that shortness basely." In the forthcoming battle, according to Hotspur, the man seeking to use his time heroically has the worthy options of either treading on kings or suffering "brave death, when princes die with us." In conclusion, he argues that "the arms are fair, / When the intent of bearing them is just." Shakespeare, however, has placed this exhortation in a context that qualifies if not undermines such heroic values. Granted, Hotspur's inability to grasp the truth about his major antagonist may be understandable (others make the same mistake), but his blindness to Worcester's machinations and his failure to see the pointlessness of the coming battle cannot be passed over so lightly. His chivalric assumptions about the honorable use of time, moreover, come about ninety lines after Falstaff's incisive catechism (V.i.127–39), a cynical speech that calls into question the essence of Hotspur's code and concludes that "Honor is a mere scutcheon."

Through this carefully crafted dramatic context, Shakespeare is forcing his audience to weigh Hotspur's claims and assumptions. Can the hero be truly honorable when not fully aware of the cause (or lack of cause) for which he is fighting? Is the "intent" of bearing arms indeed "just" in this instance? Can Hotspur, symbolically isolated from the king's offer and Hal's challenge, make meaningful statements about time and Honor, especially with Worcester, the old man who has deceived him, standing by his side? While Hal as sun-son is emerging from behind "the base contagious clouds," Hotspur's lack of control and self-knowledge is leading him to a captaincy and a battle that can only be self-defeating. Once again the dramatist has offered us comparable examples in consecutive scenes of how these two young men are using their time in a demanding arena that includes war and politics, vaunts and sophistries, heroic ideals and ugly realities. Through a range of dramatic devices comparable to those found in *Enough* or *The Trial of Treasure*, Shakespeare has fully explored for his audience the divergent paths chosen by the two protagonists as they move towards their climactic meeting.

Before discussing that confrontation, let me return to an earlier moment clearly linked to the materials presented in chapter two. Thus, in the first tavern scene, Falstaff (who believes that Prince Hal ran away at Gad's Hill) laments the withering away of true manhood and then, to castigate the prince, invokes a familiar image from the late moral plays: "A king's son! If I do not beat thee out of thy kingdom with a dagger of lath and drive all thy subjects afore thee like a flock of wild geese, I'll never wear hair on my face more. You Prince of Wales?" (II.iv.128–31). Later in the scene, when acting the part of his father, Hal describes the devil that haunts the prince "in the likeness of an old fat man"; the string of epithets climaxes with "that reverend vice, that grey iniquity, that father ruffian, that vanity in years" (ll. 431–32) and, a bit later, with "that villainous abominable misleader of youth, Falstaff, that old white-bearded Satan" (ll. 439–40). These lines need little glossing for the reader of the previous two chapters other than a reminder that Iniquity (as in "that grey iniquity" or Richard's "formal Vice Iniquity") had become in the age of Shakespeare an all-purpose name for a Vice (as in examples cited in chapter two from *Histriomastix*, *The Owl's Almanac*, and *The Devil Is an Ass*). A. R. Humphreys provides a long gloss on Falstaff's allusion to the "dagger of lath" in which he cites similar passages in *Twelfth Night*, *Henry V*, and Harsnet, as well as examples from two late moral plays, all of which suggest to him "some actual incident, apparently entirely familiar to an Elizabethan audience." For Humphreys (like Wilson) this allusion forms "part of the morality-associations" by which an audience is to know "how to take" Falstaff.[21]

Many editors, critics, and directors, however, would disagree. Indeed, one recent critic who does argue in behalf of links between *Henry IV* and the moral plays nonetheless observes that such imagistic links between Falstaff and the Vice "are such stuff as commentaries are made of, and their little life is rounded with a footnote."[22] If discussion of the dagger of lath and the reverend Vice (here or in *Richard III*) leads only to learned, ponderous glosses, I would agree. This play is richer, imagistically and conceptually, and far more complex structurally than *Richard III*, with no obvious equivalent to Richmond and no neat two phased structure akin to the late moral drama. Are there, then, any gains to be realized by investigating these allusions to the Vice and his dagger of lath with the original horizon of expectations in mind? As Falstaff says, "a question to be asked" (II.iv.392).

To provide an answer, let me turn first to weapon imagery. Except for three brief references (I.i.17–18; I.iii.32, 229), swords and daggers are mentioned only in the famous tavern scene and, as one would expect, at the climactic battle at Shrewsbury.[23] Consider the tavern scene, which contains all the references to daggers. Thus, when the prince says "do thou stand for my father," Falstaff responds: "This chair shall be my state, this dagger my sceptre, and this cushion my crown," to which Hal replies: "Thy state is taken for a joined-stool, thy golden sceptre for a leaden dagger, and thy precious rich crown for a pitiful bald crown" (II.iv.358–64). Here as elsewhere, Falstaff's weapons are played off against some higher standard—in this case, the golden sceptre of true royalty. Earlier, in a very funny moment, Sir John had described his sword-play against supposedly overwhelming odds (e.g., "Here I lay, and thus I bore my point"—l. 184). In particular, he claims to have been "eight times thrust through the doublet, four through the hose; my buckler cut through and through; my sword hacked like a handsaw—*ecce signum!*" (ll. 157–60), at that point holding up a much diminished weapon (which most actors will then display prominently throughout the remainder of the scene). Hal later gibes: "What a slave art thou to hack thy sword as thou hast done, and then say it was in fight" (ll. 247–49). With Falstaff off-stage, the prince cross-examines Peto and Bardolph ("how came Falstaff's sword so hacked?") and gets the answer: "Why, he hacked it with his dagger, and said he would swear truth out of England but he would make you believe it was done in fight" (ll. 288–92). The news from Sir John Bracy of the rebellion involving Hotspur, Douglas, and Glendower prefigures real swordplay and real blood (as opposed to the blood from noses tickled with speargrass), but the dominant images in a tavern world free from time and responsibility are a leaden dagger instead of a golden sceptre, a Vice-like dagger of lath with which the fat knight threatens to drive the prince out of his kingdom, and a visibly diminished sword that epitomizes Falstaff's unchivalric attitude towards Honor and Truth.

Consider too another relevant set of associations. Both parts of *Henry IV* display prominently the breaking of vows and the non-payment of debts, with Falstaff the most visible perpetrator. As early as the second scene, Hal reminds Sir John: "Did I ever call for thee to pay thy part?" (I.ii.48), and much of the second tavern scene is devoted to Falstaff's attempt to avoid his debt to Mistress Quickly ("I'll not pay a denier") and to pass it off on Bardolph ("let him pay"—III.iii.76, 72). Meanwhile, the rebels' critique of the king has much to do with promises and payments. In the third scene, Hotspur is furious over the nonpayment of the ransom for Mortimer, and before Shrewsbury he tells Blunt that "the king / Knows at what time to promise, when to pay" (IV.iii.52–53). In the same speech, Hotspur places great emphasis upon Henry's pledge to Northumberland during the reign of Richard II that he was returning to England "but to be Duke of Lancaster," but notes that, when opportunity came, Bolingbroke "steps me a little higher than his vow / Made to my father, while his blood was poor" (IV.iii.60–61, 75–76). In his confrontation with the king, Worcester also recounts those oaths made at Doncaster, whose violation is purportedly the basis for this rebellion (V.i.41–46, 58). But the promise-keeping of the rebel faction itself is not to be admired. Mortimer begins their council scene with: "These promises are fair, the parties sure, / And our induction full of prosperous hope" (III.i.1–2). The formal signing of indentures to solidify the alliance among the Percies, Mortimer, and Glendower is then mentioned three times during the scene that follows, while Blunt points out to Henry IV in the next scene that "a mighty and a fearful head they are, / If promises be kept on every hand" (III.ii.167–68). But in IV.i Hotspur learns that Northumberland and Glendower, despite promises and indentures, will not be fighting with him at Shrewsbury. Thus, Falstaff's consistent failure to honor debts and promises acts out a larger problem or set of attitudes widespread in this play (and in its sequel).

But Prince Hal is a notable and crucial exception. As early as the second scene he tells the audience how, at the appropriate time, he will "throw off" his "loose behavior" and thereby "pay the debt I never promisèd" (I.ii.196–97), a promise he later reaffirms with "I do, I will." At the end of the tavern scene he tells the Sheriff that "I will engage my word to thee" that Falstaff will respond to charges and be answerable for the money (II.iv.489) and, a few scenes later, reveals how he has kept his word when he tells Falstaff "the money is paid back again" (Sir John notes: "I do not like that paying back"—III.iii.171–72). Hal reconciles himself to his father by vowing to make Hotspur "exchange / His glorious deeds for my indignities"; he concludes this important speech with: "This in the name of God I promise here" and, again, "I will die a hundred thousand deaths / Ere break the smallest parcel of this vow" (III.ii.145–59). At Shrewsbury, Falstaff may owe God a death, but he is "loath to pay him before his day" (V.i.127–28). Immediately thereafter, Worcester chooses not to relay the king's offer to Hotspur because he fears that he and Vernon, "as the spring of all, shall pay for all" (V.ii.23). Everyone else in the play readily finds reasons not to pay their debts or keep their vows. But, in striking contrast, Prince Hal pays all his debts, even those he never promised, and keeps his vow to his father (by saving the king's life, killing Hotspur, and distinguishing himself at Shrewsbury), thereby breaking through the base contagious clouds at the proper moment. Hal fulfills his promises and debts: to the Sheriff, to the King, to England.

Let me return now to the climax of *1 Henry IV*, the battle at Shrewsbury, keeping in mind the allusions in the tavern scene, especially to the dagger of lath, along with Shakespeare's emphasis upon weapons in general, Falstaff's weapons in particular, and the related concepts of debt, payment, and promises. The sequence begins with Douglas killing a Sir Walter Blunt who is "semblably furnished like the king himself" (V.iii.21). Discovering Blunt's true identity, Douglas provides the epitaph: "A borrowed title hast thou bought too dear" (l. 23). Clearly, a counterfeit of a king is no match for the sword of Douglas.

After Falstaff comments briefly upon Sir Walter ("there's honor for you"—ll. 32–33), Prince Hal enters to set up a brief but telling exchange:

PRINCE.
What, stand'st thou idle here? Lend me thy sword.
Many a nobleman lies stark and stiff
Under the hoofs of vaunting enemies,
Whose deaths are yet unrevenged. I prithee
Lend me thy sword.
FALSTAFF.
O Hal, I prithee give me leave to breathe awhile. Turk
Gregory never did such deeds in arms as I have done this
day. I have paid Percy; I have made him sure.
PRINCE.
He is indeed, and living to kill thee.
I prithee lend me thy sword.
FALSTAFF.
Nay, before God, Hal, if Percy be alive, thou get'st not my
sword; but take my pistol, if thou wilt.
PRINCE.
Give it me. What, is it in the case?
FALSTAFF.
Ay, Hal. 'Tis hot, 'tis hot. There's that will sack a city.
The Prince draws it out and finds it to be a bottle of sack.

PRINCE.
What, is it a time to jest and dally now?
He throws the bottle at him.   *Exit.*   (ll. 39–54)

Note first that "lend me thy sword" is repeated three times, a
kind of emphasis (what I term "theatrical *italics*") that Shakespeare reserves for truly important images or concepts (e.g.,
"nothing" repeated five times within three lines at the opening
of *King Lear*). Hal *needs* a weapon (and we are never told where
he gets one to rescue his father and kill Hotspur); Falstaff *has* a
weapon (in my imagined staging, the same hacked sword of
II.iv). But "if Percy be alive," Sir John has no intention of giving
up whatever protection lies in his sword, so then follow the
counter offer of the pistol, Hal's discovery, and the reaction.
Note too that this vignette starts with "what, stand'st thou idle
here?" and ends with "what, is it a time to jest and dally now?"
Idleness, jesting, dalliance, all associated with the tavern world,
with freedom from time (see the beginning of I.ii), and with sack
are here rejected by the prince (as in the couplets that end
III.iii), but Falstaff, especially if he is wielding the hacked sword
of II.iv, is literally carrying the imagery of the tavern and its way
of life with him: a mangled weapon associated with his counterfeit status and a bottle of sack. Falstaff, of course, is a survivor, in
contrast to Hotspur or Blunt ("I like not such grinning honor as
Sir Walter hath. Give me life"—ll. 57–58). But Hal's values
here are keyed to his final word—"now"—which suggests a post-
tavern sense of "time" and responsibility, while the prince's
treatment of the bottle of sack is one of the most obvious symbolic actions in Shakespeare, a vivid statement in action of the
Prince of Wales's new relationship ("now") to Falstaff's world of
sack, jests, and idleness. Falstaff's dagger here poses no threat to
Hal; Falstaff's weapons can be of no help to Hal. Rather, the
prince must transcend Falstaff and his weapons and find strength
and purpose elsewhere.

In the next segment, the king urges a bleeding Hal to with-
draw, but the prince refuses, emphasizing instead the role Falstaff
had mocked in the dagger of lath speech: "And God forbid a

shallow scratch should drive / The Prince of Wales from such a field as this" (V.iv. 10–11). Henry IV then confronts a Douglas who asks the telling question: "What art thou / That counterfeit'st the person of a king?" (ll. 26–27) The question grows out of a specific battlefield situation, with apparent kings growing "like Hydra's heads" (l. 24), but, given Bolingbroke's manner of gaining the throne, the question has other dimensions as well. Just as the rebellion as a whole challenges the status of the king, so Douglas in physical combat threatens counterfeit kings and a king who may be a counterfeit.

The subsequent fight does not go well for Henry IV, but Hal's presence makes the difference, just as it will, in an analogous way, at the end of Part Two:

> *They fight. The King being in danger, enter Prince of Wales.*
> PRINCE.
>   Hold up thy head, vile Scot, or thou art like
>   Never to hold it up again. The spirits
>   Of valiant Shirley, Stafford, Blunt are in my arms.
>   It is the Prince of Wales that threatens thee,
>   Who never promiseth but he means to pay.
>   *They fight. Douglas flieth.*   (ll. 38–42)

Here Hal fulfills the promises made in III.ii, for in his father's eyes he has "redeemed thy lost opinion, / And showed thou mak'st some tender of my life, / In this fair rescue thou hast brought to me" (ll. 47–49). The key lines, moreover, underscore this fulfilling of promises and debts, for here Hal specifically names himself as the heir apparent (implying the debt he never promised) and announces: "It is *the Prince of Wales* that threatens thee, / Who never promiseth but he means to pay" (ll. 41–42, my emphasis). The Douglas, a fighting machine that has already struck down Shirley, Stafford, and Blunt and has had the king "in danger," is driven off by the Prince of Wales, the one figure who keeps his promises, pays his debts. Rather than being driven out of his kingdom with a dagger of lath (or a hacked sword), the Prince of Wales here asserts his pivotal role (both present and

future, as in ("I do, I will") and drives would-be takers of his kingdom before *him* like a flock of wild geese. Falstaff's dagger of lath
and hacked sword have no potency at Shrewsbury, but Hal's
weapon does prove potent—against both Douglas and Hotspur—while his role as Prince of Wales proves central to the pres-
ervation of the kingdom.

In both *Enough* and *The Trial of Treasure*, the two protagonists
had confronted each other in the opening scene and had then
pursued their divergent paths. In *1 Henry IV*, however, Shakespeare builds to a climax in the first and only meeting between
his two protagonists (V.iv.58–100). Typically, the initial talk is
of Honor. Although Hal grants Hotspur his due ("a very valiant
rebel"), the latter wishes that the prince's "name in arms were
now as great as mine" so that the current possessor of Honor
would have more to gain and less to lose. Again, Honor becomes
a commodity that can be engrossed up by a factor and called to
account. After his defeat, the dying warrior once more focuses
upon time, for he is forced to admit that "thoughts the slaves of
life, and life time's fool, / And time, that takes survey of all the
world, / Must have a stop." Significantly, Hotspur's heroic code
can "better brook the loss of brittle life / Than those proud titles
thou hast won of me." In striking contrast to Falstaff's two recent
prose speeches, Hotspur values Honor over life and, according to
his own rigorous interpretation, finds no Honor for himself now
that he has been defeated (an interpretation that belies the
"never-dying honor" described earlier by Henry IV). Ironically,
Hotspur's evaluation of his own Honor seems to substantiate
Falstaff's claim that Honor is only "air," "a trim reckoning," and
"insensible . . . to the dead." Although the young knight's final
broken phrase ("and food for—") is completed by his opponent
in the conventional way ("for worms, brave Percy"), the audience may remember instead Falstaff's "food for powder" and, if
so, may sense a disturbing connection between the fate of the
ragged army of IV.ii ("there's not three of my hundred and fifty
left alive"—V.iii.36–37) and the end of this chivalric hero.

Hal's epitaph suggests a different concept of Honor and chivalry, for, along with comments on "ill-weaved ambition," the

prince also refers to "brave Percy," "great heart," and "so stout a gentleman." If Hotspur were still "sensible," Hal would not be free to "make so dear a show of zeal" or indulge in such "fair rites of tenderness"—here the combination of final tribute and covering the dead knight's face with his favors. Hal's evaluation of his defeated opponent shows his ability to "know" the strengths and weaknesses of his enemy, to measure accurately the world around him, and to separate private truths from public rhetoric. By suggesting, moreover, that the dead warrior "take thy praise with thee to heaven. / Thy ignominy sleep with thee in the grave, / But not rememb'red in thy epitaph," Hal gives his former antagonist more Honor in defeat than was claimed by Hotspur himself. That the prince stands erect over this prostrate body therefore acts out not only his physical but also his intellectual superiority, for he has transcended Hotspur's limited notion of Honor in favor of a more inclusive definition that can encompass both "praise" and "ignominy." Hal's triumph is manifold.

But to grasp the full impact of this rich moment, one must consider the total stage image, particularly the presence of two and, in the original production, possibly three prostrate bodies. So Hal, whom the audience has just seen standing over the body of Hotspur, now assumes a similar stance to deliver a second epitaph over the recumbent body of Falstaff who is "counterfeiting" death. In addition, the quarto provides no evidence that the body of Sir Walter Blunt is carried off at the end of what is designated V.iii in modern editions (the quarto is not divided into scenes). In the production by the Lord Chamberlain's Men, the prince may have also stood over or near the body of a knight "semblably furnished like the king himself" and hence a counterfeit king, an image of a monarch who is less than what he appears to be. Given such an on-stage configuration, this successful young man stands over and addresses two of his symbolic antagonists—both his obvious foil, Hotspur, and the old man who sought to control him—as well as an embodiment of his father and, more specifically, an image of Henry IV's "counterfeit" status linked to his means of gaining the crown (the "borrowed title" that he "bought too dear"). Hal's erect posture over these recumbent figures is a visual summary of his total triumph, not only as a warrior who has won Honor but, more important, as a controller rather than one of the controlled, as *the* figure (like Just or Heavenly Man) who has learned to transcend the machinations of others, the deceptive surfaces around him, and even the limitations of his father in order to achieve his own goals.

One of those prostrate bodies is still to be reckoned with, for Falstaff is very much alive and, like Henry IV, has sought to protect himself by "counterfeiting" (a term repeated nine times in his big speech over Hotspur). As a further irony, Falstaff's subsequent one-sided combat with Hotspur's corpse yields the Honor that has eluded the dead knight. Even though the strange tale delivered to the two princes is scarcely believable, Hal assures his old man that "if a lie may do thee grace, / I'll gild it with the happiest terms I have" (V.iv.153–54). The action of the play has demonstrated that the Honor frantically sought by Hotspur, accepted by the king, and catechized by Falstaff is only a sham or a counterfeit—in short, a lie. Since Hal, more than any other figure, has transcended this superficial concept of Honor, he not only can see through that lie but can also control or manipulate it. Consequently, it is Hal in the final scene who can recognize Douglas's heroism (V.v.29–31) and who can give the honors of the day to Prince John,[24] just as he had awarded due Honor to Hotspur and the lie to Falstaff. Since the prince, unlike Hotspur, is not obsessed with wearing his Honor "without corrival," he can create honors for others without himself being limited by such surfaces.

To parallel the configuration of Prince Hal standing in triumph over prostrate figures, Shakespeare provides a second striking theatrical image (an image often sidestepped in modern productions), for, after Falstaff's "counterfeit" speech, the stage direction reads: "*He takes up Hotspur on his back*" (l. 127). Despite his comic bluster in the tavern, Falstaff has no power to drive the Prince of Wales out of his kingdom with a dagger of lath. Rather, in seeking a weapon, Hal rejected what the fat knight had to offer and turned instead to the traditional sword, to his own sense of debt, and to his inherited role in order to

defeat the two principal rebels. Yet Shakespeare *is* invoking here
one of the best remembered images from the moral drama, a theatrical allusion not recognized by modern readers unfamiliar with
the extant plays and nurtured instead on the usual handbook definitions of "morality play." Significantly, the figure being picked up
and eventually carried off is not Prince Hal (Every Prince) or even
a Vice-like Falstaff (who could accomplish that Herculean task?),
but rather Hotspur, the "king of honor" (IV.i. 10), who, in death,
has not only been stripped of his proud titles but has also been
subjected ignominiously to Falstaff's maiden and perhaps diminished sword ("a new wound in your thigh"—l. 126). Other
plays, including some from the 1590s, show a Vice, Worldly Man,
fool, or vicious figure being carried off to Hell in this manner.
Here, when the prince says to Sir John "come, bring your luggage
nobly on your back" (l. 152), we see how both Hal *and* Falstaff
have triumphed over Hotspur, albeit in different senses. Hal's triumph (the most significant in a series of triumphs) tells us something important about his decisive role at the climax of the play,
while Sir John's "triumph" helps to signal Hotspur's failure,
including the young man's limited and limiting definition of
Honor. Both the wound in the thigh and the carrying off of
Hotspur on the fat knight's back act out what has failed (Hotspur's myopic chivalry and impolitic values) and what has survived (Sir John's "discretion") in contrast to what is essential to
England's health (the role and values of the Prince of Wales).

   Why then does Shakespeare invoke from the late moral drama
the image of a fallen worldly figure being carried off on the back
of a tormentor? Clearly, the end of *1 Henry IV* provides no clear
moral paradigm comparable to the end of *Richard III*, for here no
Richmond acting as God's Judgment cleanses the kingdom of
Machiavellian evil. Falstaff, for one, is rewarded, not punished,
while in contrast to the imagery of II.iv, it is Hotspur, not the
Prince of Wales, who departs ignominiously. Yet the shared associations are still relevant. Just as the Vice's weapon fails him
when opposed to a superior alternative force in the second phase
of the moral play, so Falstaff's weapons (so prominent in the earlier tavern scene) are transcended by Prince Hal at Shrewsbury

when he first throws the bottle of sack at Falstaff and then drives
Douglas and Hotspur before him like wild geese to preserve his
kingdom. The triumph of the Prince of Wales at the climax of
the play moves him beyond both Hotspur's myopic chivalry and
the values of the tavern world (idleness, sack, time without responsibility). But if Falstaff's vaunts do not affect the prince,
they do, ironically, pertain to Hotspur whose reputation and
body *are* subject to the anti-chivalric sword.[25] In imagistic terms,
the dagger of lath does not drive the true prince out of his kingdom but does wound and disgrace the fallen rebel. The complete
overthrow or suppression of Falstaff in the manner of the Vice
must await the climax of Part Two, but this climactic invocation
of the moral pattern, this time through a distinctive action rather
than through a verbal allusion, helps to epitomize what has suc-
ceeded and what has failed at the end of Shakespeare's most
challenging history play.

What then does this complex and highly original play owe to
the moral drama? Certainly, the tavern scene provides evidence
that Prince Hal, for one, linked Falstaff to the Vice. To treat Hal
as Every Prince is not to exaggerate that young man's importance
for this play and for the second tetralogy. But from I.ii on, Falstaff, unlike Inclination or Covetous, is quite unsuccessful as a
tempter-controller (at the end the fat knight carries off on his
back Hotspur, not Hal), while the prince's control of himself and
his surroundings distinguishes him from most moral play protagonists (with the notable exception of Just and Heavenly Man,
whom the critics do not have in mind). Since the Hal-Falstaff
scenes, moreover, account for only part of the play's dramatic
time, to see the young man and his riotous companion as the dramatic center is to oversimplify Shakespeare's theatrical strategy.
Clearly, if *Mankind*, *Wit and Science*, and *Lusty Juventus* are to be
the yardstick, the moral play has only limited relevance to this
history play.

But if the reader's conception of "morality play" includes *The
Trial of Treasure* and *Enough*, he or she *can* note a revealing link
between *1 Henry IV* and the moral tradition. Admittedly, Shakespeare's play provides no obvious homiletic contrast like that be-

tween a Lust and a Just or between a Worldly Man and a Heavenly Man, for missing here are any black-and-white alternatives
on an absolute moral scale. Nonetheless, in performance in the
theatre both *The Trial of Treasure* and *1 Henry IV* offer their audiences a similar evolving pattern built around two contrasting figures, each epitomizing a different set of attitudes towards the
play's central questions, each with an appropriate set of companions, each undergoing analogous experiences. Thus, in nonalle-
gorical terms, Falstaff and Worcester (or Glendower and Henry
IV) play much the same role for their young men as had Inclination and Sapience or Covetous and Enough; in a sequence of moments ranging from II.iii to III.ii, Hal and Hotspur display their
politic (or impolitic) natures in a manner analogous to the much
simpler bridling and unbridling of Inclination; the results of the
choices made by these two young men then act out in Act V
their far more complex versions of the winning of Lady Trust and
Lady Treasure. Shakespeare's alternating scenes, symbolic companions, and visually analogous moments are far superior in
quality and complexity but not necessarily different in kind from
their equivalents in the late moral plays. Rather, in both moral
play and history play themes, images, contrasts, and parallels are
set in motion through a sequence of scenes built around two protagonists, a sequence that develops the dramatist's point of view
through all the verbal and visual means available.

Clearly, *1 Henry IV* is not a dramatic sermon nor does it de-
pend upon overt allegory. Nonetheless, for much of the play
Shakespeare *has* fashioned his characters, issues, and relationships along the lines of a model found in some earlier plays that
are didactic, allegorical, and obvious. Here then is evidence in
both the moral tradition and in Shakespeare of a "sense of form
by which the elements of history could be related to one another
and made to constitute a meaningful whole" but a sense of form
not dependent upon "unification in a central character." To accept the Humanum Genus paradigm as our sole model is to narrow the horizon of expectations we bring to Elizabethan drama
and, as a result, to oversimplify one of Shakespeare's finest plays.

5

O God, that right should thus
overcome might!
(V.iv.23)

The Two Phased Structure of 2 *Henry IV*

As Harry Levin notes: "Any single work which entitles itself *The
Second Part* starts from something of a disadvantage."[1] As a result, *2 Henry IV* has dwelt in the shadow of its much admired
predecessor, to the extent that a great deal of critical and scholarly attention has been devoted to the relationship (in various
senses) between the two parts rather than to investigation of the
distinctive figures, themes, images, and structure of Part Two
alone. Best remembered for its famous (to many, infamous) climactic rejection scene, Part Two has not fared well in the theatre, for many directors find the script confusing, even cluttered
(especially up through the middle of Act IV) and therefore have
made sizable cuts.[2] Both productions and critical discussions have
thus concentrated upon those facets of the play most amenable to
modern tastes and interests (Falstaff, Prince Hal, Henry IV, the
end of Act IV) and slid over other troublesome areas (the rebel
scenes, the arrest of Doll Tearsheet). Indeed, the perceived limitations of the play (like the perceived limitations of *2 Tambur-
laine*) constitute a major part of the various arguments about the
relationship between Parts One and Two, including the conjectures about Shakespeare's original plan for one play.[3]

Like most readers, I would agree that important parts of this sequel, especially in Act V, work out major themes and images set in motion in Part One (and in *Richard II* as well), most notably in Prince Hal's "I do, I will." But unlike most critics and theatrical professionals, I find in 2 *Henry IV* a distinctive thematic and structural integrity, a coherence as a dramatic unit, albeit an integrity or coherence linked to a sense of dramatic progression shared by Shakespeare, his actors, and his audience but not necessarily by us. In brief, my thesis is that in 2 *Henry IV* Shakespeare is adapting the two phased moral play strategy evident in simpler form in *Richard III* and facets of 1 *Henry IV* but here worked out on a much larger scale—indeed, the largest scale he attempted with this particular formula. Consequently, the failure to recognize the original logic of presentation (part of the theatrical legacy inherited by the Elizabethan spectator but lost today) lies at the root of much of the dissatisfaction today with the play's supposed formlessness.

To advance such a thesis is not necessarily to offer a startling new reading of the play. Indeed, although interpreters will continue to quarrel about the stature or appeal of the key figures (especially Falstaff and Prince Hal), most would agree that Shakespeare here presents a sick kingdom, associated with a tainted, troubled Henry IV, that can only be truly ordered or cleansed of stain by the accession of a new king in Act V, a necessary transition spelled out by no less of an expert than Henry IV himself in his final lecture to his son at the end of Act IV. What has *not* been fully explored, however (partly because of the preoccupation with links to Part One), is the way (or ways) Shakespeare has chosen to portray that sick kingdom in Acts I through IV (and parts of Act V) and, equally important, how the resolution under the new king both mirrors and supersedes the disorder under the old. Even when such problems have been addressed, assumptions about one kind of pattern or structure—in particular, a search for a central protagonist, whether Falstaff, the prince, or even Henry IV—have directed attention away from what the dramatist actually offers us (and thus have paved the way for various negative appraisals), for, unlike *Richard III*, *Richard II*, or even *1 Henry IV*, Part Two resists analysis and classification in the terms usually invoked by its critics.[4] What then happens when the paradigm of the two phased moral play is introduced as a potential model for Shakespeare's play? First, the expanded role allotted Falstaff (and, conversely, the diminished role allotted Prince Hal before the end of Act IV) makes a good deal more sense. If Falstaff is seen not as the tempter of Every Prince (in fact, he is on-stage with Hal-as-prince only once in the play) but rather as a much transformed version of the public Vice (who reigns as the dominant figure, the focus of dramatic emphasis, until superseded in phase two), his antics and shady successes can serve as an epitome of what is wrong in England. In addition, the function both of the rebel scenes and of various Justice or Authority figures (including Prince John) becomes clearer if one thinks of the play through IV.iii not as the development of any one central figure but rather as a panoramic (and highly theatrical) exploration of a diseased kingdom in preparation for phase two when a new Henry pays the debt he never promised, changes the mode, and transcends both his former companions and his father.

Such claims can only serve as a point of departure, for the justification for invoking such a paradigm cannot follow solely from a "historical" argument based upon available models but must be based upon an analysis of the play itself. Moreover, since numerous claims have already been made about *2 Henry IV*'s family tree, are yet more branches necessary or fruitful? But consider some advantages of viewing Part Two in terms of this model from the late moral plays. First, to focus upon the public Vice and the two phased action is to concentrate attention in the first three and a half acts not upon Prince Hal (who appears only twice) but upon the sick kingdom epitomized by Falstaff and the rebels (exactly where Shakespeare places his emphasis). Second, as in *Richard III* or *1 Henry IV*, such a working model encourages us to consider possible links or analogies between phase one (the kingdom under Henry IV) and phase two (the "new" kingdom under Henry V as presented briefly yet tellingly in Act V)—an approach that I find very revealing. Finally (and most controversially), the "logic" behind the much debated rejection of Falstaff may be clearer if the modern reader is aware not only of a general family resemblance to the Vice but, more important, of a built-in rationale behind many late moral play Vices that grants them their moments of fun and dominance with the tacit yet firm understanding that such figures will be superseded and controlled in the final movement (beaten, arrested, hanged, carried off to Hell), usually at the hands of whatever authority is singled out as the "answer" to the problem orchestrated by the moral dramatist. The same logic that pits Courage against Authority and Correction (or Richard III against Richmond), pits Falstaff (and his cohorts) against the combination of Henry V and the Lord Chief Justice, the newly chosen father to Hal's youth.

Let me turn then to phase one of *2 Henry IV*—in particular, the way in which Shakespeare presents the diseased or disordered kingdom. To bring on-stage an entity such as a kingdom, the later moral dramatists usually resorted not to a figure named Respublica or Albion Knight but rather to choric figures (e.g., Common's Cry and Common's Complaint in *Cambises*) or, more often, a cross section of social types (e.g., the petitioners at the trial scene in *All for Money*, the "estates" figures subject to Lady Lucre in *The Three Ladies of London*). In his earlier plays, Shakespeare too had brought in individual spokesmen (Exeter in *1 Henry VI*, the scrivener in *Richard III*) or groups of speakers (the three citizens in *Richard III*, II.iii, the gardeners in *Richard II*) to describe the state of England, but he also resorted to more complex actions and events to pinpoint what was wrong (the Cade rebellion in *2 Henry VI*, the repeated outrages in *3 Henry VI*). His strategy in the first four acts of *2 Henry IV* then represents his most ambitious attempt in the history plays to display on-stage a sick or tainted world.

Thus, as various critics have noted, the play's imagery and action repeatedly confront us with disease, age, the ravages of time, false or denied expectations, betrayal, venality—even Prince Hal's desire for "small beer" (II.ii.6). Starting with Rumor's Prologue and extending through the conflicting reports about Shrewsbury, Falstaff's wriggling out of debts and commitments, Northumberland's default, Falstaff's recruiting tactics, and Prince John's shady dealings at Gaultree Forest, episode after episode acts out the validity of the Archbishop's question: "What trust is in these times?" (I.iii.100) Similarly, the highly visible on-stage sickness of first Northumberland with his crutch and "sickly quoif" (I.i.145–47), then Falstaff with his real and metaphoric diseases (I.ii.1–5, 223–25, 230–35), and finally the ailing Henry IV (III.i, IV.iv–v), not to mention Falstaff's disease-ridden descriptions of Doll Tearsheet (II.iv.42–44, 315–16), provide, especially for a spectator, a physical embodiment of England's disease. This sense of a sick country is further developed in a series of major speeches: Northumberland's tirade "let order die!" (I.i.136–60); the Archbishop's account of a commonwealth "sick of their own choice" (I.iii.87–108); Henry IV's perception of "the body of our kingdom / How foul it is, what rank diseases grow, / And with what danger, near the heart of it" (III.i.38–40); and the Archbishop's justification for rebellion: "we are all diseased, / And with our surfeiting and wanton hours / Have brought ourselves into a burning fever, / And we must bleed for it" (IV.i.54–57). Many of these speeches are self-serving, for, as L. C. Knights has argued, disease in 2 *Henry IV* "is associated with disorder originating in the will." For Knights, "the land is sick because of an original act of usurpation" (as the Archbishop goes on to argue in IV.i.57–66) "and because of the further self-seeking of those who helped Bolingbroke to the throne, and because people like Falstaff think that 'the law of nature' is different from and can override the law of justice."[5]

As Knights suggests, Shakespeare's presentation of disease and false expectations encourages us to probe more deeply into causes and effects. Once we look beyond Prince Hal (who is on the fringes of the action in phase one), we can perceive a larger pattern, an almost step-by-step analysis of the limitations of Justice and Order under a symbolically sick and therefore limited Henry IV. Consider, in particular, Falstaff's activities. Except for the tavern scene (II.iv), his time on-stage is consistently linked to figures of Authority and Justice, whether the Lord Chief Justice (I.ii, II.i), Justice Shallow (III.ii, V.i, V.iii), or Prince John

(IV.iii), each of whom is clearly linked to Henry IV (for Shallow see V.iii.113). But despite his diseases, debts, and obvious violations of law and trust, Falstaff continues to be impervious to Justice and control during the reign of the ailing king, so that, thanks to "the unquiet time," he can achieve a standoff in his first confrontation with the Chief Justice ("Your day's service at Shrewsbury hath a little gilded over your night's exploit on Gad's Hill"—I.ii.140–44) and then fend off Snare, Fang, and Mistress Quickly in II.i, again despite the presence of the Chief Justice, who is "well acquainted with your manner of wrenching the true cause the false way" and comments: "You speak as having power to do wrong" (ll. 104–6, 124). Sir John's forays into Gloucestershire, both before and after battle, show his influence spreading outside the streets and taverns of London into the countryside where a Shallow, the possessor of "land and beefs," is fair prey ("If the young dace be a bait for the old pike, I see no reason in the law of nature but I may snap at him"—III.ii.305–9). Even in his one encounter with Prince Hal (who has overheard the disparaging comments), Falstaff can wriggle off the hook, for, as Poins notes: "he will drive you out of your revenge and turn all to a merriment, if you take not the heat" (II.iv.278–79).

In addition, the tavern scene provides another set of associations, for here Falstaff, except for his encounter with the prince, is presented as the reigning figure in his own element. In striking contrast to the comparable tavern sequence in Part One,[6] the bulk of this scene is devoted to Falstaff's world without Hal (and without the Lord Chief Justice or other constraints). In the theatre, the high point is then the much heralded first appearance of Pistol, Pistol's quarrel with Doll, and Falstaff's "heroic" expulsion of this rebellious figure (according to Doll, Sir John is a "valiant villain" who is "as valorous as Hector of Troy, worth five of Agamemnon, and ten times better than the Nine Worthies"— ll. 193, 203–5)—all this before Hal and Poins appear as drawers. As with the Gadshill robbery in Part One, Shakespeare here provides, albeit in raucous, comic terms, a revealing analogue to the central political action, for Falstaff's ejection of the disorderly Pistol represents an ordering of his tavern kingdom, his equivalent to Gaultree Forest. But, like the sick king's victories, little is actually accomplished. Thus, Hal's eavesdropping and subsequent encounter with Falstaff underline the gap between the two figures and the inevitable change to come when the prince becomes king, while the scene's emphasis upon death and age (Falstaff tells Doll: "Do not speak like a death's-head. Do not bid me remember mine end"—ll. 217–18) also calls attention to what lies ahead despite any short-term victories. It is no coincidence that our first view of the sick, troubled Henry IV directly follows this tavern scene, for short-term triumphs for either figure cannot resolve the deeper problems posed by time, disease, and compromised status. And, as suggested directly in the tavern and implicitly in the larger political action, the resolution of such problems for both figures is embodied in Prince Hal.

Falstaff's triumph over Pistol and his deflationary meeting with the prince are thus followed first by a troubled Henry IV who finds no comfort in Warwick's reassurances about the diseased kingdom ("It is but as a body yet distempered, / Which to his former strength may be restored / With good advice and little medicine"—III.i.41–43) and then by a full-scale display of Falstaff the recruiter and exploiter-to-be of Justice Shallow. Finally, the climax of phase one comes at Gaultree Forest where both Prince John and Falstaff achieve dubious victories that bring rebels under control without resolving any of the basic problems behind rebellion. Falstaff, moreover (the epitome of another form of rebellion), talks his way around Prince John and back to his haven in Gloucestershire, so his way of life certainly has not been changed or qualified. That the news of victory only makes the king sick[7] (IV.iv.102) is yet another comment upon the impossibility of any real "cure" for England so long as the monarch himself is the epitome of the most deeply rooted disease. At this point in the play, then, Falstaff's various encounters with the Lord Chief Justice, Justice Shallow, and Prince John have acted out how he and what he has come to represent are beyond any such control, while, even though the visible rebels have been put down, nothing has really changed in the kingdom, as epitomized in the absence of the Chief Justice, Falstaff's depredations in Gloucestershire, and the king's sickness. In particular, the sour taste left by Prince John's methods of quelling rebellion (enhanced by Shakespeare's changes in his sources)[8] heighten a sense of a tainted, suspect triumph, a questionable and disturbing placing of ends over means characteristic of the world of Falstaff and the diseased Henry IV.

What then of phase two, set up in the interview between king and prince (IV.v) and then acted out in V.ii, V.iv, and V.v? To characterize this climactic movement, let me focus upon several linked images. Throughout his history plays Shakespeare has often concentrated our attention upon children, heirs, and descent, with Prince Hal and his brothers being but one of many such sets reaching back to the sons of Edward III. Part Two starts with the reported death of a son, Hotspur, that elicits a reaction from his father that has ominous implications for the future health of the kingdom, followed by the appearance of the son of Richard II's Mowbray, a son who through his presence and pointed comments (see especially IV.i.113–29) recalls the conflicts still simmering from Bolingbroke's past, and by the appearance of a crown prince who waits in the background and discusses his problematic status with Poins in II.ii. Related references recur in the dialogue, whether in the rebels' concern "that our hopes, yet likely of fair birth, / Should be still-born" (I.iii.63–64) or Mowbray's allusion to the lives that have "miscarried under Bolingbroke" (IV.i.129) or the account of fearful omens that include "unfathered heirs and loathly births of nature" (IV.iv.122).

The most revealing passages are linked to the rhetoric of rebellion, especially when the insurgents describe the vulnerability of Henry IV. In one of his major speeches the Archbishop analyzes the awkward dilemma of the king who "hath found to end one doubt by death / Revives two greater in the heirs of life" (IV.i.199–200). In this view, each corrective action by Henry IV or his agents instead of providing a solution only adds to the problem (as epitomized by the on-stage presence of a second Mowbray). Linking correction, marriage, and children to the more familiar garden imagery, the Archbishop then sums up the dilemma of a king who knows full well he cannot "precisely weed this land." Rather:

His foes are so enrooted with his friends
That, plucking to unfix an enemy,
He doth unfasten so and shake a friend.
So that this land, like an offensive wife
That hath enraged him on to offer strokes,
As he is striking, holds his infant up
And hangs resolved correction in the arm
That was upreared to execution.   (ll. 204–14)

Similarly, just before the rebels accept John's "princely word,"
Hastings predicts that if this rebellion fails, others will "second our
attempt," and, "if they miscarry, theirs shall second them," so
that, in his terms, "success of mischief shall be born / And heir
from heir shall hold this quarrel up / Whiles England shall have
generation" (IV.ii.44–49). Although John rejects Hastings's vision of the future ("you are too shallow, Hastings, much too shallow, / To sound the bottom of the after-times"), the king too is
conscious of the problem posed by both current rebels and their
heirs in "the after-times." In his final speech to his son he admits
that the "soil" attached to his achieving the crown has "daily"
led "to quarrel and to bloodshed / Wounding supposèd peace,"
for despite all his efforts to answer the many challenges, he
recognizes that "all my reign hath been but as a scene / Acting
that argument." But the shrewd Henry IV also recognizes that,
since his own death now "changes the mode," the answer lies in
his son: "what in me was purchased / Falls upon thee in a more
fairer sort, / So thou the garland wear'st successively" (IV.v.189–
201). The dying king knows that in his own person he can never
resolve the continuing problem enunciated by Hastings and the
Archbishop. Only a new untainted king, a son who has gained
the crown or garland "successively" (rather than "as an honor
snatched with boisterous hand"—l. 191), can weed England's
garden.

In phase two, then, Henry V must come to terms with this
problem. To show this process in action in Act V, Shakespeare
provides a series of linked moments climaxing, of course, in the
famous rejection scene. One of these moments, however, has received little or no attention, in these or any other terms (and is

usually cut in performance). Thus, in the brief V. iv, one or more beadles drag on-stage Doll Tearsheet and Mistress Quickly, with the accusation against Doll that "there hath been a man or two lately killed about her" and "the man is dead that you and Pistol beat amongst you" (ll. 6, 16–17). Meanwhile, the Hostess provides her characteristic comments, including what could be a topic sentence for phase two: "O God, that right should thus overcome might!" (l. 23) Though Doll rages and the Hostess invokes the name and supposed influence of Falstaff (l. 11), these two figures are arrested, as we are reminded in the next scene just before the rejection when Pistol reveals Doll's fate to Falstaff who promises: "I will deliver her" (V. v. 39).

What is particularly striking for the spectator, moreover (although easily missed by the reader), is the stage picture of an apparently pregnant Doll who claims "an the child I now go with do miscarry, thou wert better thou hadst struck thy mother, thou paper-faced villain" (ll. 8–10). Given the various rebel allusions to heirs and unborn children, including the Archbishop's image of a wife who holds her infant up to avoid correction, Doll's claim is certainly consistent in metaphoric terms. But in response to this threat of impending miscarriage, the beadle answers: "If it do, you shall have a dozen of cushions again. You have but eleven now" (ll. 14–15). The "child," it appears, is only a cushion,[9] only another Falstaff-like trick (as with those used against the Lord Chief Justice, Hal, Shallow, or Mistress Quickly) to sidestep authority and the implications of one's actions. But, significantly, in phase two the stratagem does not work. In the context established by the rebels' speeches and imagery, not only are Doll and her accomplices arrested in the legal sense (as the rebels were arrested or attached by Westmoreland—IV. ii. 106–9), but, in addition, their way of life and, even more important, their seeds for the future are also being brought under control in an epitome of the movement of phase two. Just as many a Vice or other fallen figure had been arrested by a figure of Correction or Authority (see especially *The Tide Tarrieth No Man* and Willis's description of *The Cradle of Security*), so this epitome of the diseases and subterfuges of the world under Henry

IV is here being exposed, arrested, and metaphorically denied any progeny. In imagistic terms, an answer for phase two under Henry V is being acted out to Hastings's prophecy that "heir from heir shall hold this quarrel up / Whiles England shall have generation," for, in the Archbishop's terms, "resolved correction" has transcended the threat of the infant hostage or the continuing problem posed by "the heirs of life." Granted, the moment is comic, even anarchic in its language and action, but, especially with the paradigm of the two phased moral play in mind, there is a logic to both the arrest and the exposure of the false pregnancy that defines the "new" world under Henry V.

The other revealing moment before the climactic rejection is the new king's public vindication of the Lord Chief Justice, a figure last seen in II.i when, for a second time, he could not control Falstaff. Indeed, after coming to terms at the end of Act IV with the kingdom's most significant old man, Henry IV, Henry V's most visible actions in Act V are linked to decisions about two other old men who stand in symbolic opposition. The constant emphasis throughout this play upon false expectations has built to a climax in Henry IV's vision of the "rotten times" to come under the next regime (IV.iv.54–66) and the "wilderness" that lies ahead when "the fifth Harry from curbed license plucks / The muzzle of restraint" (IV.v.117–37).[10] The prince's explanation satisfies his father, but this private reconciliation has no effect upon the expectations of other figures in Act V, starting with Warwick, the Chief Justice, and Hal's brothers in V.ii, all of whom assume that the Justice stands "in coldest expectation" and "must now speak Sir John Falstaff fair" (V.ii.31, 33). The audience may be privy to the true Henry V, as revealed in the interview with his father, but the Chief Justice, who claims to "know" that the new king loves him not (l. 10), has no such advantage and so must rely only upon his honor, "the impartial conduct of my soul," and the first of several significant "if" clauses: "If truth and upright innocency fail me, / I'll to the king my master that is dead, / And tell him who hath sent me after him," for this principled figure will never "beg / A ragged and forestalled remission" (ll. 35–41).

The first appearance of Hal as Henry V quickly builds to the exchange between Justice and king at the heart of this play. The Chief Justice's second "if" clause ("if I be measured rightly, / Your majesty hath no just cause to hate me"—ll. 65–66) elicits the king's question how he can be expected to forgive an individual who could "rate, rebuke, and roughly send to prison / The immediate heir of England" (ll. 70–71). The Justice begins his lengthy apologia with an invocation of his authority (not much in evidence in his encounters with Falstaff) in terms of "the person of your father," "the image of his power," "the administration of his law," "the commonwealth," and "the majesty and power of law and justice, / The image of the king whom I presented" (ll. 73–79). He then climaxes his case (and, we must remember, this is a man fully prepared to join his master that is dead rather than forsake his principles) with a final "if":

> If the deed were ill,
> Be you contented, wearing now the garland,
> To have a son set your decrees at nought,
> To pluck down justice from your awful bench,
> To trip the course of law and blunt the sword
> That guards the peace and safety of your person,
> Nay, more, to spurn at your most royal image
> And mock your workings in a second body.

"Make the case yours," he goes on, continuing to emphasize the father-son inversion:

> Be now the father and propose a son,
> Hear your own dignity so much profaned,
> See your most dreadful laws so loosely slighted,
> Behold yourself so by a son disdained,
> And then imagine me taking your part
> And in your power soft silencing your son.

With all this in mind, he concludes: "sentence me, / And, as you are a king," tell me "what I have done that misbecame my place, / My person, or my liege's sovereignty." Especially after the extensive display of the limitations and vulnerability of Justice in phase one under Henry IV, this plea for Justice for future sons, as opposed to revenge for past indignities, is forceful and moving. Will the new king be any different from a Northumberland reacting to his son's fate or a Mowbray reacting to the supposed wrongs done to his father? Subjected to the power of Rumor and false expectation (like Henry IV earlier), the figures on stage, including the Chief Justice, expect the worst.

The new king's answer, more than any other single speech, then defines phase two. In a manner calculated to "mock the expectation of the world" and "rotten opinion" (ll. 126–28), he responds: "You are right, justice, and you weigh this well. / Therefore still bear the balance and the sword." Henry's subsequent commentary, moreover, like the Justice's defense (and like the rebels' analysis of the problems facing Henry IV) is linked to sons, heirs, and the future, for he wishes

> your honors may increase,
> Till you do live to see a son of mine
> Offend you and obey you, as I did.
> So shall I live to speak my father's words:
> "Happy am I, that have a man so bold
> That dares do justice on my proper son,
> And not less happy, having such a son
> That would deliver up his greatness so
> Into the hands of justice."

In a major symbolic action clearly designed to characterize the new reign, the king then commits into the hands of this newly invigorated Justice "the unstained sword that you have used to bear" (a climactic image of the sword of Justice widespread in the late moral plays) "with this remembrance, that you use the same / With the like bold, just, and impartial spirit / As you have done 'gainst me." Extending his hand (l. 117), Henry accepts this sword-bearing figure "as a father to my youth" whose voice will prompt the king's ear and whose "well-practiced wise directions" will control his intents. The man who has refused to blunt the sword of Justice (l. 87) and who "dares do justice" on the crown prince himself has been reinvested with his sword and placed on the highest level of the kingdom.

According to one familiar formulation about the two parts of *Henry IV*, Prince Hal's education involves lessons in one set of qualities in Part One (e.g., Chivalry, Temperance, Honor) and a second set in Part Two (e.g., Justice, the rule of Law). Certainly, this scene would support such an educational emphasis, for much of the king's climactic speech is a hymn to ideal Justice. But to limit the import of this scene or this speech to a lesson learned by Prince Hal is to blur the larger shape of Part Two and, in particular, to diminish the importance of this moment as an alternative to the Justice under Henry IV in phase one. Surely it is no coincidence that between the final view of the dying Henry IV and this presentation of a new, strengthened Justice under Henry V Shakespeare provides a scene that includes both Falstaff's elaborate critique of Justice Shallow (see especially his comments on the power of foolish behavior as a spreader of disease— V.i.68–71) and a revealing example of "justice" in action when Davy persuades Shallow to favor William Visor of Woncot, a known "arrant knave," over an honest man on the basis of Davy's "credit" with his master. Under the old, sick king, Justice is either hampered (the Chief Justice with Falstaff) or corruptible (Shallow's favoring William Visor) or stained (Prince John at Gaultree). But under the new king, Justice has regained its sword.

This new role for Justice (and the Chief Justice), however, is as yet unknown to Falstaff. Rather, the next scene sets up an obvious parallel to the false expectations in V.ii of the courtiers and the Justice when Pistol bursts in with his tidings of "golden times" and his news that Falstaff is "now one of the greatest men in this realm" (V.iii.94, 85–86). Shallow's futile attempt to penetrate Pistol's fustian leads eventually to the Justice's self-important claim: "I am, sir, under the king, in some authority," but when Pistol's question, "under which king, Besonian?" elicits "Harry the Fourth," the response is: "A foutra for thine office! / Sir John, thy tender lambkin now is king. / Harry the

Fifth's the man" (ll. 109–15). Nowhere are the recurrent false expectations (and the implications of those expectations) clearer: first, with Falstaff's offers to Shallow ("choose what office thou wilt in the land, 'tis thine") and to Pistol ("I will double-charge thee with dignities"); and then in one of the key speeches of the play:

> Master Shallow, my Lord Shallow—be what thou wilt, I am fortune's steward—get on thy boots. We'll ride all night. O sweet Pistol! Away, Bardolph! Come, Pistol, utter more to me, and withal devise something to do thyself good. Boot, boot, Master Shallow. I know the young king is sick for me. Let us take any man's horses; the laws of England are at my commandment. Blessed are they that have been my friends, and woe to my lord chief justice! (ll. 126–35)

If the previous scene had offered an epitome of the "new" restored Justice under Henry V, this speech (more than any other in the play) sums up the "old" way under Henry IV and, equally important, spells out clearly what the Falstaff of Part Two has actually become.

Given the magic of Falstaff's appeal (which, for many readers, takes on a life of its own that transcends the three plays in which he actually appears), many commentators ignore or play down this speech and this scene. But Shakespeare has gone to considerable lengths in Act V to provide a context for the rejection scene, a context we can ignore only at the risk of rewriting the play. For Falstaff, the Chief Justice is an enemy over whom he now expects to exult, cheered on by the new king, his tender lambkin, but, as witnesses to the previous scene, we are aware (even painfully aware) of the truth. "Let us take any man's horses" and "the laws of England are at my commandment" epitomize in two clauses the diseases of phase one, with Law clearly subservient to Knights's concept of the disordered will. Earlier figures had talked of cures for the sick kingdom (e.g., Warwick in III.i, the Archbishop in IV.i), but, as suggested in these two back-to-back scenes, that cure is linked to the king and his Chief Justice in V.ii, not the Falstaff of V.iii (who is presented in terms that no longer strike me as "comic"). Memories of the first two acts of Part One can here be very misleading, for the Falstaff Shakespeare actually gives us at the end of Part Two (like the "pregnant" Doll Tearsheet) *must* be "arrested" if the new king and the new kingdom are to supersede the old.

But we are still left with the discomfort many readers feel with the rejection scene that follows. In a provocative essay, Moody Prior observes that those who side with Henry V often treat "Falstaff as a special variant of some original prototype" (whether Vice or braggart warrior or Lord of Misrule) "who plays out an assigned role and then is dismissed without any waste of sympathy." For Prior, however, this line of argument is reductive, for no one apparently was "saddened by the routing of a Vice, or a braggart soldier, and the similarities between Falstaff and such types does not account for the differences which produce dismay in those who disapprove of the Prince's action." In Prior's view, "the appeal to prototypes and conditioned patterns of response fails because it does not give sufficient weight to the dramatist's control over the effects produced by his play." Rather, he invokes his own prototype, "the comic hero who defies time, contingency, respectability, and caution, who uses his wit and resilience to beat the odds against him." To witness the rejection scene, then, is as if "Chaplin were to be crushed to earth by the fierce looking waiter; as though the sheriff had finally caught up with Groucho's shady practices and we see him, dejected, being led away to jail; as though W. C. Fields, after his assaults on every decent sentiment, ended up not rich or heading for the Grampian Hills but instead in a D.T. ward." Prior argues that "such magnificent comic heroes were not created for such ends," so that "no matter by what critical avenues the rejection of Falstaff is approached, the unpleasantness of which so many have complained cannot be argued away."[11]

As Prior rightly observes, to introduce a prototype or conventional pattern (whether Vice or "comic hero") is to flirt with various dangers, for any convincing interpretation should be grounded in the work itself and the dramatist's art, not in material invoked from outside the play. But, like many other critics, he draws heavily upon Part One and, although admitting some changes in Part Two ("a play more sombre in tone, more serious in content"), nonetheless argues that "we are reluctant to observe any of those changes which undermine or dull the extraordinary comic achievement of Part I" (p. 166). But it is the Falstaff of Part Two who is rejected by Henry V and, more specifically, the Falstaff who has just announced that "the laws of England are at my commandment." Moreover, Prior himself notes that "the world of *Henry IV* is not that of pure comedy but of history and political power," so that "what is a disaster from the point of view of our comic involvement and response is a necessity from the point of view of the political action" (p. 168). In related terms, I would argue that the emphasis at the climax of Part Two should fall upon both the necessary reordering of England and the price that must be paid for that reordering and for becoming Henry V (as opposed to Prince Hal). When the new king states: "Presume not that I am the thing I was" (V.v.57), the message is for us as well as Falstaff. For some readers the price has seemed too high, but the more closely one regards the diseased kingdom of phase one and the Falstaff of Act V, the more one faces the "necessity" Prior admits. The prototype of the Vice who thrives until he is superseded or arrested does not "explain" Falstaff but does provide a revealing analogue that may help us to see the dramatic (or political) logic behind this controversial moment.[12]

Undoubtedly, interpreters of Part Two will continue to disagree, often vigorously, on exactly how to evaluate or describe both Falstaff and Henry V at this climactic point. The problem, it seems to me, is built into the scene, for the new king's choice strikes me as both necessary and painful. But any fair discussion should take into account the total context provided by Shakespeare. An uncontrolled, untrammeled Falstaff at the end of the play suggests to me a continuation of the world of phase one, a world of visible diseases, disordered will, and inversions of authority where a leading cleric of the realm dons armor to fight his king and where even a victory in the king's name leaves a sour taste behind. After the interview between the dying king and the king-to-be, we see no more political rebels, but we do see an arrant knave favored over an honest man by the old king's Justice and the symbolic choice of another kind of Justice by the new king. Any defense of Falstaff must then confront the placement of V.ii, with its public display of the new status of the Chief Justice, *before* V.iii, with its summary presentation of Falstaff's view of Law ("let us take any man's horses") and the Law's representatives ("woe to my lord chief justice"). Can one read these two scenes in sequence and, regardless of the memories of Part One, conclude that what Falstaff has come to stand for can continue without subverting the new regime? Herein lies the importance of the "arrest" in V.iv, not only of Doll and Mistress Quickly but also of the supposed child, the future associated with Falstaff and Pistol, "the heirs of life" associated with a continuing threat to Henry V and to England.

Those uncomfortable with Henry V and the rejection also point to Prince John's closing lines in which this suspect figure from Gaultree Forest praises "this fair proceeding of the king's" in that "his wonted followers / Shall all be very well provided for" (ll. 98–100). As one critic notes: "I do not think I am being fanciful in suggesting that I would not care to be 'very well provided for' by John of Lancaster; the statement from his mouth conjures up for me visions of thumbscrews and gibbets."[13] But in his subsequent speech John predicts "that, ere this year expire, / We bear our civil swords and native fire / As far as France" (ll. 106–8), a prophecy or set of expectations that, unlike so many in phase one, proves true. The earlier situation under Henry IV that had provided a context for John's misleading "princely word" at Gaultree Forest has now given way to a changed (or changing) society under an untainted king, so John's statements at the end of the play, delivered to a corroborating Chief Justice, strike me as straightforward and factual. At this point all the figures from phase one are "under arrest"—rebels, Falstaff and companions, even presumably Justice Shallow (the Chief Justice says: "Take all his company along with him"—l. 93), so John's terms, tone, and point of view should be revaluated in this new context.

Prince John's "fair proceeding" and "very well provided for" should also be viewed in terms of the difference between the use of language in phases one and two. In the world of the sick Henry IV, language itself was called into question and was not to be trusted. In the comic scenes, individual words are shown to be losing their force or meaning, not only in Mistress Quickly's highly audible malapropisms but also when Doll criticizes Pistol for his use of *captain*, comparing such a decline in meaning to the already corrupted *occupy*, (II.iv.126–36) or when Bardolph dazzles Shallow with his use of *accommodated* (III.ii.63–77). Elsewhere, words that out of context could sound meaningful, moving, or heroic appear only comic or hollow in this sick world, most notably the protestations of "courageous Feeble," the woman's tailor, in the recruiting scene (e.g., "A man can die but once. We owe God a death. I'll ne'er bear a base mind"— III.ii.153, 221–25). As in Part One, Falstaff's verbal obfuscations are a major key to his success, whether with the Chief Justice (when he turns *gravity* into *gravy*—I.ii.153–54) or with Mistress Quickly (when he redefines *swaggerer* as *tame cheater* to gain admittance for Pistol—II.iv.90) or with Shallow or Prince John, while in the political action, to paraphrase the Archbishop's question, there is no trust in words, most obviously those of Northumberland and John of Lancaster. Shakespeare provides a climactic (and very funny) example after Davy announces "there's one Pistol come from the court with news" (V.iii.78–79), for despite the general anticipation (and much prodding from Falstaff), it still takes almost forty lines for the fact of Henry IV's death to break through Pistol's fustian.

But Prince Hal is the obvious alternative. After the first of the dying king's prophecies of what will follow his death, Warwick defends the prince as a student of language, one who "but studies his companions / Like a strange tongue, wherein, to gain the language, / 'Tis needful that the most immodest word / Be looked upon and learned" even though such words thereafter may only "be known and hated." According to Warwick, "in the perfectness of time" Hal will reject his present companions "like gross terms" so that "past evils" will serve "as a pattern or a measure" (IV.iv. 68–78). Although unappealing to Hal's detractors, this rationale fits well with what we are shown in both parts of *Henry IV*. Equally important, in contrast to a wide range of comic and political speakers in phase one, a sense of a chaster, clearer language emerges in the prince or new king's major speeches in Acts IV and V: "You won it, wore it, kept it, gave it me. / Then plain and right must my possession be" (IV.v.221–22); "You are right, justice, and you weigh this well. / Therefore still bear the balance and the sword" (V.ii.102–3).

In the context of this "new" language of phase two, John's "this fair proceeding" and "very well provided for" can more readily be taken at face value (as the Chief Justice appears to accept them), for, despite much cynicism among modern critics, there *is* now trust in these times. Moments earlier, moreover, in a more significant moment, Henry V had prevented Falstaff from using his vaunted verbal dexterity to defend himself. In their only previous meeting in Part Two the prince had overheard "how vilely" Falstaff had spoken of him, but in his "no abuse" speech Sir John had argued (rather lamely) that "I dispraised him before the wicked, that the wicked might not fall in love with him," disparaging Bardolph, Doll, and the Hostess as "the wicked" (II.iv.280, 298–317). But in phase two, after Henry V has noted that "the grave doth gape / For thee thrice wider than for other men" and Falstaff apparently has started to respond (one can almost hear the joke coming), the words are cut off: "Reply not to me with a fool-born jest" (V.v.54–56). Detractors of Henry V may conclude only that they have been cheated out of another bit of vintage Falstaff, but the logic of phase two demands a new king in command of language and tone, a Chief Justice empowered to "arrest" not only Falstaff but also language (see ll. 94–96), and a Falstaff whose words to Shallow now ring hollow, whether about the thousand pounds or being sent for in private by the king or "I will be the man yet that shall make you great." Significantly, it is after Falstaff has been cut off by the Chief Justice ("I cannot now speak. I will hear you soon") that we hear John's speech that climaxes not with "very well provided for" but with the proviso that the king's former companions "all are banished till their conversations / Appear more wise and modest to the world" (ll. 101–2). Wise and modest "conversation" (a term that links language and behavior) is the ticket to the world of phase two.

What then are the advantages for an analysis of 2 *Henry IV* of invoking the public Vice and the two phased paradigm from the moral plays? As Prior notes, use of such prototypes can be reductive and can subject Shakespeare's richness of character and imagery to moral formulas. But for reasons I do not profess to understand, many readers of this play, including those who reject the Falstaff-as-Vice argument, have indulged in their own reductive approach and have substituted the Falstaff of Part One for the figure actually presented here, have ignored or played down Part Two's distinctive images and emphases, and, especially in my phase one, have focused upon the limited role of Prince Hal at the expense of Shakespeare's scenes and actions. Although I have not sought to provide an exhaustive analysis of this play, the pattern I have developed does take into account the entire scope of Part Two and does explain the progression epitomized in the sequence of scenes in Act V that displays the conflict between old and new, Justice reinstated, a series of "arrests," and the new king's public confrontations with two formidable old men. Granted, no one today can speak for that original audience, but, as with the contrasting protagonists in *The Trial of Treasure*, the public Vice and the two phased action *did* exist in the 1590s as one option for a dramatist looking for an appropriate form or paradigm for a history play. My "historical" reading is therefore linked to a model available in the age of Shakespeare, as opposed to a response that invokes Charlie Chaplin, Groucho Marx, and W. C. Fields.

In conclusion, Falstaff is not a Vice; 2 *Henry IV* is not a moral play. Yet events and relationships in Part Two *are* structured in a manner analogous to the moral plays described in chapter two (a group rarely invoked in such discussions). My goal has not been to use this part of Shakespeare's dramatic heritage to distill his message or sermon or even to uncover the archaeological strata beneath his surface but to provide yet another instance of how he used, adapted, and transcended his inherited materials, whether from the moral plays, Plautus, Holinshed, or Plutarch. In this case, moreover, emphasis upon the public Vice and the two phased action takes us a step closer to the distinctive images and structure of the play Shakespeare actually wrote, as opposed to that play about Prince Hal that many readers would have preferred. Falstaff's one allusion to the moral plays is only a joke on Shallow's physique ("And now is this Vice's dagger become a squire"—III.ii.297–98). Nonetheless, the modern interpreter in tune with the late moral drama is in a position better to appreciate Shakespeare's achievement in this ambitious, meaningful history play.

6

When you find him out, you
have him ever after.

III.vi.84–85

The Logic of Bertram's "Conversion"
in *All's Well That Ends Well*

To move from *2 Henry IV* to *All's Well That Ends Well* is apparently to leave behind ugly political realities and difficult compromises in favor of a sunnier world characterized by respected noble figures and a much admired romance heroine. Yet, like *2 Henry IV*, this comedy has a sick king, a hero whom many interpreters find objectionable, and a comic pretender to valor and influence who struts through much of the play only to be publicly exposed and brought under control near the end. Like Part Two, moreover, *All's Well* climaxes with a striking confrontation between its hero and a second figure equally important to the play, a confrontation that has occasioned controversy among both academics and theatrical professionals. Like Henry V's rejection of Falstaff, Bertram's reconciliation with Helena has puzzled and antagonized readers and playgoers who have found such a "conversion" underdeveloped or unconvincing. Critics, as a result, often second Dr. Johnson's complaint that Bertram "is dismissed to happiness."[1] A. P. Rossiter, for one, argues that the traits Bertram reveals in Act V "are *not* those of a puppet-hero about to live happily ever after; but those of a weak, cowardly, mean-spirited, false, and ill-natured human being," so, for him, "Bertram's vices are buried hugger-mugger."[2]

To account for both this problematic moment and the general shape of the play, some scholars have invoked the traditional "morality play" paradigm and have treated Bertram as a Humanum Genus figure who must choose between two symbolic companions, Parolles and Helena, who embody opposing sets of values.[3] Parolles's part in such a paradigm is then supported by comments from various spokesmen within the play. Thus, the countess calls Parolles "a very tainted fellow, and full of wickedness," adding that "my son corrupts a well-derivèd nature / With his inducement" (III.ii.85–87); Diana points to Parolles as "that same knave / That leads him [Bertram] to these places" (III.v.80–81); and Lafew tells the countess that her son had been "misled with a snipped-taffeta fellow there" (IV.v.1–2). In addition, Shakespeare provides one scene that can be interpreted as a tug-of-war or psychomachia (II.v) in which the newly wed Helena unsuccessfully begs a kiss, only to be rejected by an unyielding Bertram (who has already made his plans to leave her) while a silent Parolles is standing by, presumably at his side. Indeed, in a recent production in which the director was striving for a less culpable Bertram,[4] an exiting Helena blew a kiss to a Bertram who was almost ready to yield only to have Parolles step in front of him, intercept the kiss, and literally brush it away. From the virginity debate in the opening scene through this moment, Helena and Parolles do function as polar opposites who epitomize alternative choices for the comic hero.

After Act II, however, the paradigm of a Humanum Genus figure attended by tempter and good angel can provide a model for the action only in the most general terms. Unlike Desdemona with Othello, Helena has no real on-stage contact with her husband again until the final moments (she does see him from a distance in III.v), while after II.v Bertram is progressively distanced from a Parolles who has been replaced by the two Dumaines. Moreover, as R. L. Smallwood notes, the final scene prevents us from seeing Parolles as "the wicked angel responsible for leading Bertram astray," for, long after the comic hero has seen through his former companion, he demonstrates himself to be "independently capable of his most objectionable behaviour, in that long demonstration of weakness, cowardice, and lying."[5] Finally, whether the interpreter invokes the traditional "morality play" or modern psychology, the comic hero's reconciliation with his wife remains a problem, for few readers are comfortable with the new or changed Bertram that seems to be called for in the spirit of romance. Rather, as Alexander Leggatt notes: "We are still not entirely sure that the solving of a riddle can make one person love another."[6] Like the rejection of Falstaff, this climactic moment poses a continuing problem for any interpretation of *All's Well*, whether that interpretation be historical or modernist, psychomachic or psychoanalytic.

Granted, for some readers the solution to this problem is relatively simple. Thus, Kenneth Muir suggests that our difficulties with *All's Well* result from the poor state of the text and imperfect re vision on Shakespeare's part. For Muir, "if the Clown were giver. better jokes and Bertram a better speech at the end, the play would leave us with feelings of greater satisfaction," as opposed to having Bertram's capitulation delivered "in an absurd couplet."[7] To be less charitable, one can join the long tradition, well documented by Joseph G. Price, of treating this play as a failure or, more recently, as Shakespeare's bold but largely unsuccessful experiment in making the transition from the romantic comedies to the final plays.[8] Considering the various options, Rossiter observes that we can conclude that "Shakespeare is inept: he might have given us a convertible Bertram, and he has not"; or that "Shakespeare is cynical about his audience: he relies on their being crass or unreflective"; or "that he was aware of what he had done, even if it was the best he could do with it."[9] The difficulty may therefore lie in the text, the revisions, some unsuccessful experiment, some lost convention, or Shakespeare's failure this time to depict accurately that piece of work, man, but for almost all of today's interpreters, the difficulty persists.

Consider the roots of this problem. As Dr. Johnson and generations of subsequent readers have attested, Bertram is *not* an appealing figure throughout much of the play, especially when compared with Helena, the countess, the king, and Lafew. Some of his least attractive moments, moreover, come in the final scene where he lies, slanders Diana, and, in general, behaves despicably in his unsuccessful attempt to defend the indefensible. Then, as Muir suggests, his capitulation and apparent conversion after Helena's appearance are, by our standards, *very* quick, with Bertram given a total of only two and a half lines and with much of the dramatic time of this concluding movement devoted elsewhere (to Parolles, Lafew, the king, and Diana). The modern reader or actor therefore cries out for some clearer signals of this change that is so important to the climax of the comedy, whether a bigger speech, an aside, or some revealing stage action. With regard to the play as a whole, *our* conditioning leads us to expect more emphasis upon Bertram's learning process (as with the standard view of the education of Prince Hal), so modern interpreters look for a clearly charted progression from the callow youth who rejects Helena in Act II to the romance hero of the finale. Such expectations, however, are not satisfied (at least in our terms) either in Bertram's behavior with Diana in Act IV or in his lies and evasions in front of his mother, the king, and Lafew in Act V. All in all, Bertram (like the Falstaff of Part Two) is not the hero (or the husband for Helena) that most readers of the play would prefer nor has his rapid capitulation and conversion proved convincing or palatable. Particularly for the believer in psychological realism, "the realistic quality in Bertram is at odds with his theatrical redemption."[10]

Such problems, moreover, are compounded when the play is compared with its putative sources, Boccaccio and Painter.[11] Putting aside Shakespeare's significant additions (e.g., figures such as Parolles, the countess, Lafew, and the clown), one is left with the same two key events or phases of the story (Giletta-Helena's curing of the king to gain a husband and her winning back of Beltramo-Bertram by satisfying two apparently impossible conditions through a "bed-trick"), but Shakespeare appears to have gone out of his way to make his Bertram more culpable and less attractive than Beltramo. In particular, in the story Shakespeare inherited, Giletta appears at the end with the ring and with twin sons to be accepted as wife by a Beltramo who is both the husband who set the conditions and an impartial judge equivalent to the king in *All's Well*. Bertram's wriggling and squirming under the cross-examination of his mother, the king, and Lafew is therefore Shakespeare's addition or insertion, not an obligatory part of the story. In short, the ending as we have it appears a product not of the source but of the dramatist's design, presumably an essential part of his strategy.

Granted, one can still argue that our problems with the ending may be occasioned by a poor text, faulty revision, or even careless writing (Shakespeare, like Homer, may nod), but comparison of V.iii with the events narrated by Boccaccio and Painter suggests to me a conscious design, a change (or series of changes) with some end in mind. The problem therefore may lie not in the text itself but rather in the logic of interpretation wittingly or unwittingly being used as the basis for analysis. Are we indeed asking the right questions and looking at the appropriate evidence? In particular, is the psychological approach to character, motivation, and change that we take for granted in Shakespeare's tragedies (or in modern fiction) fully applicable to the climax of this comedy?[12] And if there *is* an alternative logic at work here, wherein lie its components or terms and how are we to grasp the relationships?

As I have already noted, one set of clues is provided by the gaps between sources and play. The first movement that builds to Helena's curing of the king does not deviate significantly from the story Shakespeare inherited. But Helena's success only creates a new set of problems rooted in Bertram's intransigence and his disdain for the poor physician's daughter, so the next two acts are devoted to Bertram's victories in Italy, his wooing of Diana, Helena's quest, and Parolles's adventures and exposure, all of which feed into the complex denouement in V.iii. What is especially instructive is how much of the material in this part of the play (the scenes that fall between the cure and the conversion) Shakespeare did *not* find in his sources (outside of the bed-trick to satisfy the two conditions). If indeed there *is* an Elizabethan dramatic logic that could explain the various puzzles of *All's Well*, that logic should be evident in the figures and scenes Shakespeare chose to figure forth this part of his story. In contrast, modern interpreters primarily interested in Helena and Bertram often have not taken this material into account (especially the Parolles scenes) except in the most general terms and have therefore neglected the moments Shakespeare included to enhance and clarify the major events and characters as *he* understood them. These additions to the inherited story may not be as jarring as those made by earlier moral dramatists (e.g., R. B.'s introduction of Conscience, Justice, and Haphazard the Vice to dramatize the story of Apius and Virginia). Nonetheless, herein lies one obvious place to look for clues to Shakespeare's conception of what he was doing.

At the risk of minimizing the importance of Helena's quest (a major part of both source and play), let me focus upon the function of the two Parolles scenes in Act IV. Shrewd observers like Helena and Lafew have already grasped the truth about Parolles, but only in Act IV (and just after his apparent success with Diana) does Bertram finally share this awareness of his companion's cowardice, folly, and unreliability. Since Bertram does not reappear on-stage until the final scene, in what sense can his new insight into Parolles be seen as a preparation for his reconciliation with Helena, especially since this new insight follows so closely his attempted seduction of Diana and giving away his monumental ring? Most critics would agree with M. C. Bradbrook that at the climax of the play "the unmasking of Bertram re-echoes the unmasking of Parolles,"[13] for this progression (first understand and properly value Parolles, then similarly understand and properly value Helena) appears to be basic to the comic hero's education. Nonetheless, according to the logic of psychological realism, there is no clear link between the Bertram who recognizes the truth about the blindfolded Parolles ("damnable both-sides rogue!"—IV.iii.208) and the Bertram who (presumably) finally recognizes the true value of Helena. Moreover, if this new understanding of Parolles is an important stepping-stone, why is Bertram's next appearance in Act V so full of Parolles-like lying and posturing?

To raise such questions is to get to the heart of the problem, for our logic based upon post-Elizabethan notions of psychology, education, and dramatic progression may not be adequate, in this instance, to describe what Shakespeare is actually present-ing. Herein lies the advantage of introducing an alternative logic of presentation from the late moral plays, even as a general ana-logue (as opposed to a close working model). Granted, Parolles stands at several removes from the public Vice (and Shakespeare in this play provides no allusions as signposts as he did in *Richard III* and both parts of *Henry IV*), but to link him to such a proto-type is to open up various avenues that can expand the modern interpreter's sense of how a "comic character" can function. For example, such a model encourages us to consider not only Parolles's personal failings and his adverse influence upon Bertram but also his role as an epitome of a larger disease or set of false values found in both Bertram and the court as a whole.[14]

Consider some early scenes. At his first appearance Helena characterizes Parolles as "a notorious liar" and "a great way fool, solely a coward"; she then twits him about being born when Mars was retrograde because "you go so much backward when you fight" (I.i.96–97, 194). Moments later, although he speaks no lines, Parolles is included when Bertram makes his first appear-ance at court (I.ii.17.s.d.) and thus is present to hear the king's long description of Bertram's father, a hymn to the true soldier and courtier who "might be a copy to these younger times / Which, followed well, would demonstrate them now / But goers backward" (ll. 46–48). The Parolles who goes "so much back-ward" as a warrior is therefore linked metaphorically to the "goers backward" who represent the new breed of courtiers. The king notes also that the former count rejected those "younger spirits, whose apprehensive senses / All but new things disdain; whose judgments are / Mere fathers of their garments; whose constancies / Expire before their fashions" (ll. 60–63). The king need only glance at an outlandishly attired Parolles to make the obvious connection (and much depends too on how the other courtiers are costumed).

Parolles's first lines at court come when he and two departing lords urge Bertram to "steal away bravely" to the wars (advice Bertram does not take until after the enforced marriage); typically, Parolles here brags of his martial experience ("I have seen those wars") and the wound he supposedly gave Captain Spurio (II.i.29, 26, 41–45). Most significant, especially after the king's speech on courtly virtue, is Parolles's lecture to Bertram on courtship after the two lords have departed:

> Use a more spacious ceremony to the noble lords, you have re-strained yourself within the list of too cold an adieu. Be more expres-sive to them; for they wear themselves in the cap of the time; there do muster true gait, eat, speak, and move under the influence of the most received star; and though the devil lead the measure, such are to be followed. After them, and take a more dilated farewell.
>
> (ll. 50–57)

Here Shakespeare neatly epitomizes the values of the world of fashion, for, in contrast to the king's critique of faulty judgment or lack of constancy, Parolles argues that those in fashion who "wear themselves in the cap of the time" should be taken as mod-els "though the devil lead the measure." Given an appropriate costume for Parolles (and perhaps for Bertram and the two lords as well) along with suitably affected manners or behavior, this speech sets up a world of surfaces and postures epitomized in this bizarre figure but also permeating the court, described by the king as composed of "goers backward," figures "whose constan-cies / Expire before their fashions."

Like the Vice, then, Parolles is both a colorful, entertaining figure and a signpost pointing to what is wrong with the court (and with Bertram). So long as Bertram believes in him, how-ever, his status remains unchanged,[15] even though more and more figures begin to see through him. In particular, Lafew (like Helena earlier) holds up for our comic scrutiny Parolles's lies, evasions, cowardice, and absurd adherence to fashion (with spe-cific attention to his scarves and bannerets—II.iii.202, 221–22). The witty old lord asks: "Why dost thou garter up thy arms o' this fashion? Dost make hose of thy sleeves?" (ll. 244–46) and concludes: "You are more saucy with lords and honorable person-ages than the commission of your birth and virtue gives you heraldry" (ll. 255–57). Significantly, just after this critique Parolles supports Bertram's plan to leave Helena ("I'll to the Tuscan wars, and never bed her"—l. 267). At his next appearance, Lafew seems to accept Bertram's assurances that Parolles "is very great in knowledge and accordingly valiant" (II.v.7–8), but another look, particularly at his clothes ("Pray you, sir, who's his tailor?"—l. 15), causes Lafew to revert to his original estimate. As he sums up his critique for Bertram and for us: "there can be no kernel in this light nut; the soul of this man is his clothes. Trust him not in matter of heavy consequence" (ll. 42–44). Bertram's continued acceptance of Parolles, regardless of these comments, is immediately followed by his parting from Helena (and the denial of a kiss), so nowhere in the play are Bertram's choices, values, and particular form of blindness more clearly defined. Throughout Act II and especially in this scene, Shakespeare is using Parolles for a variety of purposes, not all of which can be encompassed by our sense of "comic character."

One further motif from Act II is useful as groundwork for the second half of the comedy. Early in his first encounter with Parolles, Lafew states: "I have now found thee; when I lose thee again, I care not" (II.iii.204–5). For this shrewd figure (as opposed to Bertram), "finding" or "finding out" Parolles is no difficult task. In the next scene, after the clown has skewered Parolles, the latter retorts: "Go to, thou are a witty fool; I have found thee," to which Lavatch responds: "Did you find me in yourself, sir, or were you taught to find me? . . . The search, sir, was profitable; and much fool may you find in you, even to the world's pleasure and the increase of laughter" (II.iv.31–35). Lavatch is an obvious fool, readily identified by his costume, his manner of speaking, and his role in the play, so to find the fool in him is not difficult. But to find the fool in oneself (whether for Parolles or Bertram) is a far more demanding task, especially if the goal is not merely "the world's pleasure and the increase of laughter" but, more significantly, the exorcism or transcending of that fool or folly within. Finding the fool in the clown is easy, axiomatic; finding the fool or the truth in Parolles is easy for Helena, Lafew, and the clown but so far impossible for Bertram (as indicated also in the dismissal of Helena); finding (and transcending) the fool in Bertram is by far the most challenging task and must await the climax of the play.

The first two acts thus set up a Parolles who functions in several related yet discrete ways: as an entertaining comic figure; a false companion who brings out the weaker side of Bertram; an epitome of the false values and fashions of the court; and an embodiment of the folly within that must be "found" or transcended if Bertram is to recognize Helena's value. Although Shakespeare provides glimpses of him in III.iii and III.v, his next and most significant sequence begins in III.vi when the two lords, echoing Lafew's earlier critique, call Bertram's attention to Parolles's limitations ("a most notable coward, an infinite and endless liar, an hourly promise-breaker, the owner of no one good quality worthy your lordship's entertainment"—ll. 9–11), warning Bertram not to trust him lest "he might at some great and trusty business in a main danger fail you" (ll. 13–14). Again, the emphasis is upon "finding," "knowing," and "seeing": "If your lordship finds him not a hilding, hold me no more in your respect" (ll. 3–4); "when his disguise and he is parted, tell me what a sprat you shall find him, which you shall see this very night" (ll. 94–95); and, most elaborately: "You do not know him, my lord, as we do. Certain it is that he will steal himself into a man's favor, and for a week escape a great deal of discoveries; but when you find him out, you have him ever after" (ll. 82–85). Clearly, finding out or discovering the truth about this pretender is to be the focus for this part of the play.

In the two highly entertaining scenes that follow, Parolles is captured, blindfolded, threatened, and exposed, with much appropriate commentary from the onlookers (e.g., "is it possible he should know what he is, and be that he is?"—IV.i.42–43). But the choric commentary is also directed at Bertram. The two lords note "the worthy blame laid upon him" for his treatment of Helena and comment upon his seduction of Diana upon whom "this night he fleshes his will in the spoil of her honor" (IV.iii.5, 14–15). The two Dumaines marvel at the "rebellion" of appetites in man, what Helena calls Bertram's "idle fire" (III.vii.26) and

Bertram himself refers to as "my sick desires" (IV.ii.35): "As we are ourselves, what things we are!" (ll. 18–19) for, like a traitor, Bertram "in this action contrives against his own nobility, in his proper stream o'erflows himself" (ll. 20–24). Linking Bertram's lapses to Parolles, the second lord concludes: "I would gladly have him see his company anatomized, that he might take a measure of his own judgments, wherein so curiously he had set this counterfeit" (ll. 29–32). Both the sequence of scenes (in which Bertram's wooing of Diana is encased between the capture and exposure of Parolles) and these comments link Bertram's faulty judgment, both past and present, with Parolles, so that the exposure in IV.iii would seem to represent a major step forward for the comic hero, an anatomy not only of a false companion but also of some significant part of himself. To discover the truth about Parolles is to gain some insight into manners and pretense ("I will never trust a man again for keeping his sword clean, nor believe he can have everything in him by wearing his apparel neatly"—ll. 136–38), but Bertram has yet to confront the full lesson, the presence of the fool or folly in himself.

Unlike Bertram, however, Parolles has been forced to face up to what he truly is, what he has become. Left alone, he comes to terms with his new status in a soliloquy that has endeared him to many readers. "Captain I'll be no more," he realizes, but still he can survive, for "simply the thing I am / Shall make me live" (an interesting echo of the king's comment on Helena's status and honor: "The property by what it is should go, / Not by the title"—II.iii.129–30). Discovery, he admits, was inevitable, so now he can "live / Safest in shame; being fooled, by foolery thrive. / There's place and means for every man alive" (ll. 307–17). In this instance, discovery or finding out has led not only to public humiliation and loss of status but also to self-recognition and greater self-understanding, a process that should be relevant to Bertram as well, especially in the final scene.

Clearly, the comic hero has learned something important about his former companion ("what a past-saving slave is this!"—l. 131) and, indirectly, something about himself. But despite the initial suggestion that in reading the letter from his mother "he changed almost into another man" (ll. 3–4), Bertram in this scene exhibits no profound changes as a result of such new under-standing of Parolles. Rather, his values had been acted out tell-ingly in the previous scene when he gave his ring to Diana and told her: "My house, mine honor, yea, my life be thine, / And I'll be bid by thee" (IV.ii. 52–53). As Helena had predicted (III.vii.25–28), Bertram's "sick desires" easily outweigh the "honor 'longing to our house, / Bequeathèd down from many an-cestors" (ll. 42–43). Nor is a "new" Bertram evident in the final scene, for although he starts with a smooth and believable speech that describes how his attraction to Maudlin had blinded him to Helena's virtues ("well excused" says the king—V.iii.55), this initial impression is quickly undercut by the recognition of Helena's ring, the obvious lies, and the subsequent charges brought by Diana (Lafew reacts: "I will buy me a son-in-law in a fair"—l. 148). Although Parolles is introduced as a witness, the modern interpreter finds no clear and compelling link between this final movement and the exposure in IV.iii, nor, as Muir notes, does Shakespeare give Bertram a speech equivalent to Parolles's soliloquy of self-recognition and growth. Rather, once Diana starts her buildup of tragicomic paradox and confusion, Bertram has only 5 lines in the last 110 of the play.

Yet the more closely one views these two important sequences in tandem, the more one sees suggestive links and parallels (analogous to the two phased moral plays). In general terms, Parolles's loss of his drum that led to his capture and exposure becomes Bertram's loss of his ring that leads to the same results; similarly, Parolles standing blindfolded in front of three figures who pass judgment upon him (Bertram and the two Dumaines) becomes Bertram on trial before the king, the countess, and Lafew (wearing not a blindfold[16] but the velvet patch described by the clown at the end of IV.v). Just as Parolles had been taken off under guard at the end of IV.i midway in the sequence, so too Bertram is taken off under guard midway in the last scene; in both sequences, moreover, Diana then comes on-stage to place strong emphasis upon the ring. Just as Parolles initially had con-vinced Bertram of his valor and reliability, so Bertram too initially mollifies the king and Lafew; then, just as Parolles's abject revelations got him in deeper and deeper trouble, so do Bertram's lies and evasions (and Bertram's aspersions on the on-stage Diana recall Parolles's comments on Bertram and the two Dumaines). Rather than setting up a clear cause-and-effect sequence (first understand Parolles, then, on that basis, understand Helena and oneself), Shakespeare is presenting analogous or parallel actions whereby both figures go through the same process of public exposure that leads eventually to a new understanding. Our logic of cause-and-effect has been superseded by a logic based upon analogy or patterned action.

To clarify and support such patterning, Shakespeare provides other kinds of analogous links as well. Consider, for example, the connection between Lavatch and Parolles. Thus, when dispatched to the court, the clown exhibits his courtly answer to all questions, a comic turn built around his repeating "O Lord, sir!" in response to the countess's queries (see II.ii.40, 43, 45, 47, 56). Moments later, we see and hear Parolles playing the courtier by punctuating Lafew's lines not with "O Lord, sir!" but with "so I say" (four times) or "so would I have said" or other variants (see II.iii.11–38) for a total of seven such usages (later Parolles does use "O Lord, sir!" as well—IV.iii.288). Then, as noted earlier, when Parolles and the clown meet at court, the latter wittily emphasizes the finding of the fool in oneself ("and much fool may you find in you"—II.iv.34). At this point, Parolles can dismiss Lavatch without finding the fool in himself ("a good knave, i'faith, and well fed"—l. 36), but his terms here, whether literal or proverbial, are later echoed by Lafew who eventually takes pity on the discredited Parolles: "though you are a fool and a knave, you shall eat" (V.ii.51). Throughout the play Lavatch may amuse, challenge, or offend various figures, but he never deceives anyone. Rather, soon after Parolles's exposure, Lafew describes the clown as "a shrewd knave and an unhappy" (IV.v.59), and the countess reveals that, despite his "sauciness," the clown has his place in her household on the authority of her husband who "made himself much sport out of him" (ll. 60–63). Like Lavatch, then, at the end of the play Parolles too has become a known and recognized fool who has found a home with Lafew ("the first that found me"—V.ii.41–42), so that in the penultimate speech of the final scene the witty lord concludes: "Wait on me home; I'll make sport with thee. Let thy curtsies alone; they are scurvy ones" (V.iii.319–20).

What then is gained by noting the links between the fool and the foolish Parolles? In the final scene, the latter figure achieves the new status he had predicted in his soliloquy where he had rejected his false captaincy and chose instead to live, even thrive "by foolery," for "there's place and means for every man alive." Having been exposed in front of Bertram (the last still to believe in him and the source of his support), the braggart and impostor comes to terms with his status as a fool and, like Lavatch, finds "place and means" with a worthy figure who has recognized his limitations all along but nonetheless will value him as "simply the thing I am." The foolery of Lavatch is contained or sheltered within the benign control of the countess. The foolery of Parolles has been recognized, controlled, and contained by Lafew ("let thy curtsies alone; they are scurvy ones"). By the logic of analogy, the foolery of Bertram (associated with both his trust in Parolles and his rejection of Helena) is now to be transcended through a reaffirmation of his marriage to a rediscovered Helena who has met his conditions and, in symbolic terms, proved herself worthy. Lavatch and particularly Parolles thus act out versions of Bertram's folly and prepare us for the transcending of the central foolery of the play, Bertram's disdain for Helena. After witnessing the exposure of Parolles, Bertram had left behind a foolish part of himself. At the end of the play, in the presence of the "new" Parolles, he completes the process.

Such an explanation based upon analogy and phased action still does not answer the question that troubles many interpreters of *All's Well*: if Shakespeare indeed wanted to display a transformed Bertram at the climax of the play, why did he not provide a major speech (equivalent perhaps to Henry V's rejection of Falstaff) or some other decisive signal? One answer is that Bertram's relative silence during the last hundred lines is to be attributed (as in *2 Henry IV*) to a new control of language as opposed to the abuse of words throughout much of the comedy. Obviously, Parolles (as suggested by his name) talks too much, so that his "I love not many words" (III.vi.76) is a very funny line. To reinforce the motif, Lafew tells Parolles "you are not worthy another word" and asks: "is it not a language I speak?" (II.iii.257–58, 188), while Lavatch notes that "many a man's tongue shakes out his master's undoing" (II.iv.22–23). Like his costume, Parolles's words (especially those delivered to Bertram in Act II) are a major symptom of what is wrong. The plot against Parolles, designed to test "the utmost syllable of your worthiness" (III.vi.62–63), then involves an invented tongue complete with interpreter because Parolles has "a smack of all neighboring languages" (IV.i.15–16) and is "the manifold linguist" (IV.iii.221–22). In the final scene, the emphasis switches to Bertram, for initially the king accepts his apology ("not one word more"—V.iii.38) but soon turns prosecutor ("thou speak'st it falsely"; "You boggle shrewdly"—ll. 113, 232). But after Parolles is characterized as "a naughty orator" (l. 253) and Diana's riddles seem to "abuse our ears" (l. 291), Helena resolves all ambiguities by presenting the ring, quoting the words from Bertram's letter in this new context, and emphasizing plainness and simple truth in a summary couplet: "If it appear not plain, and prove untrue, / Deadly divorce step between me and you" (ll. 314–15). That Parolles has no words here (and is even prevented from doing his curtsies) and Bertram has few (as opposed to his wooing of Diana or his Parolles-like verbiage earlier in this scene) is then a signal that language and behavior are now under control, so that every word should weigh heavily and ring true.

If language alone does not provide that decisive signal for Bertram's transformation, consider instead the role of stage imagery—in particular, the potential interpretative significance of Bertram's patch. At the end of Act IV Lavatch describes the arrival of Bertram off-stage "with a patch of velvet on's face," adding: "whether there be a scar under't or no, the velvet knows, but 'tis a goodly patch of velvet; his left cheek is a cheek of two pile and a half, but his right cheek is worn bare." Lafew's comment—"a scar nobly got, or a noble scar, is a good livery of honor; so belike is that"—then elicits Lavatch's rejoinder: "But it is your carbonadoed face" (IV.v.88–95). Here, as I read the passage, Shakespeare uses what I term theatrical *italics* to prepare the audience for something soon to be seen and provides in advance three different ways to evaluate that image. Most obvious is Lafew's inference that the velvet patch worn by "the young noble soldier" (l. 97) covers "a noble scar" or "a good livery of honor," a worthy emblem of heroic deeds (the kind of scar one associates with Coriolanus). In contrast, Lavatch's cynical reference to "your carbonadoed face" suggests that under the patch lurks a scar of less worthy origins, an incision "made to relieve syphilitic chancres" (G. K. Hunter's gloss in his New Arden edition, p. 124). The third (and, for me, the most suggestive) possibility is supplied in the clown's comment: "Whether there be a scar under't or no, the velvet knows, but 'tis a goodly patch of velvet." Bertram's left cheek, like his right, may be bare of any scar at all.

In the absence of any further references to patch or scar, what are we to conclude? Parolles, under extreme pressure, describes Bertram as "a dangerous and lascivious boy, who is a whale to virginity" and is "very ruttish" (IV.iii.206–7, 201) but does not associate him with venereal disease. Lafew's "noble scar" is in keeping with Bertram's martial exploits in Florence, but the verbal emphasis, starting in II.iii, has been upon the comic hero's less than honorable behavior. Thus, in a major speech after Bertram's rejection of Helena, the king comments at length upon "dropsied honor" (II.iii.127), while the countess notes that her son's "sword can never win / The honor that he loses" by deserting Helena (III.ii.91–92). Repeatedly, Bertram's honor is called into question in Act IV, especially in his dialogue with Diana about the ring that is associated with "an honor 'longing to our house, / Bequeathèd down from many ancestors, / Which were the greatest obloquy i'th'world / In me to lose" (IV.ii.42–45). Note too that Parolles, who is associated with "snipped-taffeta," "villainous saffron" (IV.v.1–2), scarves, and fashions ("the soul of this man is his clothes"), tries to fake an honor he has not earned: "I would the cutting of my garments would serve the turn, or the breaking of my Spanish sword" (IV.i.44–45). Both the general comments on honor and the specific analogy to Parolles seem to me to preclude Lafew's generous inference about the velvet patch and to suggest instead a Bertram who is using that patch to direct attention away from his shameful treatment of Helena (and his loss of the ring).

At the end of IV.v, before we see the returning Bertram, Shakespeare thus signals the presence of a velvet patch and provides three possible interpretations, one of which (that it, like Parolles's scarves and military bearing, covers nothing of substance) follows from a well developed cluster of images. But no further mention of patch or scar is to be found in the Folio. As a result, critics and editors rarely comment upon the patch's presence or function in the final scene; directors either ignore the problem completely or cut the Gordian knot by eliminating Lavatch's lines in IV.v or provide some token resolution (in the 1977 Stratford Festival Canada production, Nicholas Pennell wore a tiny black spot the size of a "beauty mark"). But what if Bertram *is* wearing such a patch, particularly a patch large enough to recall Parolles's blindfold of IV.iii? If then at some point during the climactic scene that patch should fall off or be taken off (by Bertram, by Helena, by someone else) to reveal no scar beneath, this loss of the last symbol of "dropsied honor" would be juxtaposed with the "new" Bertram who accepts Helena and transcends his former self, just as Parolles's blindfolded state, once transcended, had led to new insight and new status. The loss of the patch, moreover, would be offset by the regaining of the ring, the symbol of true, lineal honor, and with the restitution of Helena as wife, thus undoing the sin against honor that, as noted by various figures, had offset any chivalric gains (so I can envisage Helena putting the ring on Bertram's finger and taking off the patch). Reunion with Helena, not a velvet patch covering a nonexistent scar, brings honor back to Bertram. An italicized presence and removal of the patch would reinforce key images, ideas, and analogies and buttress the change in Bertram that troubles so many readers.

Let me reconstruct my "Elizabethan" version of Bertram's conversion. To heighten what I take to be the basic analogy, the configuration offered to the spectator in the final scene should resemble as much as possible the configuration seen in Act IV, so that the king, the countess, and Lafew should be placed on-stage so as to echo the placement of Bertram and the two Dumaines, and Bertram's exit under guard should be handled so as to echo Parolles's exit in IV.i. Diana's speeches to the king and her handling of the ring should bring to mind her similar behavior with Bertram in IV.ii, and, perhaps most important, the beleaguered Bertram, wearing a highly visible patch, should be clearly analogous to the beleaguered, blindfolded Parolles. At Helena's entrance, the king's surprised reaction ("is't real that I see?") elicits her "'Tis but the shadow of a wife you see, / The name and not the thing," to which Bertram responds (in what amounts to his "major speech" of the scene):[17] "Both, both; O pardon!" (comparable in its brevity and significance to Prince Hal's "I do, I will"). As opposed to their last on-stage meeting in II.v, Helena here confronts a Bertram without Parolles at his side, a Bertram, moreover, who has both witnessed the public exposure of that Parolles and just suffered through an analogous public display of his own folly. Helena's "the name and not the thing" echoes Parolles's "simply the thing I am / Shall make me live," but Bertram's "both, both" gives her back not only "the name" of wife but also "the thing" itself (again, remember the king's comment in II.iii that "the property by what it is should go, / Not by the title").

Helena's display of Bertram's letter and ring ("this is done") then leads to her telling question: "Will you be mine, now you are doubly won?" For me "doubly won" refers both to her satisfying of his two conditions and to her winning him back as a second achievement linked to her original task performed in Act II (so a second "cure"). His response (Muir's "absurd couplet") is: "If she, my liege, can make me know this clearly, / I'll love her dearly—ever, ever dearly." Helena's parallel couplet, also based upon the magical "if" (remember Touchstone's "much virtue in if"), pushes us forward quickly: "If it appear not plain, and prove untrue, / Deadly divorce step between me and you." Their future is linked to her ability to prove the truth of her claims, to make him "know this clearly." The claims, we know, are true (so the image here is far different from that provided by the "pregnant" Doll Tearsheet in Part Two); moreover, the last attempt to make Bertram "know" something led to the successful exposure of Parolles. Significantly, after Helena devotes one line to the countess, Lafew calls our attention back to Parolles ("Wait on me home; I'll make sport with thee. Let thy curtsies alone; they are scurvy ones"). At this climactic point, Shakespeare displays Parolles under Lafew's wing, Bertram and Helena united, and (to pursue my hypothesis) Bertram's highly visible velvet patch coming off to show an unblemished face. Helena has "cured" Bertram (and I would have *her* remove the patch), just as she has cured the king (hence the extra meaning in "doubly won"). But, especially if the removal of the patch clearly echoes the removal of Parolles's blindfold, part of the force or logic of the moment comes from an awareness of both the analogous exposure of Parolles that led to new self-knowledge and the presence of that figure now under the control of Lafew (in striking contrast to the last time Bertram, Helena, and Parolles had been on-stage together in II.v where Bertram moments earlier had ignored Lafew's critique). The fool is under control. More important, the fool within Bertram has been exposed, cured, and transcended.

Admittedly, my analysis relies heavily upon analogy and metaphor and posits staging that, although consistent with the Folio text, cannot be proved. Readers wedded to psychological realism may therefore argue in response that Shakespeare could have provided all that I have suggested and *still* have given us more evidence of Bertram's change in a big speech (or even a more revealing couplet). The case advanced by Muir and others for a poor or imperfectly revised text, moreover, is supported by various anomalies in the Folio (e.g., the inconsistent naming of the two Dumaines; the presence of a "ghost" figure, Violenta, at III.v.o.s.d.). Yet unless we are prepared to discard the play or (as Shaw did with *Cymbeline*) to rewrite the last scene to suit ourselves, we can only deal with the text as we have it. What we *do* have, moreover, *does* have a logic of its own, albeit a logic that may not be readily accessible to many modern interpreters, especially theatrical professionals. The problems posed by the final scene, whether in Elizabethan or modern terms, are certainly not insurmountable (as witnessed by successful productions in recent years by Stratford Festival Canada, BBC Television, and the Royal Shakespeare Company), but various gaps or anomalies will persist so long as we interpret the final movement and the conversion by means of a modern logic that cannot accept analogy and metaphor as a basis for explaining "character."

Note then the advantages of including in one's horizon of expectations the public Vice and the two phased moral play. Even though that paradigm may not provide an exact model, nonetheless the moral play logic of presentation or dramatic progression is closer to that of *All's Well* than the other models wittingly or unwittingly invoked by modern interpreters from Shakespeare's tragedies or modern fiction. Parolles's status and influence early in the play provide a comment both upon Bertram and upon the courtly world described by the king (after all, in what kind of a world would a Parolles thrive?), so much of this phase is devoted to a world of surfaces and fashions. The key early scene between Bertram and Helena, moreover, is strongly conditioned by the presence of Parolles. But after Parolles's exposure, the play enters a new phase that moves beyond false courtly values and behavior and is dominated by figures opposed to this Vice-like figure such as Helena, Diana, Lafew, the countess, and the king. In the final scene, Bertram's Parolles-like actions recapitulate both the exposure of Act IV and the movement of the comedy as a whole. With the epitome of false influence and folly "arrested" and exposed, the way is cleared for Bertram's new understanding and transcending of the folly within himself in a final phase familiar to readers of romance but also analogous to the climactic movement of many late moral plays. The paradigm from the moral drama therefore provides an overall rationale that encompasses both Parolles and the "new" Bertram.

My goal in this chapter has not been to mount a full-scale attack upon modern "character" analysis or psychological realism but rather to suggest the limitations of a post-Elizabethan logic of interpretation for problematic moments such as the climax of *All's Well*. As noted throughout this chapter, the roots of this particular problem may be manifold, for not only may the Folio text be imperfect but also various stage images or configurations of considerable interpretative importance remain in doubt.[18] But the essence of the problem remains conceptual, for the demonstration of analogous or metaphoric links between IV.iii and V.iii or between Parolles and the fool within Bertram will not "explain" Bertram's conversion to a modern consciousness shaped by Ibsen, Henry James, and Freud. Yet these analogues and metaphors *are* there in the play as we have it; moreover, such a climactic action in a final phase, with a Vice-like pretender now under control and new order being established, *does* correspond to a paradigm available in the late moral plays, a paradigm Shakespeare had already adapted to his purposes in *Richard III* and *2 Henry IV*. As John Shearman has argued in his discussion of the many anomalies found in Mannerism: "In decoding messages from the other side we get more meaningful results if we use their code rather than ours."[19] If we approach *All's Well* with Shakespeare's own "code" in mind, we can more fully appreciate both the nature of his experiment and his distinctive achievement.

7

Moral Play Components
in Shakespeare's Scenes

Close attention to the final movements of *All's Well*, *Richard III*, and *2 Henry IV* demonstrates how a horizon of expectations linked to the late moral play figures and strategies outlined in chapter two can shed light on problematic moments. Rather than pursuing other distant cousins of the public Vice and the two phased action (e.g., Pistol in *Henry V*, Lucio in *Measure for Measure*, Autolycus in *The Winter's Tale*), let me turn now to other features of the moral plays also of interest to interpreters of Shakespeare. First, in general terms, the moral drama provides an obvious example of how theme or thesis can take precedence over our sense of plot or character. Joanne Spencer Kantrowitz, for one, has argued forcefully for the special nature of allegorical characters and the primacy of theme over fable in such plays. The true action of a didactic work, she notes, "is not the surface events, but the action of the unfolding argument," so that "anything can, and often does, happen," not because the works are diffuse and undisciplined, but because "episodes are invented and ordered for the sake of the thesis."[1] Similarly, John Weld argues that "the audiences for which Shakespeare and his contemporaries wrote had been trained to expect a unifying theme"; he notes that "unity of action is almost non-existent" in plays like *All for Money* and *The Three Ladies of London*, "but unity of theme is rigorously observed." For Weld, "the point is not that all scenes in all morality plays were tightly bound in thematic unity, but that whatever unity the plays possessed was thematic."[2] Both Kantrowitz and Weld therefore single out the presence in the moral drama of a different logic of presentation or organization, a logic geared to thesis, theme, or homiletic intent rather than to our notions of psychological realism or narrative credibility.

Such an allegorical or thematic logic is familiar to readers of *The Faerie Queene* or Book II of *Paradise Lost*. What has not been addressed, however, is the interpretative problems and anomalies that result from the presentation of allegorical figures, theses, and action on a stage as opposed to on a page. Thus, most scholars have accepted Bernard Spivack's formulation that, except for an occasional throwback, the period after 1590 "marks the dead end and dissolution of the allegorical drama, at least on the popular stage."[3] Such a conclusion, however, is based primarily upon reading rather than seeing the plays, a process that gives undue prominence to the speech prefixes in the printed texts. In contrast, Arnold Williams has noted that an audience watching a performance of *Mankind* would see not a parade of abstractions but "four small-time hoodlums, a priest, a real, live devil, who, however, is invisible to the actors on stage, and a good hearted but weak and somewhat dim-witted English peasant. We would hear a good bit of sermonizing by the priest and a good bit of underworld jargon from the vices." According to Williams, the critic can easily be misled by "the names of the characters and the fact that the play has been labelled a morality."[4] Similarly, John Weld emphasizes that "the speech headings that loom so large in the italics of print are non-existent on the stage" (p. 38). For Weld, the failure to "see" the moral plays "accounts both for a serious misunderstanding of the way they work and for the critical disregard of the morality as genre ever since antiquarians began to reprint them." Rather, "what the audience sees is not so many abstractions, but people—red-faced, tall, short, fat, greasy, grotesque, and sly; and they are not involved in inter-abstractional relationships; they hit each other, brawl, kiss, ring bells, and chase each other around the stage" (p. 14). Both Williams and Weld remind us that, in performance, the moral plays may have seemed less blatantly allegorical, a reminder that could narrow the gap that seems to separate them from the later "realistic" plays.

Consider, for example, some earlier and later figures that perform comparable functions. For a spectator as opposed to a reader, how much actually would separate Fellowship (*Everyman*) or Riot (*The Interlude of Youth*) from later good fellows or riotous companions with names like Pistol and Bardolph? How different are the unnamed murderers of Clarence in *Richard III* or Banquo in *Macbeth* from the villains who kill Smirdis in *Cambises*, even though the latter figures are called Murder and Cruelty? How large is the gap, again from the perspective of an audience in the theatre, between the Good Counsel figure of the moral plays, usually dressed as a clergyman, and the many friars or moral spokesmen in later plays, figures like the Old Man in *Doctor Faustus* or Friar Francis in *Much Ado about Nothing*? In *The Castle of Perseverance* Greed is dramatized in the person of Avaricia, one of the seven deadly sins, but in the 1570s Wapull displays this sin in *The Tide Tarrieth No Man* by means of a grasping usurer named Greediness who acts out the pernicious influence of the Vice. How different, then, would be a viewer's experience of an actor playing a merchant or usurer named Greediness, whose behavior is linked to the central thesis of the play, from that viewer's experience of an actor playing Corvino, the covetous merchant in *Volpone*, whose behavior is also linked to Jonson's satiric thesis about gold and human values? Especially in the late moral plays (as opposed to *The Castle of Perseverance*, *Everyman*, or *Wit and Science*), the names of various personae in the printed texts may cloak a similarity in kind between nominally allegorical figures and later characters like Corvino (or Parolles or Kent), a similarity easily missed by the reader when dealing with playscripts designed for a spectator.

My purpose here is not to allegorize Marlowe, Jonson, and Shakespeare but rather to suggest how moral abstractions that leap out at us from printed speech prefixes can become considerably less abstract when conditioned by the realities of stage performance. When a human actor takes on an allegorical role, something immediately happens that distinguishes the event from *The Romance of the Rose* or *The Faerie Queene*, a distance that becomes even greater when the actor is playing not the concept itself (as with figures such as Goods or Good Deeds in *Everyman*) but a social type that acts out that concept (a greedy merchant, a pious clergyman, a conscienceless murderer, a riotous tavern companion). Consider too the corollary: that not only may the late moral plays have seemed less "allegorical" in the theatre but also that many supposedly "literal" or "real" dramatic characters and actions in the age of Shakespeare may have had more in common with Wager, Wapull, Lupton, and Wilson than with Ibsen and Henry James. The absence of clear allegorical signposts may not, in fact, denote "the triumph of realism," especially in an age when Shakespeare could introduce such figures as Rumor (*2 Henry IV*) and Time (*The Winter's Tale*) and allegorical personae could appear in plays from the 1590s such as *A Knack to Know a Knave, Old Fortunatus, A Warning for Fair Women,* and *Two Lamentable Tragedies.*

For some seventeenth-century evidence that suggests such similarity or continuity, consider two allusions cited earlier. First, in his collection of epigrams published in 1610, John Heath describes a foolish playgoer: "Now at the *Globe* with a judicious eye, / Into the Vice's action doth he pry."[5] Standing alone, this reference to a Vice at the Globe in the first decade of the seventeenth century sounds anomalous to our ears (and could be interpreted as a thrust at the satirized Momus, whose "judicious eye" sees not what is in front of him but instead conjures up a figure a generation out of date). But consider as well a passage some fifteen years later, the comments of Jonson's choric gossips in the second intermean of *The Staple of News* (1626):

MIRTH.
How like you the *Vice* i' the Play?
EXPECTATION.
Which is he?

MIRTH.

Three or four: *old Covetousness*, the sordid *Pennyboy*, the *Money-bawd*, who is a flesh-bawd too, they say.

TATTLE.

But here is never a *Fiend* to carry him away. Besides, he has never a wooden dagger! I'ld not give a rush for a *Vice*, that has not a wooden dagger to snap at everybody he meets.

MIRTH.

That was the old way, Gossip, when *Iniquity* came in like *Hokos Pokos*, in a Juggler's jerkin, with false skirts, like the *Knave* of *Clubs*! but now they are attir'd like men and women o' the time, the *Vices*, male and female! *Prodigality* like a young heir, and his *Mistress Money* (whose favors he scatters like counters) prank't up like a prime *Lady*, the *Infanta* of the *Mines*. (ll. 5–20)

Here Jonson is glossing his own play to explain how moral play personae are being clothed in "modern" (1626) dress. The old-style Vice, who had snapped his wooden dagger at his victims until carried off by the Devil, now is "attir'd like men and women o' the time." In this formulation, "the old way" associated with figures like Covetousness, Iniquity, and Prodigality has been replaced by a new way that metamorphoses the old-style allegorical figure into a contemporary social type (a young heir, a usurer) whose function in society in some way is analogous. Such a formulation may or may not be relevant to Jonson's best-known comedies[6] that lack either allegorical personae or choric exegesis and may, moreover, be distant from Shakespeare's practice. Nonetheless, one of the major writers of the period both remembers the distinctive features of the late moral plays and, even more revealing, finds a way to incorporate some of those features into his own satiric strategy (as he also incorporated the Vice's exit to Hell on the Devil's back as noted in chapter two).

Two isolated passages do not justify a total reassessment of all the potential Vice-like figures in Jacobean drama. Nonetheless, these allusions *do* indicate a continuing awareness of the Vice and late moral play practice in the context of ongoing dramatic activity in the seventeenth century, just as the allusions to the morall cited in chapter one also suggest *some* kind of generic continuity. Our notions about "character" or realism therefore may not be fully in tune with the horizon of expectations assumed by Shakespeare, his actors, and his audience. Remember, for roughly two hundred years the moral drama, in one form or another, ruled the English stage. Although neglected or scorned by subsequent devotees of "the triumph of realism" (many of them readers rather than spectators of plays), that drama clearly had developed considerable expertise or knowhow, especially for putting ideas into action on a stage. Many features of this moral drama were then superseded or rejected in the age of Shakespeare (and no one laments the passing of fourteener couplets as the poetic norm), but, as argued throughout this book, some features or paradigms were still available as models to be adapted for later use by Shakespeare and his contemporaries (e.g, Humanum Genus, dual protagonists, the public Vice and the two phased action). Particularly in the late moral drama of Shakespeare's boyhood, other resources also were available for solving various problems in theatrical presentation, problems that did not disappear in the 1590s. Admittedly, Shakespeare and his fellow dramatists could have found some of these devices in nondramatic poems like *The Faerie Queene*, but the less sophisticated moral plays had the advantage of offering allegorical techniques geared to the exigencies of the stage rather than the province of the page.[7]

My purpose in introducing such possibilities is not to mount a full-scale assault upon all modern interpretation of Shakespeare's characters but rather to expand the options available to the reader or theatrical professional. As noted in chapter two, twentieth-century treatments of the Vice have been influenced by a preference for that figure's comedy over the homilies provided by the virtues and by a keener interest in the temptation of Man than in the allegorical display of the health of a kingdom. Similarly, when reading Shakespeare's plays we give privileged status to those features that do make sense in our terms, even when they are obvious nonrealistic conventions like the soliloquy, but inevitably we play down or screen out other devices that do not conform to our horizon of expectations. Here is where an awareness of the knowhow of the moral drama, particularly the late moral drama, can be useful.

Consider in particular one of the major assets of this kind of drama—its ability to break down a subject or entity into component parts. Thus, one of the earliest scholars to write at length about the moral drama notes that in *The Castle of Perseverance* "the subjective forces that in reality belong to man himself in the most personal sense were transformed by the poet into visible, external forces" so that, in effect, "the motives and impulses of man's own heart were taken from him, and, clothed in flesh and blood, given him again for companions."[8] In A. C. Bradley's terms, the moral dramatists deployed their stage figures "to decompose human nature into its constituent factors,"[9] a process that gives external stage life to internal forces and thereby uses the special advantages of the theatre to provide psychological insights, moral lessons, and entertainment.

Unlike the soliloquy, this approach to the on-stage display of the workings of the mind is not readily compatible with the expectations of many modern readers or playgoers. Nonetheless, such a technique does have various assets, especially if the emphasis is upon the moral geography of the soul. Thus, in his discussion of the Good and Evil Angels in *Doctor Faustus* Wilbur Sanders argues that such a stage psychomachia is not "clumsily primitive" but rather "an immensely dramatic procedure." As he describes a representative scene: "The first effect of the interruption is to arrest all action on the stage, and to focus attention on the protagonist, suspended in the act of choice. Not until he speaks do we know to which voice he has been attending. It is the act of choice in slow motion, a dramatisation of his strained attention to the faint voices of unconscious judgment."[10] To some modern readers such an effect may seem a blemish in a complex psychological tragedy, but in the theatre such a suspension or slowing down of the process of choice can serve as a meaningful equivalent to a soliloquy or to a novelist's presentation of interior states of consciousness, especially for an audience attuned to such a technique.

In the earlier and more familiar moral dramas, this breaking down of the entity Man served as a strategy to organize an entire play. When the later moral dramatists turned to other strategies or paradigms, they still found use for such a device to display at length a significant decision in an individual scene. Perhaps the most revealing example is to be found in R. B.'s *Apius and Virginia* where after Apius agrees to the Vice's plan (that will wrest Virginia from her family), the stage direction reads: "*Here let him make as though he went out and let Conscience and Justice come out of him, and let Conscience hold in his hand a lamp burning and let Justice have a sword and hold it before Apius' breast*" (l. 500). Although Conscience and Justice have no lines while Apius is on-stage, the judge himself supplies their half of the argument:

> But out I am wounded, how am I divided?
> Two states of my life, from me are now glided,
> For Conscience he pricketh me contemned,
> And Justice saith, judgment would have me condemned:
> Conscience saith cruelty sure will detest me:
> And Justice saith, death in the end will molest me,
> And both in one sudden me thinks they do cry,
> That fire eternal, my soul shall destroy.   (ll. 501–8)

Haphazard the Vice, however, mocks Conscience and Justice ("these are but thoughts"—l. 510) and argues instead: "Then care not for Conscience the worth of a fable, / Justice is no man, nor nought to do able" (ll. 521–22). After Apius agrees to forgo his scruples ("let Conscience grope, and judgment crave . . ."), Conscience and Justice are left alone on-stage to lament his decision in psychological terms (e.g., Conscience complains: "I spotted am by willful will, / By lawless love and lust / By dreadful danger of the life. / By faith that is unjust"—ll. 538–41).

To act out the central decision in his play, R. B. has not resorted to a soliloquy or even to straightforward temptation by the Vice but has chosen to break down Apius's choice into its component parts. Somehow, at the moment when the judge is leaving the stage under the influence of the Vice and his own lust,

Conscience and Justice are to "come out of" Apius (or "glide" from him, according to the dialogue), whether from behind his cloak or through some stage device (as in the genealogy of sin sequence in *All for Money*). The theatrically emphatic presence of these two figures (with their striking entrance, their emblems, and their gestures) is then linked verbally to Apius's own conscience and sense of justice. Apius's subsequent exit with the Vice acts out his choice and spells out how he has abandoned his conscience and sense of justice in favor of his lust. Both the stage direction that indicates that Conscience and Justice are to "come out of" Apius and the Vice's insistence that "these are but thoughts" underscore how the inner workings of the protagonist's mind have been orchestrated in a fashion particularly suited to on-stage presentation.

As I have argued elsewhere,[11] the late moral dramatists regularly used such stage psychomachias to display at length pivotal decisions, whether the choice of Faith over Despair (*The Tide Tarrieth No Man*) or the effect of Knowledge of Sin upon Infidelity (*The Life and Repentance of Mary Magdalene*) or the choice of Covetous over Enough (*Enough Is as Good as a Feast*). The technique survives in the 1590s, as witnessed by the Good and Evil Angels of *Doctor Faustus* and one or more angels who flank a despairing figure in *A Looking Glass for London and England*. Consider in particular *A Warning for Fair Women* (1599), where a pivotal event, the seduction of Mistress Sanders, is presented not through dialogue among the characters but by means of a dumb-show:

> *next comes Lust before Brown, leading Mistress Sanders covered with a black veil: Chastity all in white, pulling her back softly by the arm: then Drury, thrusting away Chastity, Roger following: they march about, and then sit to the table: the Furies fill wine, Lust drinks to Brown, he to Mistress Sanders, she pledgeth him: Lust embraceth her, she thrusteth Chastity from her, Chastity wrings her hands, and departs: Drury and Roger embrace one another: the Furies leap and embrace one another.* (D1r)

To underscore the effect, Tragedy as presenter explicates this dumb-show for the spectator (e.g., "Now blood and *Lust*, doth

conquer and subdue, / And *Chastity* is quite abandoned").
Clearly, the anonymous dramatist has not opted for the temptation scene expected by a modern reader but instead has provided
a breaking down of the event into components that include both
"real" figures (wife, seducer, bawds) and allegorical forces (Chastity, Lust, the Furies). In place of a soliloquy or a speech of ac-
quiescence for the protagonist, the dramatist provides as major
signals the thrusting away of Chastity and the embracing of Lust.
Like R. B., Wapull, and Wager (or Marlowe with his two angels), this dramatist felt that such an orchestration of component
parts was a workable method of putting on theatrical display at
an important moment the mind of his protagonist.

Such a breaking down into component parts could be used for
other entities as well. For example, some moral plays that scholars have criticized as shapeless seem so because they present not a
Humanum Genus protagonist but rather a wide range of figures
that, especially for a spectator, add up to a cross section of society. In such plays the entity being broken down for theatrical
analysis is not Mankind but England or the kingdom, often by
means of a cross section of "estates" figures who, taken together
(often as victims of the Vice), represent a larger whole (the title
page describes *The Three Ladies of London* as "A Perfect Pattern
for All Estates to look into"—p. 246). Several of the plays
cited in chapter two (e.g., *Like Will to Like, The Tide Tarrieth No
Man, The Three Ladies of London*) employ such a thesis-and-
demonstration structure in which the thesis is linked to the Vice
(and often to the proverbial title as well) and the demonstration
is provided by some set of components of the kingdom, whether
"estates" figures (e.g., a farmer, a clergyman, a courtier, a scholar,
a soldier) or some other configuration (Wealth, Health, and Liberty; the three ladies—Love, Conscience, and Lucre).

As with the psychomachia, such a breaking down of the kingdom into component parts for exploration on-stage could be
adapted to an individual scene as well as to an entire play (although here the limited personnel available to perform many of
these scripts provided obvious constraints). The best example is
to be seen in one of the major scenes in Thomas Lupton's *All for
Money* (1577) where a series of petitioners (presumably played by

only two actors) parade before the magistrate, All for Money, who has instructions to grant only those suits approved by Money. The audience watches as this corrupt magistrate favors an admitted thief and ruffian, a woman who has murdered her child, a bigamist who seeks to replace his legal wife with a younger one, a foolish priest, a litigious landowner who exploits his poor neighbor, and an old crone who buys false witnesses to snare a young husband. The only figure refused by All for Money (who is flanked by Sin the Vice) is Moneyless-and-Friendless, a hapless figure too poor to provide a bribe. In a play with the announced goal of "plainly representing the manners of men and fashion of the world nowadays" (p. 145), Lupton has used a corrupt magistrate, a Vice, and a group of social types or "estates" to act out in one extensive scene how venality in various parts of society can undermine justice. As with Apius's decision, the key to the technique lies in the breaking down of an entity into component parts suitable for a theatrical presentation that can fully develop the dramatist's thesis or point of view.

Shakespeare, however, does not incorporate into his plays anything as obvious as the Conscience and Justice who come out of Apius or the Good and Evil Angels who flank Doctor Faustus, nor does he resort to a clear "estates" formulation, although a moment such as 3 Henry VI, II.v (in which Henry VI laments the horrors of civil war along with a son who has killed his father and a father who has killed his son) comes close. Still, the principle of breaking down an entity or a decision into component parts for fuller display in the theatre was certainly not unknown to him, as witnessed by Launcelot Gobbo's parody of the stage psychomachia where the decision whether or not to leave Shylock is orchestrated in terms of the voices of Conscience and the Devil (The Merchant of Venice, II.ii.1–29). Let me turn then to a few representative scenes to demonstrate, as in my previous chapters, how an expanded horizon of expectations in tune with late moral play practice can aid the modern interpreter.

First, consider once again Richard III where Shakespeare repeatedly calls to our attention both the workings of the protagonist's mind and the health of the kingdom. Thus, at the climax of the play Richard's reaction to the eleven ghosts ("O coward conscience, how dost thou afflict me!"—V.iii.180) sets up a sense of internal division (in which self is pitted against self) in a fashion much more amenable to the modern interpreter than R. B.'s presentation of Apius's internal strife ("But out I am wounded, how am I divided? / Two states of my life, from me are now glided"):

> What do I fear? Myself? There's none else by.
> Richard loves Richard: that is, I am I.
> Is there a murderer here? No. Yes, I am:
> Then fly. What, from myself? Great reason why—
> Lest I revenge. What, myself upon myself?
> Alack, I love myself. Wherefore? For any good
> That I myself have done unto myself?
> O no! Alas, I rather hate myself
> For hateful deeds committed by myself.
> I am a villain. Yet I lie, I am not.
> Fool, of thyself speak well. Fool, do not flatter.
> My conscience hath a thousand several tongues,
> And every tongue brings in a several tale,
> And every tale condemns me for a villain. (ll. 183–96)

Although the sense of internal division and even some of the specific terms (especially the emphasis upon Conscience) are similar to R. B.'s formulation, clearly Shakespeare's soliloquy sets forth Richard's state of mind without recourse to on-stage personae equivalent to Haphazard, Conscience, and Justice. The moral dramatist's breakdown of a major decision into visible component parts therefore seems distant from this climactic speech couched in terms in tune with our sense of psychological realism.

But this orchestration of a division within Richard linked to the voice of conscience is the culmination of a series of choices made by a wide range of figures who are not realized this fully (or granted introspective soliloquies). Of particular interest is the interchange between the two murderers of Clarence both before and after the murder. In his brief interview with these two figures, Richard had praised the absence of pity in their faces ("Your eyes drop millstones when fools' eyes fall tears"), while the first murderer had assured his employer that "we will not stand to prate" with Clarence, for "talkers are no good doers." Rather, he assures Richard: "We go to use our hands, and not our tongues" (I.iii. 349–52). The reader or spectator may then be surprised at the amount of talking provided by these two figures in the next scene (roughly two hundred lines) along with the actual "doing," with a substantial part of that talking not linked to Clarence's plea for his life. By modern standards, the length of the discussion between the two murderers before Clarence awakes may seem out of proportion to the scene or the play as a whole, for few interpreters today value highly this display of qualms of conscience by minor figures who will not reappear. But if that interpreter has in mind the options available in the moral plays, this sequence makes excellent sense and, like R. B.'s configuration, spells out (albeit without overt allegory) the forces at work behind other more significant but less fully orchestrated decisions to follow.

First, before the murderers even begin their debate, Brackenbury accepts their commission and announces: "I will not reason what is meant hereby, / Because I will be guiltless from the meaning" (I.iv.93–94). Like many figures to follow (e.g., the Mayor, the scrivener, various figures of religion, Stanley in III.iv), this chooser opts for willful blindness over dangerous knowledge, so that conscience or principle is superseded by profit or self-preservation. The fifty lines that follow then orchestrate at length the forces at work behind such decisions (forces much in evidence thereafter, building to Richard's soliloquy in V.iii). Initially, it is "the urging of that word 'judgment'" that breeds "a kind of remorse" in the second murderer, not a fear of killing Clarence ("having a warrant" to do so) but a fear of being "damned for killing him, from the which no warrant can defend me" (ll. 106–11). The earthly sense of "warrant" linked to Richard's power and plotting is here played off against a higher sense of "warrant" or Justice (an opposition that prefigures the superseding of Richard by Richmond in Act V). When the first murderer threatens to inform their employer of such backsliding, the second murderer holds him back in the hope that "this passionate humor of mine will change," for "it was wont to hold me but while one tells twenty." Any "dregs of conscience" that remain "yet within" are then expelled when this wavering figure is reminded of the payment awaiting him ("Zounds, he dies! I had forgot the reward"—ll. 112–23).

The subsequent lines more than any other passage in the play italicize the role of Conscience (and prepare us for Richard's "coward conscience" soliloquy in V.iii as well as the dilemmas faced by Hastings, Buckingham, Stanley, and others):

1 MURDERER.
Where's thy conscience now?
2 MURDERER.
O, in the Duke of Gloucester's purse.
1 MURDERER.
When he opens his purse to give us our reward, thy conscience flies out.
2 MURDERER.
'Tis no matter; let it go. There's few or none will entertain it.
1 MURDERER.
What if it come to thee again?
2 MURDERER.
I'll not meddle with it; it makes a man a coward. A man cannot steal, but it accuseth him; a man cannot swear, but it checks him; a man cannot lie with his neighbor's wife, but it detects him. 'Tis a blushing shame-faced spirit that mutinies in a man's bosom. It fills a man full of obstacles. It made me once restore a purse of gold that (by chance) I found. It beggars any man that keeps it. It is turned out of towns and cities for a dangerous thing, and every man that means to live well endeavors to trust to himself and live without it.

1 MURDERER.
Zounds, 'tis even now at my elbow, persuading me not to
kill the duke.
2 MURDERER.
Take the devil in thy mind, and believe him not. He
would insinuate with thee but to make thee sigh.
1 MURDERER.
I am strong-framed; he cannot prevail with me.

(ll. 124–46)

This extended acting out of a decision (to murder or not to murder Clarence) may seem far removed from Apius's choice or even
Launcelot Gobbo's comic version of the psychomachia (where
the two voices also were labeled Conscience and the Devil).
Readers today, moreover, impatient to get back to scenes involving Richard, may encounter here more than they want to know
about such negligible "characters" (e.g., that one of them once
restored a purse of gold found by chance). But if we remember
how in the moral plays thesis regularly supersedes "character" or
"realism," this extended debate makes excellent sense, not as an
investigation of these two figures (or even of Clarence) but
rather as an orchestration of a debate or conflict at work within a
sequence of major and minor figures (Lady Anne, Clarence,
Hastings, the Mayor, the Cardinal, Buckingham) building to
Richard's soliloquy in V.iii that clearly echoes this passage. Particularly through the qualms of the second murderer, Shakespeare
is adapting the breakdown technique of the late moral plays in
order to spell out in some detail the moral coordinates behind a
series of choices central to this play.

The brief coda to this scene again underscores the two voices or
alternatives. Apparently (as Richard had predicted), Clarence's
pleas have had some effect, for he says to the second murderer:
"My friend, I spy some pity in thy looks" (l. 258). The resolute
first murderer, however, kills Clarence and exits with the body
("I'll drown you in the malmsey butt within"), leaving his cohort
on-stage to lament this "bloody deed" so "desperately dispatched"
and to wish that he, Pilate-like, could "wash my hands / Of this

most grievous murder!" (ll. 265–68). Upon his return, the first murderer berates the second, who, in turn, renounces his "fee," adding: "For I repent me that the duke is slain" (l. 273). "So do I not," concludes the murderer, who labels his colleague (who has just exited) a "coward" (a clear prefiguration of Richard's "coward conscience" in V.iii). The exit with the body by the first murderer (who has chosen Profit, as epitomized by Richard's purse, over Conscience) leaves the second figure, identified with Conscience, alone on-stage to lament what has happened. In this instance, the appetite for the gold in Richard's purse overrides Conscience, which then is left behind, powerless. With the return of the first murderer, the spokesman for Conscience or Repentance ("For I repent me . . .") has one more speech, but his choice to forgo the fee comes too late to avert the murder, so that the scene's final speech is given to the figure who has chosen "meed" (l. 277) or profit over Conscience or principle. These two figures may not stand out as memorable "characters" in this rich and densely populated play, but the alternatives they body forth are central to the entire action. The subject here is no one figure but a way of thinking, a set of moral coordinates, for Shakespeare is adapting the resources of his theatre, including his legacy from the moral plays, to exhibit and develop the internal voices at work within more significant figures, including eventually Richard himself.

A subtler yet analogous effect is to be found in another preparatory moment, the galley scene of *Antony and Cleopatra*. Modern productions often provide a party so raucous that the dialogue is buried under sounds of bacchanalian revelry, but Shakespeare has gone to some lengths to set up a series of options or voices that, like the interchange between the two murderers, orchestrates issues central to what is to follow, especially key decisions by Mark Antony. As with *Richard III*, I.iv, moreover, the reader or spectator anxious to move forward to Antony's return to Cleopatra, the battle of Actium, and the tragic events that follow may grow impatient at the amount of dramatic time here devoted to apparently negligible figures soon to be eclipsed (Lepidus, Pompey, Menas). But, again, our sense of dramatic economy or mainstream event may block us off from Shakespeare's use of such figures, in a manner in keeping with his legacy from the moral plays, to explore more fully Antony's situation, especially the reasons for his vulnerability to Octavius Caesar and Cleopatra. Close attention to the choices and values of Lepidus and Pompey reveals (at least for the reader or spectator in tune with such a technique) how Shakespeare is displaying essential elements in Antony's "character" without recourse to overt allegory (or even to the kind of quasi-allegorical speeches about Conscience provided by the murderers of Clarence).

The scene starts with comments from two servants that sum up the plight of Lepidus, who has been tricked into drinking more than his share ("They have made him drink alms-drink") to the extent that a "greater war" has been raised "between him and his discretion" (II. vii. 5, 9–10). As the Pelican editor notes, the two speakers view the drunken and out of control Lepidus as "a little man in a part too big for him" (p. 1187). With the entrance of the revelers, the focus remains upon Lepidus, who continues to respond to toasts until he passes out, while various observers provide shrewd comments (Antony remarks: "These quicksands, Lepidus, / Keep off them, for you sink"—ll. 58–59). While Menas tries to pull Pompey aside, the bulk of the dialogue is devoted to Antony's account of Egypt for the benefit of the increasingly drunken Lepidus, an account that climaxes with a witty tautological description of the crocodile:

LEPIDUS.
What manner o' thing is your crocodile?
ANTONY.
It is shaped, sir, like itself, and it is as broad as it hath breadth; it is just so high as it is, and moves with it own organs. It lives by that which nourisheth it, and the elements once out of it, it transmigrates.
LEPIDUS.
What color is it of?
ANTONY.
Of it own color too.

LEPIDUS.
'Tis a strange serpent.
ANTONY.
'Tis so, and the tears of it are wet.
CAESAR.
Will this description satisfy him?
ANTONY.
With the health that Pompey gives him; else he is a very
epicure.   (ll. 40–51)

"'Tis a strange serpent" is Lepidus's last line in this scene and
his next-to-last speech in the play (see III.ii.65–66), for when
Pompey pledges this hapless figure once again, Antony responds:
"Bear him ashore. I'll pledge it for him, Pompey" (ll. 83–84).
The disposition of this drunken triumvir is spelled out by Enobarbus's quip to Menas that the servant who bears off Lepidus is
"a strong fellow" because he "bears the third part of the world"
(ll. 87–90). Lepidus's abject position is then described at length
at the beginning of III.ii by Enobarbus and Agrippa, who emphasize his fulsome expressions of love and praise for both Antony
and Octavius. A few scenes later, the downfalls of both Lepidus
and Pompey are quickly summed up by Eros (III.v.4–18).
    Few interpreters of this tragedy have troubled to focus upon
the fall of Lepidus. But note that the dominant image of the
galley scene as a whole and of Lepidus's part in it is drinking
and revelry, an image associated throughout the play not with
Lepidus but with Antony (and it is Antony in line 84 who assumes the burden of the last toast directed at Lepidus and thereby
takes on the role of this fallen figure). Similarly, except for the
toasting calculated to get him drunk, the dialogue involving
Lepidus is devoted to Egypt, the Nile (ll. 17–23), "strange serpents" (l. 24), the pyramids, and, in the lines cited above, the
crocodile—again, features linked not to Lepidus but to Antony
(soon to return to his "serpent of the Nile," Cleopatra—an
epithet hovering around the edges of Antony's description of
Egypt).
    Consider then, with the moral play breakdown into compo-

nent parts as an analogue, how Lepidus functions here as one window into the more important figure, Antony. Thus, the first ninety lines of this scene present in effect two plays-within-the larger play (with the Pompey-Menas interchange in counterpoint to the Lepidus story). The prologue with the servants establishes Lepidus as vulnerable to drink and to the machinations of his comrades and so, as a result, ill-equipped to function in the "huge sphere" (l. 14) of world politics. An increasingly drunken and thereby vulnerable figure is then entranced by things Egyptian, as epitomized by his credulous acceptance of the nonsensical description of the crocodile, while summary comments are provided by Antony's "these quicksands, Lepidus, / Keep off them, for you sink" and Caesar's incredulous "will this description satisfy him?" The scene has displayed the literal and metaphoric fall of a figure who has failed to recognize the quicksands on which he stands, here associated both with drink and with manipulation by those around him. Indeed, Lepidus-Antony is vulnerable both to things Egyptian (the accounts of the Nile, serpents, pyramids, and crocodiles) and things Roman (almsdrink, the code implicit in the toasts), and therefore can be manipulated in a variety of ways. For Antony in scenes to come, the equivalent to the toasting and alms-drink is the "dare" to fight at sea rather than on land at Actium, as opposed to Caesar's refusal of the challenge to single combat, a refusal Antony can never understand (see IV.ii.1–2). The later and far more significant equivalent to a drunken Lepidus's being "satisfied" with the description of the crocodile is Antony's accepting Cleopatra's various defenses of her actions. In particular, after his long tirade based upon her reception of Thidias, Antony acquiesces yet again to the protestations of his serpent of the Nile with the response: "I am satisfied" (III.xiii.167) and ends the scene with a call for "one other gaudy night" in which he and his followers will "fill our bowls once more" and make "the wine peep through their scars" (ll. 183–84, 191). This Lepidus-like moment, moreover, tips the scales for the wavering Enobarbus, who concludes this scene with the announcement: "I will seek / Some way to leave him." Eventually, the Antony who has made these Lepidus choices about wine, Egypt, and being "satisfied" is also carried off the stage, not drunk but mortally wounded. The fall of Lepidus, however, is only one facet of the galley scene, for Shakespeare presents in counterpoint the equally telling choices made by Pompey (an episode, unlike the drunken collapse of Lepidus, drawn from North's Plutarch). While Pompey plays host (and, more specifically, the pledger of toasts to Lepidus), Menas seeks (at first unsuccessfully) to draw his master aside. Menas's repeated question ("Wilt thou be lord of all the world?") immediately follows Antony's reference to "these quicksands" and finally gets Pompey's attention ("How should that be?"—ll. 60–62). In keeping with the predominant image of the scene, Pompey's initial reaction is that Menas must be drunk ("Hast thou drunk well?"), but the latter's response reveals that at least one figure has avoided those quicksands ("No, Pompey, I have kept me from the cup"—l. 65). The promise to make Pompey "the earthly Jove" who will control "whate'er the ocean pales, or sky inclips" arouses more interest ("Show me which way") and sets up another revealing exchange:

MENAS.
    These three world-sharers, these competitors,
    Are in thy vessel. Let me cut the cable;
    And when we are put off, fall to their throats.
    All there is thine.
POMPEY.
                    Ah, this thou shouldst have done,
    And not have spoke on't. In me 'tis villainy,
    In thee't had been good service. Thou must know,
    'Tis not my profit that does lead mine honor;
    Mine honor, it. Repent that e'er thy tongue
    Hath so betrayed thine act. Being done unknown,
    I should have found it afterwards well done,
    But must condemn it now. Desist, and drink.
MENAS.
    [aside] For this,
    I'll never follow thy palled fortunes more.

Who seeks, and will not take when once 'tis offered,
Shall never find it more.
POMPEY.
This health to Lepidus!   (ll. 69–83)

Here the final collapse of Lepidus is juxtaposed with Pompey's failure to take the offered opportunity (and Menas's verdict on Pompey clearly anticipates Enobarbus's conclusions about Antony late in Act III). This potential Jove figure, it should be noted, does not totally reject the proposition, for "being done unknown, / I should have found it afterwards well done," but since Menas has "spoke on't" rather than done the deed without advance consultation, this chooser "must condemn it now." The reasoning here may strike us as suspect, but for this figure Honor (however murkily defined) takes precedence over Profit (one thinks of Hotspur or Hector). Menas's summary can then serve as Pompey's epitaph: "Who seeks, and will not take when once 'tis offered, / Shall never find it more" (and one need only conjecture how Octavius would have reacted given the same choice). "Desist, and drink" brings us back to the quicksands of Lepidus, the world of the senses and immediate gratification, the world so much enjoyed by Antony.

Like Lepidus, Pompey is a figure of some significance in Act II and negligible thereafter, but, also like Lepidus, he functions in this scene as a window into a far more important chooser, Antony. However muddled his reasoning may be, Pompey, like Antony, does operate by a code of Honor that takes precedence over personal profit or advantage. Like Lepidus with the toasts or alms-drink, such a figure is vulnerable to others who do not share that code but can recognize and manipulate it. Like Antony, moreover, Pompey inspires strong loyalties based upon personal appeal and military prowess, but that appeal can be lost or undercut (with a Menas or an Enobarbus) when the leader fails (or seems to fail) to grasp a golden opportunity.

Both Lepidus and Pompey thus act out significant facets of Antony's tragic situation. No Haphazard, Conscience, and Justice (or Despair and Faith) are needed here, for, even more than the anonymous murderers of Clarence, these two "historical" Romans are "characters" in their own right who earn their part in the story. Nonetheless, the interpreter aware of the moral play technique of breaking down entities into components can appreciate how these two subordinate actions are not ends in themselves (or material Shakespeare was obliged to include) but rather function as his way of exploring in depth key values or ways of thinking to be displayed in subsequent scenes by the tragic hero. Individually, Lepidus and Pompey provide various revealing analogies to Antony. Taken together they act out his key weaknesses or vulnerabilities in a fashion not possible in a soliloquy or choric commentary. Like Pompey, Antony is not ruthless enough to counter Caesar; like Lepidus, he is vulnerable to the serpent of the Nile, to drink and the life of the senses, and to manipulation by a shrewd opponent who understands his weaknesses and can exploit them. Antony too is easily "satisfied" by Egyptian stories and is therefore vulnerable to quicksands and to the loss of his equivalents to Menas (especially after Actium). And, by way of coda to this sequence, we discover that Caesar, although he grudgingly complies with the drinking code and "the conquering wine" (l. 106), still maintains his distance and composure ("our graver business / Frowns at this levity"—ll. 119–20), in the process setting himself off from Antony and the other revelers, just as later he stands aloof from Antony's code and choices. If Lepidus and Pompey give us facets of Antony, Caesar (and, for a time, Menas) give us an alternative.

For a third example of Shakespeare's skillful adaptation of the moral play approach to component parts, consider the Trojan council scene of *Troilus and Cressida*. Unlike my previous two examples, this scene has received its fair share of commentary, for most interpreters would agree that Shakespeare here sets forth the values that characterize this society and eventually lead to its deterioration and ultimate demise (as signaled in Act V by the death of Hector and the disillusionment of Troilus). Less attention has been paid, however, to the way in which the individual contributions of Priam, Cassandra, and the four debaters (Hector, Helenus, Troilus, and Paris) add up to the display of a larger entity—this time not a single figure like Antony but rather a composite view of Troy or the kingdom as embodied in the Trojan mind or way of thinking.

As a point of departure, consider the on-stage configuration presented to the spectator for most of this scene. Priam, who introduces the topic for discussion (II. ii. 1−7), is presumably either on his throne or in some centrally located position—an old, revered king (in modern productions, often physically decrepit) who as king−father−aged figure should be the symbol of order and control in Troy. But with the exception of a brief comment to Paris later in the scene (ll. 142−45), Priam says nothing thereafter but leaves the fate of Helen (and Troy) to his sons. He could be listening intently, following the alternating speakers with his head; he could be frozen in place; he could even nap (as does Revenge during Act III of *The Spanish Tragedy*). Regardless, as king-order-reason figure he remains on-stage (as does Helenus the priest) not as an active force but as a representative of qualities or faculties that carry little weight in this society.

In contrast to Priam's passivity, the spectator sees, on one side, two young men, Troilus and Paris, who argue vigorously for keeping Helen and, on the other side, Hector and, briefly, Helenus, who counter such arguments. The positions espoused by these four figures cannot be labeled as neatly as those articulated by the two murderers of Clarence. Nonetheless, Paris (for obvious reasons) is closely linked to Appetite; Helenus as priest (presumably in some distinctive costume) introduces through his brief remarks and his continuing presence larger considerations that, for the most part, are ignored; Troilus serves as spokesman for Will and for the siren call of Honor; and Hector, for much of the scene, speaks for Reason. The first movement (before the entrance of Cassandra) pits the "fears and reasons" (l. 32) of first Helenus and then Hector against Troilus's emphasis upon "the worth and honor of a king" and "the past proportion of his infinite," a conflict that climaxes in the disagreement between Hector and Troilus over the source of Value. For Hector, "value dwells not in particular will"; rather, Helen or any object holds its "estimate and dignity" to the degree "'tis precious of itself." In contrast, Troilus invests Helen with value, emphasizes "the conduct of my will," and, in a long speech, uses various analogies to stress the Honor that will be lost if Helen is returned under coercion ("O theft most base, / That we have stol'n what we do fear to keep!"). Clearly, Troilus is the spokesman not only for Trojan Honor but also for the Trojan Will, that drive for the Infinite that will not be bounded by Reason, limit, or sordid reality. As he later tells Cressida: "the will is infinite and the execution confined; . . . the desire is boundless and the act a slave to limit" (III.ii.75–77).

Cassandra's startling appearance breaks the scene in half. Her "prophetic tears" and vision of the future climax in her dire warning: "Troy burns, or else let Helen go" (l. 112). But, as in V.iii, the prophetess is doomed not to be believed, for what Hector describes as "these high strains / Of divination in our sister" that should appeal to "discourse of reason" are instead seen by Troilus only as "brainsick raptures" that cannot "deject the courage of our minds" or "distaste the goodness of a quarrel / Which hath our several honors all engaged / To make it gracious." For the spectator who knows the outcome of the Trojan story, Cassandra's appearance has a special poignancy, for it calls to mind the momentous nature of the decision being made here and therefore should make us particularly attentive to the forces at work.

After Cassandra's departure and Paris's defense of himself and Helen, this elaborate display of the Trojan mind at work reaches its climax in Hector's long speech (ll. 163–93). In keeping with his posture throughout the scene, this voice of Reason and reasonableness links his two youthful adversaries "to the hot passion of distemp'red blood" and invokes in opposition "this law / Of nature," "a law in each well-ordered nation / To curb those raging appetites that are / Most disobedient and refractory," and "these moral laws / Of nature and of nations." In answer to the argument advanced by Troilus and Paris about the "disgrace" in returning Helen "on terms of base compulsion" (ll. 150–53), Hector notes: "Thus to persist / In doing wrong extenuates not wrong, / But makes it much more heavy." Here, more than any other place in the scene (or the play), the voice of Reason and Law appears to prevail.

What then follows (to the surprise of many interpreters) is the pivotal moment in the scene (and perhaps in the play):

> Hector's opinion
> Is this in way of truth; yet ne'ertheless,
> My spritely brethren, I propend to you
> In resolution to keep Helen still;
> For 'tis a cause that hath no mean dependence
> Upon our joint and several dignities.

Regardless of what has gone before, here and in his speech that ends the scene (ll. 206–13) Hector's values cannot be distinguished from those of his "spritely brethren" (a category that, presumably, does not include Helenus). If the focus of the scene were solely upon Hector's train of thought as a pivotal "character," this moment would indeed be puzzling, for Shakespeare provides little or no evidence for the switch from the "way of truth" to the way of Honor (what Troilus describes a moment later as the "rich advantage of a promised glory"—l. 204). But the interpreter aware of late moral play technique can recognize that the focus here is not upon the mind of Hector but upon the mind of Troy. Like Priam's passivity or the quick putdown of Helenus, this figure's about-face is not an end in itself, a display of "character" in twentieth-century terms, but rather a means to a larger end—in particular, a demonstration of the vulnerability of Reason, Law, and Truth to the siren call of Honor in Troy and Trojan thinking. In my imagined staging, during one of his final speeches Hector would cross the stage to join Troilus and Paris, thereby breaking the configuration of Reason standing off Will and Appetite. Similarly, the *Exeunt* that ends the scene cloaks many potentially striking effects. For example, Troilus, Paris, and Hector could stride off-stage, arm in arm, while an aged, decrepit Priam is slowly helped off by an ashen-faced, tight-lipped Helenus. As with the two murderers in *Richard III* (or with Apius, Conscience, and Justice), figures who exit and figures who remain behind can, for an audience in the theatre, act out the relative power of competing forces or principles.

With or without my conjectured staging, the reader or spectator should recognize that the protagonist in this rich scene has been no one character but Troy itself. For more than two hundred lines the most fateful decision in the play has been slowed down and physically acted out so that a viewer can witness and fully grasp the larger mind at work (with Cassandra's prophecy italicizing the implications). The behavior of the individual participants, especially Hector and Troilus, is not inconsistent with their "characters" in the rest of the play, but, at least for this sequence, such individual personae are in the service of a larger design or rationale. If Hector's about-face surprises us, that impression is central to Shakespeare's strategy, for, whether in this scene or elsewhere in the play, the stance of Reason within Troy or individual Trojans is shaky and can easily be undermined by Will, Appetite, or the call to Honor. Hector's sudden shift may appear inconsistent (or "unreasonable") by the yardstick of psychological realism, but the interpreter aware of the moral play approach to components can recognize how the collapse of Reason (or the failure of the way of Truth) climaxes a meaningful display of a larger entity that supersedes any single figure.

In a suggestive passage, Bernard Beckerman notes that once we recognize a device as a dramatic convention (his example is Shakespeare's eavesdropping or concealed observation scene), we become conscious how a dramatist could "select dramatic activity from artistic tradition, thereby gaining readily accepted dramatic tools." Such a convention, he goes on to argue, builds upon "theatrical practice not life activity," for "the observation scene is an artificial formulation, obeying its own rules, following its own forms, and judged according to its own context."[12] Not all such conventions, however, are as easily recognized today as the observation scene, the soliloquy, and the aside, especially those conventions at odds with twentieth-century assumptions about psychological realism and dramatic economy (as with the function of seemingly peripheral figures such as the two murderers, Lepidus, and Pompey). The modern interpreter therefore

has little difficulty grasping the meaning and function of a soliloquy by Richard III, Antony, or Troilus or commentary by choric
spokesmen (e.g., the three citizens in *Richard III*, II.iii; the two
lords in *All's Well*, IV.iii). But, as noted throughout this book,
those conventions or techniques linked (in Beckerman's terms)
to the "theatrical practice" of another age and divorced from
"life activity" as we understand it today can easily be ignored or
missed completely.

My purpose in this chapter has been to expand our horizon of
expectations so to encompass techniques available to an Elizabethan or Jacobean dramatist but easily missed by the modern
reader. Even though the critic who prizes irony, subtlety, and realism finds little merit in the late moral drama, these plays did
bequeath to the age of Shakespeare solutions to various presenta-
tional problems, solutions geared to the practical assets and lia-
bilities of Elizabethan stages and staging. In particular, what a
modern interpreter expects to *infer* about "character" (e.g., in a
novel, a film, or a naturalistic play) could be spelled out or orchestrated, both in the moral plays and in Shakespeare, in a
manner that interpreter may not recognize. Indeed, where is it
written down that the on-stage display of the workings of the
mind must be limited to the soliloquy and the aside? Few readers
today expect Shakespeare to body forth on his stage the interaction of Ego, Superego, and Id (to cite but one set of modern
coordinates), but why should we *not* expect him to display, by
whatever method, the interaction of Conscience, Will, Appetite, and Reason—terms well developed in his dialogue and
familiar to *his* audience through many avenues outside of his
plays? To recognize available tools or conventions in the late
moral plays is not to pluck out the heart of Hamlet's mystery but
nonetheless to move a step closer to a sense of what was shared
among dramatists, actors, and spectators in the age that gave
birth to this impressive body of drama.

8

If you have writ your annals true . . .
Coriolanus, V.vi.112

Conclusion:
Shakespeare and the Late Moral Plays

Interpreters of Shakespeare—on the page, on the stage, in the classroom—continue to ply their trade, often oblivious to the claims and strictures of editors and historical scholars. Formulations about what Shakespeare and his audience "believed" or "took for granted" are easy to resist or ignore, especially when those shared values and assumptions (e.g., about divine right, marriage, authority, and psychology) are remote from our twentieth-century horizon of expectations.[1] Such disdain for "historicism," moreover, gains formidable support from the selective tradition, for works and authors well known then are obscure today, while works not available to Shakespeare (e.g., *The Castle of Perseverance, Everyman*) have been canonized in our anthologies and learned journals. To cite two examples, in *2 Henry IV* Pistol twice calls out "have we not Hiren here?" (II.iv.145, 158–59), apparently a famous line from a lost play, a line as well known then as "to be or not to be" now but, for us, only fodder for a footnote. In contrast, consider the anthology that served for several decades as the basis for the study of the early drama—Joseph Quincy Adams's *Chief Pre-Shakespearean Dramas*[2]—with its bowdlerized version of *Mankind*, its erratic sampling of Corpus

Christi pageants (that includes all the admired "comic" figures but lacks a Crucifixion play), and its preponderance of "classical" or "elite" sixteenth-century plays (e.g., *Gorboduc*, *Ralph Roister Doister*, *Damon and Pythias*, *Supposes*) at the expense of the "popular" tradition.

Any attempt to redress the balance—to buck the selective tradition, fill in various gaps, and present a balanced "historical" assessment—inevitably will encounter strong resistance, especially from those comfortable with the received formulation. In the case of the late moral plays, this resistance is reinforced by the nature of the evidence. Both the Roman drama of Plautus, Terence, and Seneca and the fifteenth century moral plays are much better known today than the interludes of Wapull, Fulwell, Lupton, and Wager; most readers would argue, moreover, that the earlier plays, both Roman and English, are superior as works of dramatic art. Certainly, Shakespeare (as witnessed by *The Comedy of Errors*) knew some of the Roman comedies, perhaps many or even most (and, as noted in chapter one, Jonson owned a manuscript of Terence's plays). So, given the twin criteria of availability (at least for Plautus, Terence, and Seneca) and quality, the historian can argue in behalf of the importance of such antecedents for the genesis of Shakespeare's plays. In contrast, I can present no evidence that Shakespeare, Jonson, or other dramatists had read any of the specific late moral plays upon which I have based my analysis. Such plays *were* printed or reprinted between the 1560s and 1590s (and so have survived as texts available for study today) but, with a few notable exceptions (e.g., *Cambises*, *The Three Ladies of London*), subsequent references to the extant plays are hard to find.

But, as reflected in a wide range of allusions, Shakespeare and his fellow dramatists remembered vividly the Vice, the dagger of lath, the exit to Hell on the Devil's back, and other stock features of the late moral plays. I suspect that such awareness on the part of Shakespeare, Nashe, Jonson, and others came from *seeing* such plays in performance (perhaps plays no longer extant) rather than *reading* them. Remember, many of the interludes with allegorical titles cited in court records as having been performed during the reign of Queen Elizabeth have not survived; *The Cradle of Security*, also lost, had a lasting impact upon at least one viewer; some version of *Like Will to Like* was performed at the Rose as late as 1600.[3] Unlike Roman drama or *Everyman*, these late moral plays had an on-stage life for several decades that made them well known as a form during the boyhoods of the major Elizabethan dramatists. Indeed, along with romances like *Common Conditions* and *Clyomon and Clamydes* (both of which contain a Vice), for roughly thirty years these late moral plays *were* English popular drama. We may *read* Marlowe, Shakespeare, and Jonson, but they *saw* plays like *The Trial of Treasure*, *The Tide Tarrieth No Man*, and *Apius and Virginia*.

Regardless of such historical considerations, the power of the selective tradition (that started with the strictures of Sidney) remains formidable. The reader today therefore has no difficulty finding reasons to disdain the late moral drama: the quality of the verse; the heavy-handed didacticism; the allegorical personae. But if the focus is to be Shakespeare's legacy from his past, should we let our literary or dramatic tastes block out significant parts of the historical situation? Must the late moral plays satisfy our aesthetic standards (or our penchant for "realism") to qualify as significant factors in Shakespeare's equations, especially when we are talking about the possible relationship between one set of plays in the popular tradition and another? What does the *quality* of the material (according to our yardsticks) have to do with that material's potential importance for later Elizabethan form or procedure?

What then are the gains for that interpreter who does not confuse aesthetic judgments with historical assessment and therefore resists the power of the selective tradition? Rather than recapitulate all the claims made in this book, let me focus in this conclusion upon questions of genre. First, in dealing with comedy, comic form, and comic structure in the plays of Shakespeare and his contemporaries, interpreters today draw upon a wide variety of models and formulations (e.g., from Suzanne Langer, Northrop Frye, and C. L. Barber), but few have drawn upon the moral plays and even fewer (given the absence of a Humanum

Genus figure) upon the late moral plays. Similarly, those who link the moral drama to subsequent histories and tragedies have emphasized "unification in a central character" as the key element that connects the earlier prototypes to what follows. But do such formulations actually take into account all or even most of the evidence? Especially given the allusions to the morall set forth in chapter one, is our sense of the available genres consistent with the horizon of expectations shared by Shakespeare, his fellow dramatists, and their audience?

Consider one final set of allusions. Historians today distinguish between "Old Comedy" (associated with Aristophanes) and "New Comedy" (associated with Menander, Plautus, and Terence), a distinction also familiar in the sixteenth century. Thus, one verse satirist defending his craft notes "how far the ancient Comedy / Pass'd former Satires in her liberty,"[4] for "ancient" or "old" comedy was known for its "liberty"—in particular, the singling out of specific contemporary personages. Although some Elizabethan allusions to "old comedies" do indeed refer literally to out-of-fashion or dated English comedies,[5] many references do support an Elizabethan sense of the term as we understand it. For example, in the Induction to Jonson's *Every Man Out of His Humour*, Cordatus hails this unusual play as "strange, and of a particular kind by itself, somewhat like *Vetus Comedia*" (ll. 231–32).[6]

But several other allusions, including another from Jonson, point in a different direction. Thus, several allusions to "Vetus Comedia" turn up in the Marprelate controversy with reference to plays staged in the 1580s. In one tract (usually attributed to Nashe) the author writes: "Me thought *Vetus Comedia* began to prick him at London in the right vein, when she brought forth *Divinity* with a scratched face, holding of her heart as if she were sick, because *Martin* would have forced her, but missing of his purpose, he left the print of his nails upon her cheeks, and poisoned her with a vomit which he ministered unto her, to make her cast up her dignities and promotions."[7] Here (and less specifically in other allusions),[8] "Vetus Comedia" is used to describe an allegorical play of a topical or controversial nature, with the "liberty" associated with Aristophanes transferred to a dramatic form closer to home. Even more specific is the use of the term by Jonson in his description to Drummond in 1618 (cited in chapter two) of how he inverted the Vice's traditional exit in *The Devil Is an Ass*: "according to Comedia Vetus, in England the devil was brought in either with one Vice or other, the Play done the devil carried away the Vice." Here Jonson (who owned an edition of Aristophanes) has singled out a characteristic feature of the late moral plays and attached the label "according to Comedia Vetus."

As with the allusions to the morall, I find such conflation of "old comedy" and the moral plays suggestive but elusive, for many references to Vetus Comedia are not linked to the moral drama. Nonetheless, the fact that such a link or conflation was possible, especially for Jonson as late as 1618, suggests to me a large gap between the Jacobean view of early Elizabethan drama and our perspective today. Whether here or with the morall (or the pastoral or the "nocturnal," another term that turns up in various lists), are our assumptions about dramatic genre in tune with the sense of available forms held by the dramatists actually writing the plays? More specifically, should the late moral plays (as seen from Jonson's vantage point in 1618) somehow be housed under the rubric "Comedy," whether that rubric be linked to Aristophanes or the Roman dramatists? In the case of the Vice, dominant for most of the play but ultimately superseded and "arrested," are we dealing with a variation on New Comedy with its underlying sense of an impasse overcome and a newly ordered society at the close?

So long as the selective tradition dominates our anthologies and scholarship, the current codification of dramatic genres will remain unchallenged, so such questions remain not only unanswered but unposed. Rather, most critics, editors, and teachers would agree with Robert Grams Hunter that "anyone who has read an example of the form knows perfectly well what a morality is."[9] But, as I have argued throughout this book, that confidence is based upon evidence filtered through the selective tradition and is linked to assumptions about "unification in a central character" often at odds with the plays available to be read or performed in Shakespeare's boyhood. Breaking through the image of "the morality play" accepted by most modern interpreters is a necessary first step towards a fuller understanding of what the moral drama had to offer dramatists in the age of Shakespeare. Dual protagonists, the public Vice, the two phased action, the single-scene breakdown of Man or the kingdom into component parts—features not associated with "the morality play" but present in the late moral plays—should be recognized as potential paradigms or tools available to Shakespeare, Jonson, and other dramatists.

Perhaps the strongest argument in favor of a historical approach that takes into account the techniques and strategies of the late moral drama is that the logic of theatrical presentation that emerges *is* significantly different from the logic of realism we instinctively supply. Indeed, why should we expect Shakespeare always to follow *our* assumptions about plot, structure, and character? Although we may automatically take for granted various propositions about realism or motivation and although these propositions often may work (or appear to work) when applied to Shakespeare's plays, need such concepts pertain to every situation throughout the canon? Need figures such as Lepidus, Pompey, Hector, and the two murderers always function as consistent, fully rounded "characters" in our terms or can they serve other functions as well? Undoubtedly, Jonson's "old way" associated with the late moral plays (by the choric gossips in *The Staple of News*) seemed old-fashioned by the 1590s (like the movies of the 1930s today), but these older plays *were* part of Shakespeare's dramatic tradition (as the Western is part of ours). The options found in the moral drama would then be a likely source of models or paradigms, especially for the playwright fashioning a history play, a dramatic form (unlike comedy and tragedy) with no clear "classical" precedent. Obviously, Shakespeare and his contemporaries have moved several significant steps beyond the achievements of Wapull, Lupton, Wager, and Fulwell, but both chronologically and, I suspect, in subtler ways as well, Shakespeare was closer to the moral plays than we are to him, even though his plays seem to speak directly to us across the wide gap of time.

One key to my overall argument is therefore the *and* in my title, a conjunction that provides much room to maneuver (to paraphrase Touchstone: "much virtue in *and*"). Certainly, I am not presenting to the reader a didactic Shakespeare or an allegorical Shakespeare (or a slavish Shakespeare who merely followed in the footsteps of the moral dramatists), nor do I support any reductive treatment of his characters and images (as in Spivack's conclusions about Richard III and Iago). Many other paradigms were available to Shakespeare, moreover, whether from classical literature, popular drama, or his own extrapolation. The scholar embarking upon such an investigation of antecedents or roots must first demonstrate the availability of a given model and then provide a convincing account of its relevance to the later drama (hence the importance of my *and*). Nonetheless, the various components and the overall logic of presentation invoked in the preceding chapters *did* exist and, as reflected in allusions, *were* remembered by Shakespeare and his contemporaries. The Shakespeare plays I have singled out for analysis, moreover, have caused continuing problems when interpreted on the basis of post-Elizabethan assumptions. Regardless of twentieth-century distaste for the rigidity of the moral drama, is it not reasonable to postulate *some* connection between the late moral plays and Shakespeare, especially in *Richard III* and *1 Henry IV* where the interpreter need only follow the signposts set up by Richard, Falstaff, and Prince Hal?

As noted in chapter one, any study of the literature of an earlier age is vulnerable to the twin pitfalls of "naive historicism" and "blind modernism." Throughout this book I have sought to display the advantages of an enlightened historicism by bringing to bear upon a series of Shakespeare plays some paradigms not familiar to most modern interpreters. At this point, only the reader can judge whether Richard's allusion to "the formal Vice Iniquity" and Falstaff's invocation of the dagger of lath are merely "such stuff as commentaries are made of" or, in contrast, are Shakespearean clues that can lead the modern detective to a satisfying solution.

Notes

Chapter 1

1. Edgar Schell, *Strangers and Pilgrims: From "The Castle of Perseverance" to "King Lear"* (Chicago and London, 1983), p. 1. Schell has in mind the studies by Potter, Spivack, Bevington, and Farnham to which I will be referring in my first four chapters.

2. *2 Henry IV*, V.ii.126. Unless otherwise noted, quotations from Shakespeare are drawn from *The Complete Pelican Shakespeare*, gen. ed. Alfred Harbage (Baltimore, 1969). For the editions used for other plays, see the list at the end of this book. To avoid invidious comparisons between modern-spelling Shakespeare and old-spelling contemporaries, I have chosen to modernize the spelling when quoting from both plays and nondramatic sources.

3. "Literary History as a Challenge to Literary Theory," *New Literary History*, 2 (1970), 18–19. See also Jauss's "The Alterity and Modernity of Medieval Literature," *New Literary History*, 10 (1979), 181–227. For an extended debate on the problems posed by literary history, see the Autumn 1975 issue of *NLH* (vol. 7, no. 1), especially Quentin Skinner's essay on "Hermeneutics and the Role of History" (pp. 209–32) and Alastair Fowler's essay on "The Selection of Literary Constructs" (pp. 39–55). See also Anthony Savile, "Historicity and the Hermeneutic Circle," *NLH*, 10 (1978), 49–70.

4. The case for Senecan influence was made at length by J. W. Cunliffe, seconded by a host of figures (most notably H. B. Charlton, F. L. Lucas, and T. S. Eliot), challenged by Willard Farnham and Howard Baker, and put in perspective by Peter Ure and G. K. Hunter. For an overview, see Anna Lydia Motto and John R. Clark, "Senecan Tragedy: A Critique of Scholarly Trends," *Renaissance Drama*, n.s. 6 (1973), 225–29.

5. See "Sir Amorous Knight and the Indecorous Romans; or, Plautus and Terence Play Court in the Renaissance," *Renaissance Drama*, n.s. 6 (1973), 3–27; and "Toward the Rediscovery of Tragedy: Productions of Seneca's Plays on the English Renaissance Stage," *Renaissance Drama*, n.s. 9 (1978), 3–37.

6. For an account of the books and manuscripts known to have been in Jonson's library, see *Ben Jonson*, ed. C. H. Herford and Percy and Evelyn Simpson, 11 vols. (Oxford, 1925–52), 1:250–71; 11:593–603. Jonson's debt to Plautus is most evident in *The Case Is Altered*, where the two plots clearly are drawn from *Aulularia* and *Captivi*.

7. *The Long Revolution* (New York and London, 1961), pp. 49–52.

8. "Comments on H. R. Jauss's Article," *New Literary History*, 10 (1979), 370–71.

9. *From "Mankind" to Marlowe: Growth of Structure in the Popular Drama of Tudor England* (Cambridge, Mass., 1962), p. 1.

10. Ibid., p. 3.

11. For both an allusion to *The Three Ladies of London* and the only mention of the rebuttal, see Stephen Gosson, *Plays Confuted in Five Actions* (1582) in *The English Drama and Stage under the Tudor and Stuart Princes, 1543–1664*, ed. W. C. Hazlitt (London, 1869), p. 185. In 1598, Everard Guilpin refers to "the old moral of the comedy, / Where Conscience favors Lucre's harlotry." See *Skialetheia*, ed. D. Allen Carroll (Chapel Hill, 1974), Satire I, ll. 33–34 (p. 64). Originally printed in 1584, *The Three Ladies of London* appeared in a second quarto in 1592, one of the few late moral plays to be reprinted (along with *King Darius* in 1577, *Like Will to Like* in 1587, and undated editions of *Impatient Poverty*, *Nice Wanton*, *Lusty Juventus*, and *Cambises*).

12. For arguments on behalf of the significance of Aristophanes for the age of Shakespeare, see Leo Salingar, *Shakespeare and the Traditions of Comedy* (Cambridge, 1974); for Euripides, see Emrys Jones, *The Origins of Shakespeare* (Oxford, 1977).

13. *Mannerism* (Middlesex, 1967), p. 136.

14. *The English Morality Play* (London and Boston, 1975), pp. 197–211.

15. Thus, *All for Money* (1577) is described on its title page as "A Moral and Pitiful Comedy"; the 1647 Folio of Beaumont and Fletcher's plays includes *Four Plays, or Moral Representations, in One*; in Marston's *What You Will* (1601), the duke rejects a proposed entertainment, saying: "The itch on *Temperance* your moral play!" (p. 290).

16. *Documents Relating to the Office of the Revels in the Time of Queen Elizabeth*, ed. Albert Feuillerat, *Materialen*, vol. 21 (Louvain, 1908), pp. 286, 349. Throughout my discussion, I retain the spelling "morall" because (1) it is the most common Elizabethan rendition (along with "morrall") and (2) therefore helps to distinguish the word as a dramatic kind from various other terms with which it can so easily be confused. For a fuller discussion of the problem and the evidence, see Alan C. Dessen, "The Morall as an Elizabethan Dramatic Kind: An Exploratory Essay," *Comparative Drama*, 5 (1971), 138–59.

17. *The English Drama and Stage*, ed. Hazlitt, p. 165.

18. *An Addition; or, Touchstone for the Time*, p. 24v; affixed to *A Mirour for Magestrates of Cyties* (1584), STC no. 25341.

19. Ed. G. B. Harrison for the Bodley Head Quartos (London and New York, 1923), p. 34.

20. *The Works of Thomas Nashe*, ed. Ronald B. McKerrow, 5 vols. (Oxford, 1905), 1:275, 2:99.

21. *The Seven Deadly Sinnes of London*, ed. H. F. B. Brett-Smith (New York and Boston, 1922), p. 54.

22. *Mount Tabor; or, Private Exercises of a Penitent Sinner* (London, 1639), p. 114.

23. *The English Drama, 1485–1585* (New York and Oxford, 1969), p. 46.

24. *Works*, 3:114.

25. Ed. R. B. McKerrow (London, 1904), p. 54.

26. Ed. Richard H. Perkinson, Scholars' Facsimiles and Reprints (New York, 1941), A3v–A4r, F4r.

27. For the relevant documents for the King's Men and the other companies, all of which contain such references to the morall, see the Malone Society *Collections* (Oxford, 1909), I, iii, 262–84.

28. Middleton not only refers to his book as "my politick Morall"

and "a harmless *Morall*" (A3v, F3r), but, in addition, before his verse prologue he places the heading "A Morall" in large type (B1r) and has a running title "A *Morall*" on each of the next three pages.

29. Ed. William S. Woods (Columbia, S.C., 1950).

30. My conjecture is supported by a possible allusion in the final scene of *Eastward Ho* where Touchstone begins his summary of what has happened to "the careful father," the "thrifty son," the usurer, and "the prodigal child" with: "Now, London, look about, / And in this moral see thy glass run out" (V.v.219–23). Throughout my discussion, however, I have chosen not to build upon such passages in which the speaker may be referring either to *morall* as dramatic kind or *moral* as "moral meaning." For an analogous argument about didactic comedy (but based upon the traditional notion of "morality play" and with no reference to the evidence about the morall), see Sylvia D. Feldman, *The Morality-Patterned Comedy of the Renaissance* (The Hague, 1970).

31. Quoted by William V. Shannon in "Controversial Historian of the Age of Kennedy," *New York Times Magazine* (November 21, 1965), p. 135.

Chapter 2

1. *Elizabethan Drama and the Viewer's Eye* (Chapel Hill, 1977), pp. 126–56.

2. *A Dictionarie of the French and English Tongues* (1611), ed. William S. Woods (Columbia, S.C., 1950).

3. *Queen Anna's New World of Words; or, Dictionarie of the Italian and English Tongues* (London, 1611), STC no. 11099.

4. *A Dictionarie in Spanish and English*, by Richard Percivale, enlarged by John Minsheu (London, 1599), STC no. 19620.

5. *The Historie of the World Commonly Called, The Naturall Historie of C. Plinius Secundus*, trans. Philemon Holland (London, 1601), STC no. 20029, p. 181 (book 7, chap. 48).

6. Ed. Gladys Doidge Willcock and Alice Walker (Cambridge, 1936), p. 84.

7. *Hay Any Worke for Cooper* (1589), p. 4; rpt. in *The Marprelate Tracts* (1588–1589) (Menston, 1967). See also *Alphonsus Emperor of Germany* (1594), E4v; and Nashe's *Summer's Last Will and Testament*, ll. 341–46.

8. Ed. Frederick J. Furnivall for the New Shakespere Society (London, 1877–79), pp. 145–46.

9. *Works*, ed. Alexander B. Grosart, 3 vols., the Huth Library (1884); rpt. AMS Press (New York, 1966), 2:127; 1:189.

10. *A Refutation of Sundry Reprehensions* (Paris, 1583), p. 523; rpt. in *English Recusant Literature, 1558–1640*, ed. D. M. Rogers (Scolar Press, 1975), vol. 263.

11. *The Complete Works of Thomas Nashe*, ed. Alexander B. Grosart, 4 vols. (1883–84), 1:166.

12. *A Declaration of Egregious Popish Impostures* (London, 1603), pp. 114–15.

13. Ed. Don Cameron Allen (Baltimore, 1943), p. 43.

14. Our information about this lost play is drawn from the account provided by R. Willis in *Mount Tabor; or, Private Exercises of a Penitent Sinner* (London, 1639), pp. 111–13. Further references to *The Cradle of Security* are from this passage.

15. *Works*, ed. McKerrow, 2:99.

16. *A Declaration of Egregious Popish Impostures*, pp. 114–15.

17. *Ben Jonson*, ed. C. H. Herford and Percy and Evelyn Simpson, 11 vols. (Oxford, 1925–52), 1:143–44, ll. 410–12. For the passages from *The Devil Is an Ass* and *The Staple of News* see 6:262, 303.

18. In the preceding pages I have introduced only those allusions that supply some useful or revealing associations with the Vice and have therefore omitted many passages that merely acknowledge the existence of the figure. Of the allusions omitted, the most intriguing for me remains John Heath's description of the foolish Momus as playgoer: "Now at the *Globe* with a judicious eye, / Into the Vice's action doth he pry" (*Two Centuries of Epigrammes*, London, 1610, STC no. 13018, E3v). A Vice at the Globe in 1610? Also of interest to the interpreter of *The Winter's Tale* is the possible allusion in Leontes's rejection of Hermione's defense in the trial scene: "I ne'er heard yet / That any of these bolder vices wanted / Less impudence to gainsay what they did / Than to perform it first" (III.ii.53–56). Unlike most modern editions (including the Pelican, from which I am quoting), the Folio presents the phrase as "bolder Vices."

19. *Shakespeare and the Allegory of Evil* (New York and London, 1958), pp. 306–7.

20. For this term and a useful description of the Vice and his play,

see J. A. B. Somerset, "Falstaff, the Prince, and the Pattern of '2 Henry IV,'" *Shakespeare Survey*, 30 (1977), 39–40.

21. "Dangerous Sport: The Audience's Engagement with Vice in the Moral Interludes," *Renaissance Drama*, n.s. 6 (1973), 53. Similarly, Charlotte Spivack calls attention to the presence throughout the moral drama of "repeated emphasis on the dangers of what *seems* to be innocent merriment," so that "often the humor of what appears to be merely congenial party spirit is itself a condemnation of a serious threat to salvation" (*The Comedy of Evil on Shakespeare's Stage* [Rutherford-Madison-Teaneck, N.J., for Fairleigh Dickinson University Press, 1978], p. 80).

22. *Shakespeare and the Allegory of Evil*, p. 229.

23. Douglas Cole, *Suffering and Evil in the Plays of Christopher Marlowe* (Princeton, 1962), p. 34.

24. *Works of Nashe*, ed. Grosart, 1 : 181.

25. B. Spivack, *Shakespeare and the Allegory of Evil*, p. 210.

26. Herford and Simpson, *Ben Jonson*, I : 169.

27. "The Origin of the Figure Called 'the Vice' in Tudor Drama," *Huntington Library Quarterly*, 22 (1958), 28. In the same vein, Sidney Thomas describes the Vice as "in almost every play in which he appears, predominantly a comic character" (*The Antic Hamlet and Richard III*, New York, 1943, p. 18).

28. B. Spivack, *Shakespeare and the Allegory of Evil*, p. 200.

29. *Selected Essays* (New York, 1960), p. 144.

30. *Allegorical Imagery: Some Mediaeval Books and Their Posterity* (Princeton, 1966), pp. 6, 9.

Chapter 3

1. Katherine Haynes Gatch, "Shakespeare's Allusions to the Older Drama," *Philological Quarterly*, 7 (1928), 27.

2. For extensive glosses on this passage, see the original Arden edition, ed. A. Hamilton Thompson (London, 1907), pp. 91–92; the New Variorum edition, ed. Horace Howard Furness, Jr. (Philadelphia, 1908), pp. 200–203; and Bernard Spivack, *Shakespeare and the Allegory of Evil* (New York and London, 1958), pp. 393–95.

3. *A Commentary on Shakespeare's Richard III*, trans. Jean Bonheim (London, 1968), p. 125.

4. *The Antic Hamlet and Richard III* (New York, 1943), p. 32.

5. Introduction to his New Arden edition (London and New York, 1981), p. 101. See also Anne Righter (Barton), *Shakespeare and the Idea of the Play* (London, 1962), pp. 95–96.

6. *Shakespeare and the Allegory of Evil*, pp. 393–407. The passages quoted here are to be found on pp. 394, 395, 397, 401, and 405.

7. For a recent and very useful discussion of Senecan elements in this play, with an emphasis upon Shakespeare's eclecticism, see Harold F. Brooks, "'Richard III,' Unhistorical Amplifications: The Women's Scenes and Seneca," *Modern Language Review*, 75 (1980), 721–37.

8. Thus, Richard's mother laments "that deceit should steal such gentle shape / And with a virtuous visor hide deep vice" (II.ii.27–28), using terms that, according to Spivack, "belong to the unmistakable vocabulary of the moral play, and go straight to the heart of the formula that created the theatrical stereotype of the Vice" (*Shakespeare and the Allegory of Evil*, p. 399). Although the Folio capitalizes "Deceit" and "Visor" but not "vice," in his New Arden edition (p. 195) Anthony Hammond does print "Vice" so as "to remind one of the association with the theatrical role Richard is playing." Here, at least for the reader of this edition, is another clear verbal signal of this link before the obvious allusion in III.i.

9. Hammond (p. 216) describes "with all my heart" (l. 111) as "one of Richard's best jokes: he would, with all his heart, love to give young York a dagger—thrust into the child's vitals." See also Hammond's gloss on "greater gift" (l. 115).

10. *Holinshed's Chronicles of England, Scotland, and Ireland*, 6 vols. (London, 1808), 3:403, 447.

11. *The Letting of Humours Blood in the Head-Vaine*, A2r in *The Complete Works of Samuel Rowlands*, 3 vols (Glasgow, 1880), vol. 1.

12. *Patterns of Decay: Shakespeare's Early Histories* (Charlottesville, 1975), p. 81.

13. *The Dramatist and the Received Idea: Studies in the Plays of Marlowe and Shakespeare* (Cambridge, 1968), pp. 79, 83–84, 87. For example, Sanders describes minor characters like the scrivener as "not great apostates, nor great cowards, but the small moral casualties of the fray in which others lose their heads" (p. 83); he also argues that "the potency of Richard's evil" rests, at least in part, "upon the moral cowardice of a

Brackenbury, the moral laxity of an Edward, and the moral impotence of an Anne" (p. 87).

14. *Angel with Horns and Other Shakespeare Lectures*, ed. Graham Storey (London, 1961), pp. 15–16. Rossiter concludes (p. 21) that Shakespeare converted the "ready-made Senecan tyrant" he found in popular myth "into a quite different inverter of moral order: a ruthless, demonic comedian with a most un-Senecan sense of humour and the seductive appeal of an irresistible gusto, besides his volcanic Renaissance energies."

15. Ibid., p. 20.

16. See Robert C. Jones, "Dangerous Sport: The Audience's Engagement with Vice in the Moral Interludes," *Renaissance Drama*, n.s. 6 (1973), 45–64.

17. "Shakespeare's Halle of Mirrors: Play, Politics, and Psychology in *Richard III*," *Shakespeare Studies*, 8 (1975), 126.

18. *The Dramatist and the Received Idea*, pp. 72–73, 93, 95–97, 109.

19. *Dramatic Documents from the Elizabethan Playhouses*, 2 vols. (Oxford, 1931), 1:x.

Chapter 4

1. See, for example, John Webster Spargo, "Interpretation of Falstaff," *Washington University Studies, Humanistic Series*, 9 (1922), 119–33; John W. Shirley, "Falstaff, an Elizabethan Glutton," *Philological Quarterly*, 17 (1938), 271–87; Daniel C. Boughner, "Vice, Braggart, and Falstaff," *Anglia*, 62 (1954), 35–61; Bernard Spivack, "Falstaff and the Psychomachia," *Shakespeare Quarterly*, 8 (1957), 449–59; and Eben Bass, "Falstaff and the Succession," *College English*, 24 (1963), 502–6. For some suggestive links between Falstaff and Wrath, see Lawrence L. Levin, "Hotspur, Falstaff, and the Emblem of Wrath in 1 *Henry IV*," *Shakespeare Studies*, 10 (1977), 43–65.

2. Thus, almost seventy years ago Sir Arthur Quiller-Couch argued that Hal "is poised on the balance. In the one scale is Hotspur, challenging him to honour with a provocation purposely made exorbitant; in the other, packed into Falstaff, all that is sensual—this also exorbitant, the very bulk of the man helping our impression of the weight that would drag the Prince down." He concludes that "the whole of the

business is built on the old Morality structure imported through the Interlude" and "might almost be labelled, after the style of a Morality title, *Contentio inter Virtutem et Vitium de anima Principis*" (*Notes on Shakespeare's Workmanship*, New York, 1917, pp. 125–27). See also Spargo, "Interpretation of Falstaff," pp. 130–33; and Robert Adger Law, "Structural Unity in the Two Parts of *Henry the Fourth*," *Studies in Philology*, 24 (1927), 240–42.

3. *The Fortunes of Falstaff* (Cambridge, 1943), pp. 14, 22.

4. *The Medieval Heritage of Elizabethan Tragedy* (Berkeley, 1936), pp. 209, 242. For similar views see Irving Ribner, *The English History Play in the Age of Shakespeare* (Princeton, 1957), p. 43; and Bernard Spivack, *Shakespeare and the Allegory of Evil* (New York and London, 1958), p. 307 and passim. In his recent full-length study of the moral drama, Robert Potter characterizes this "untidy dramatic genre" in the 1560s and 1570s by its "inexplicable dumb shows, satirical invective, a scattering of hilarious moments, and an habitual belaboring of the obvious" (*The English Morality Play*, London and Boston, 1975, pp. 108, 110). For plot summaries, pertinent facts, and bibliography for fifty-nine moral plays, see Peter J. Houle, *The English Morality and Related Drama: A Bibliographical Survey* (Hamden, Conn., 1972).

5. *Annals of English Drama, 975–1700*, ed. Alfred Harbage, rev. S. Schoenbaum (London, 1964), pp. 34–55. Dates attached to plays throughout my text are drawn from this work.

6. For a list of moral plays performed at court, see E. K. Chambers, *The Elizabethan Stage*, 4 vols. (Oxford, 1923), 3:178, n. 2. The titles of lost plays include *The Marriage of Mind and Measure*; *Beauty and Huswifery*; *Loyalty and Beauty*; *Error*; and *Truth, Faithfulness and Mercy*. A. P. Rossiter points to the performance of *Liberality and Prodigality* "as an example of quite unambiguous Morality in the highest of high places in Shakespeare's mature manhood" (*English Drama from Early Times to the Elizabethans*, London, 1950, p. 101).

7. For a description of this lost play, in which Life led away from Delight and Recreation by Zeal becomes subject to Glut and Tediousness, see Stephen Gosson, *Plays Confuted in Five Actions* in *The English Drama and Stage Under the Tudor and Stuart Princes, 1543–1664*, ed. W. C. Hazlitt (1869), pp. 201–3. Chambers (*Elizabethan Stage*, 1:294–95) describes another lost play in which Martin Marprelate ap-

peared "dressed like a monstrous ape on the stage, and wormed and lanced to let the blood and evil humours out of him" while "Divinity appeared with a scratched face, complaining of the assaults received in the hideous creature's attacks upon her honour."

8. *Endeavors of Art* (Madison, 1954), p. 6.

9. *From "Mankind" to Marlowe* (Cambridge, Mass., 1962), p. 3.

10. Ibid., p. 4.

11. Ibid., p. 158.

12. *The English History Play in the Age of Shakespeare*, pp. 40–41.

13. *The Tudor Interlude: Stage, Costume, and Acting* (Leicester, 1962).

14. Chambers notes that although 307 plays are extant for the period between 1586 and 1616, there is reason to suppose that this total "only represents a comparatively small fraction of the complete crop" (*Elizabethan Stage*, 3:182). The percentage of lost plays could be even higher for early Elizabethan drama, so that the historian must tread warily when drawing inferences from the existing evidence. Nonetheless, as Bevington points out (*From "Mankind" to Marlowe*, p. 10), "almost all pre-Marlovian plays of the sixteenth century which bear convincing evidence of popular commercial production are in fact moralities or hybrids." The presence of dual protagonists in two such plays therefore could be quite significant.

15. To see the trap set up by the Humanum Genus paradigm, consider two divergent analyses of *Jack Straw*. First, according to Ribner (*The English History Play*, p. 76), Jack Straw makes "the same choice as a typical morality hero, and he undergoes much the same consequences" as he pursues to his destruction a chosen path of rebellion. In contrast, Mary G. M. Adkins argues that the king, not Jack Straw, is the dramatic focus, for "Richard may be said to dominate the play not only in dramatic conception of character, but also in dramatic emphasis, both in the scenes in which he actually appears and those in which he is talked about" ("A Theory about *The Life and Death of Jack Straw*," *University of Texas Studies in English*, 28, 1949, 79). Both views share the same fallacy, that unity and emphasis demand a single focus, a king or a rebel.

16. *Shakespeare's Festive Comedy* (Princeton, 1959), p. 200.

17. For useful discussions of Shakespeare's adaptation of his sources

in this play, see A. R. Humphreys's introduction to his New Arden edition (London and Cambridge, Mass., 1961), pp. xxi–xxxix; and Kenneth Muir, *The Sources of Shakespeare's Plays* (New Haven, 1978), pp. 91–103. On Hotspur's "unhistorical youthfulness," see Humphreys, pp. xxvi–xxviii; Muir points out (p. 97) that, historically, Hotspur actually "was older than Henry IV."

18. For example, John Shaw argues that Lady Percy's long speech in II.iii amounts to "a kind of stage direction for Hotspur: MOVE ABOUT." For Shaw, it is this arbitrary movement "that Francis unknowingly mimicks in the next scene," a mimicry that then establishes an analogy between the two figures ("The Staging of Parody and Parallels in 'I Henry IV,'" *Shakespeare Survey*, 20, 1967, 71).

19. This scene is particularly valuable in assessing Shakespeare's dramatic strategy, for it represents his imaginative expansion upon a neutral, unprepossessing sentence in Holinshed, who relates that these negotiations were carried out by agents, not by the principals, and that Northumberland, not Hotspur, was to gain a third of the kingdom. For the passage, see Humphreys's New Arden edition, pp. 170–71. Muir notes (*Sources of Shakespeare's Plays*, p. 98) that "Shakespeare adds Hotspur's temperamental irritation with Glendower, the quarrel about the division, and the language barrier between Mortimer and his wife."

20. This scene clearly establishes the age of both Henry IV and Worcester (see V.i.13, 23–25). On the king's age, see Humphreys's edition, p. xxviii, and Muir, *Sources of Shakespeare's Plays*, p. 97.

21. See his New Arden edition (London, 1960), p. 64.

22. J. A. B. Somerset, "Falstaff, the Prince, and the Pattern of '2 Henry IV,'" *Shakespeare Survey*, 30 (1977), 36. Similarly, a recent book length study devoted to Shakespeare and the moral play describes "Hal's epithets for Falstaff" as "merely allusive and decorative." See Edmund Creeth, *Mankynde in Shakespeare* (Athens, Ga., 1976), p. 164.

23. For example, see V.ii.92–95; V.iii.9, 26, 39, 43, 48, 50; V.iv.79, 128–29, 149.

24. Muir notes (p. 98) that "the freeing of Douglas without a ransom" in Holinshed "is done by the King"; giving the disposition to Hal provides "a final touch of knightly magnanimity, already apparent in his epitaph on Hotspur."

25. For a suggestive treatment of Falstaff's encounter with Hotspur

(without reference to the moral plays), see James Black, "*Henry IV*: A World of Figures Here," in *Shakespeare: The Theatrical Dimension*, ed. Philip C. McGuire and David A. Samuelson (New York, 1979), pp. 178–81. Black notes (p. 180) that "Hotspur's great and informing vision of himself," associated with being on horseback in chivalric splendor, "has dwindled to this physical degradation," so that the spectator finally does see Hotspur "mounted" but "only upon the back of Falstaff" in what Black sees as "a tragic final answer to the question asked of him earlier and answered so flippantly: 'What is it carries you away?'" (as opposed to Hal, who supposedly was "violently carried away" by Falstaff—II.iii.72, II.iv.424).

Chapter 5

1. "Falstaff's Encore," *Shakespeare Quarterly*, 32 (1981), 5.

2. For example, see "Preparing the Text: *The History of Henry the Fourth, Part Two*," *On-Stage Studies*, the Colorado Shakespeare Festival, Number 4 (1980), pp. 53–67, where director Tom Markus describes both his extensive cuts and the logic behind them.

3. Of the many studies of the relationship between the two parts the most influential remains Harold Jenkins's *The Structural Problem in Shakespeare's "Henry the Fourth"* (London, 1956). For critiques of this argument, see A. R. Humphreys's introduction to his New Arden edition of Part Two (London, 1966), pp. xxv–xxviii; and Sherman H. Hawkins, "*Henry IV*: The Structural Problem Revisited," *Shakespeare Quarterly*, 33 (1982), 278–301.

4. A notable exception is to be found in J. A. B. Somerset's argument in "Falstaff, the Prince, and the Pattern of '2 Henry IV,'" *Shakespeare Survey*, 30 (1977), 35–45. Stressing at the outset the self-sufficiency of Part Two, Somerset argues that the familiar moral formula based upon a Humanum Genus protagonist "is inapplicable to *2 Henry IV*, and to think of the play in its terms is misleading" (p. 37). Rather, he turns to various features of the late moral plays (which he terms "morality variety shows"), including the Vice, "estates" figures, and the "separability" of vices and virtues (who, owing to doubling problems, often never meet) in order to suggest links to Shakespeare's play. The paradigm from the moral plays invoked in Somerset's article is quite dif-

ferent from the one proposed in this chapter, but the interpretation of Part Two that results is provocative and fruitful.

5. *Some Shakespearean Themes* (London, 1959), p. 61. For other helpful discussion of themes and images, in addition to Knights's fine essay, see the Hawkins and Somerset articles cited above and Clifford Leech, "The Unity of *Henry IV*," *Shakespeare Survey*, 6 (1953), 16–24.

6. For a recent comparison between the two scenes, with an emphasis upon the increasing distance between Falstaff and Hal as a preparation for the rejection in Part Two, see J. McLaverty, "No Abuse: The Prince and Falstaff in the Tavern Scenes of 'Henry IV,'" *Shakespeare Survey*, 34 (1981), 105–10.

7. Knights (*Some Shakespearean Themes*, p. 56) notes the parallel to the bad tidings brought to Northumberland about Hotspur's death that "have in some measure made me well" (I.i.139).

8. For example, in Holinshed Prince John plays no significant role at Gaultree Forest (or at Shrewsbury in Part One). Rather, Westmoreland is responsible for the strategem, a Westmoreland, moreover, faced with a numerically superior rebel army (a fact not used by Shakespeare), so that his resorting to such questionable tactics is, if not palatable, at least more understandable. For additional comments and context, see Humphreys's New Arden edition, especially p. xxxii and Appendix V (pp. 237–40).

9. An alternative interpretation is that the beadle is wrong and Doll actually *is* pregnant. Thus actress Martha Henry, who provided a remarkable "deathshead" diseased Doll in the Stratford Festival Canada production of 1979, suggested to me that the offspring of such a tainted mother and an old, vice-ridden Falstaff would be truly sick, even diabolic (an effect comparable to the devil's child spawned in the novel and film *Rosemary's Baby*). To "arrest" such a mother and future child would also epitomize the new world of phase two. In *The Cobbler's Prophecy*, one of the major symbols of the diseased Boeotia of phase one is a Venus pregnant by Contempt, the allegorical prime mover of the play, whose comments link the child to disease and corrupted love.

10. For a suggestive treatment of Henry IV's speeches in this scene, see Edgar T. Schell, "Prince Hal's Second 'Reformation,'" *Shakespeare Quarterly*, 21 (1970), 11–16. Schell argues (p. 16) that Shakespeare here presents not "the difference between what Hal is and what he

ought to be" but "rather the dramatically analogous difference between what he is and what he appears to Henry to be." For Schell, Hal's "reformation" in Part Two "is the closing of that gap . . . but before the gap can be closed it must first be opened as wide as possible"—hence the violence or extravagance in the king's language that conveys his (false) expectations.

11. "Comic Theory and the Rejection of Falstaff," *Shakespeare Studies*, 9 (1976), 159–60, 166–67. For a balanced and well argued treatment of this climactic scene (with much reference to previous criticism), see Edward I. Berry, "The Rejection Scene in *2 Henry IV*," *Studies in English Literature*, 17 (1977), 201–18.

12. Another factor often omitted from discussions of the rejection scene is the pivotal role that can be played by choices in the staging. For example, what tone or posture is to be used by the actor playing Henry V? Pious? Taunting? Reluctant? As to costume, are we seeing (here or in V.ii) the familiar Prince Hal or a very different Henry V? Is the actor to provide a pregnant pause before "I know thee not, old man" (or before the king's climactic speech to the Chief Justice in V.ii)? Is the king's first line ("My lord chief justice, speak to that vain man") an attempt to avoid a public confrontation with (and humiliation of) Falstaff, only to have Falstaff in his hubris brush the intervening figure aside, or does Henry V seek out, even relish this moment? Given the absence of stage directions or clear signals in the dialogue, interpreters of very different persuasions have had no difficulty imagining or staging this important scene in a fashion that suits them.

13. John Pettigrew, "The Mood of *Henry IV, Part 2*," *Manner and Meaning in Shakespeare*, Stratford Papers, 1965–67, ed. B. A. W. Jackson (Shannon, 1969), p. 166.

Chapter 6

1. *Samuel Johnson on Shakespeare*, ed. W. K. Wimsatt, Jr. (London, 1960), p. 84. The full passage reads: "I cannot reconcile my heart to Bertram; a man noble without generosity, and young without truth; who marries Helen as a coward and leaves her as a profligate; when she is dead by his unkindness, sneaks home to a second marriage, is accused by a woman whom he has wronged, defends himself by falsehood, and is dismissed to happiness."

2. *Angel with Horns* (London, 1961), p. 91. For a useful review of the criticism up to the early 1960s, including many negative comments about Bertram and the final scene, see Joseph G. Price, *The Unfortunate Comedy: A Study of "All's Well That Ends Well" and Its Critics* (Toronto, 1968), pp. 75–129. One of the few critics to defend Bertram's repentance is Robert Grams Hunter, who argues for a theatrical convention at work that draws "upon the shared beliefs of an audience"—in this case, "a belief in the reality of the descent of grace upon a sinning human" (*Shakespeare and the Comedy of Forgiveness*, New York and London, 1965, pp. 130–31). For a discussion of this moment in relation to other contemporary last scene repentances, see Robert Y. Turner, "Dramatic Conventions in *All's Well That Ends Well*," PMLA, 75 (1960), 497–502.

3. For discussions of Bertram and the Humanum Genus figure, see E. M. W. Tillyard, *Shakespeare's Problem Plays* (Toronto, 1950), pp. 108–9; M. C. Bradbrook, "Virtue Is the True Nobility: A Study of the Structure of *All's Well That Ends Well*," *Review of English Studies*, n.s. 1 (1950), 301; G. K. Hunter's Introduction to his New Arden edition (London, 1959), p. xxxiii; Robert Grams Hunter, *Shakespeare and the Comedy of Forgiveness*, passim; and Jonas A. Barish's Introduction to his Pelican edition, pp. 365–66. For an iconoclastic argument (in which Shakespeare is described as taking an "anti-genre" approach in order to offer "a refutation of the Morality ethic"), see W. L. Godshalk, "*All's Well That Ends Well* and the Morality Play," *Shakespeare Quarterly*, 25 (1974), 61–70. Many critics would admit, with various qualifications, that "the pattern is certainly in the background" (R. L. Smallwood, "The Design of 'All's Well That Ends Well,'" *Shakespeare Survey*, 25, 1972, 58) or that it functions as a "blueprint" (Barish, p. 366).

4. Oregon Shakespearean Festival, 1974, directed by Jon Jory. To make Bertram less offensive, Jory also cut his line at Helena's entrance: "Here comes my clog" (II.v.52). Richard David notes that in Michael Benthall's Old Vic production of 1953–54 "it was Parolles whose nods and becks strengthened Bertram in his first resistance to the King's command that he should marry a commoner. Having married her, he appeared to soften towards her, and would have given her the kiss she so pathetically begs at parting had not a 'Psst!' from Parolles recalled him to his previous resolution" ("Plays Pleasant and Plays Unpleasant," *Shakespeare Survey*, 8, 1955, 136). The stage business added by both

directors reinforces a point made by various critics. For example, Robert Grams Hunter (*Shakespeare and the Comedy of Forgiveness*, p. 119) notes that if Parolles "could be found to function in the play as a surrogate for the audience's dislike of his master," then "the difficulty of forgiving Bertram at the play's end would be considerably eased"; while S. Nagarajan argues that "the dramatic function of Parolles's character is to protect Bertram from damaging reproach" ("The Structure of 'All's Well That Ends Well,'" *Essays in Criticism*, 10, 1960, 24).

5. "The Design of 'All's Well That Ends Well,'" p. 49. Similarly, Robert Grams Hunter notes (*Shakespeare and the Comedy of Forgiveness*, p. 121) that "if Parolles had been previously responsible for Bertram's ignoble actions, we would be justified in expecting Bertram to begin acting decently once he had been removed from the influence of his bad angel," but "nothing of the sort happens."

6. "*All's Well That Ends Well*: The Testing of Romance," *Modern Language Quarterly*, 32 (1971), 40.

7. *The Sources of Shakespeare's Plays* (New Haven, 1978), p. 174. Similarly, Rossiter (*Angel with Horns*, p. 91) notes that "Bertram is silent until Helena arrives, when all he is given is four words and a very lame couplet."

8. See chapter six of *The Unfortunate Comedy* (pp. 87–109) for Price's account of the "analysis of failure" by the critics on the basis of psychological realism. Of the many treatments of the play as an experiment, I find Alexander Leggatt's discussion of "the testing of romance" especially instructive.

9. *Angel with Horns*, p. 92.

10. Ibid.

11. For suggestive treatments of Shakespeare's use of his sources, see ibid., pp. 82–89; G. K. Hunter's Introduction, pp. xxv–xxix; Muir, *The Sources of Shakespeare's Plays*, pp. 170–74; R. L. Smallwood's essay; and Howard C. Cole, *The "All's Well" Story from Boccaccio to Shakespeare* (Urbana, Chicago, and London, 1981).

12. Thus Robert Grams Hunter (decidedly in the minority among modern critics) argues that although Bertram's recalcitrance is central to the play, "there is little reason to believe that Shakespeare therefore felt called upon to account for it either with strict psychological realism or by providing any of the tidy 'motives' which some academic critics

still naively regard as explanations for human action." Rather, for Hunter, "Bertram's intransigence is Shakespeare's donné. He dramatizes it, considers it, comments on it, but he does not explain it" (*Shakespeare and the Comedy of Forgiveness*, p. 122). Leggatt ("*All's Well That Ends Well*," p. 36) poses the same problem in different terms: "Will Bertram's repentance be purely conventional and arbitrary, stemming entirely from the symbolic consummation of the marriage? Or will the playwright try to show that a real psychological adjustment is taking place, preparing the ground, so that when Helena fulfills the task, Bertram will be able—both symbolically and literally—to accept her?" Leggatt then finds the ending to be "an honest reflection of the tensions created by the play as a whole," for he sees Bertram as "a realistic character being acted on by a romantic convention whose power is not fully established" (p. 40).

13. "Virtue is the True Nobility," p. 293. For suggestive discussions of the links between the unmasking of Parolles and Bertram, see especially Smallwood, "The Design of 'All's Well,'" pp. 49, 59–60, and Robert Grams Hunter, *Shakespeare and the Comedy of Forgiveness*, pp. 121–22, 126–27. W. L. Godshalk ("*All's Well That Ends Well* and the Morality Play," pp. 66–68) develops the analogy between Parolles's drum and Bertram's ring. A dissenting voice is provided by Bertrand Evans (*Shakespeare's Comedies*, Oxford, 1960, pp. 160–61), who argues "that the unmasking of Parolles and the single-handed reclamation of Bertram by Helena are incompatible elements." Perhaps the most unusual link between Acts IV and V is suggested by James L. Calderwood, who argues that the final moments provide "a gloss on the bed-trick" in that "Bertram is stripped of his pretensions in the final scene as he was stripped of his clothes earlier" ("Styles of Knowing in *All's Well*," *Modern Language Quarterly*, 25, 1964, 293).

14. Here my argument overlaps to some extent with that of Robert Grams Hunter, who sees Parolles as "a symptom rather than a cause of Bertram's disease" and "as the fistula, the symptom by which Bertram's malady can be recognized." Thus, for Hunter, Parolles's most important function "is as symptom and as analogue, rather than as tempter" (*Shakespeare and the Comedy of Forgiveness*, pp. 121–22).

15. Here Parolles is analogous to the Vice Inclination in *The Trial of Treasure* who early in the action is bridled by Just, the virtuous pro-

tagonist, but nonetheless retains his power and influence so long as Lust (like Bertram) unbridles him and continues to indulge him.

16. At the 1977 Stratford Festival Canada production director David Jones set up an even more obvious link between Parolles and Bertram by having the latter wearing a blindfold (as part of a romantic game) when led in by Diana in IV.ii. Quite a few critics have called attention to the figurative link between Parolles's blindfold and Bertram in Act V. For example, Ann Pasternak Slater points out that "the trial scene in which Parolles is *literally* unblindfolded and made to face up to his own lies is thus the stage equivalent of Bertram's interrogation in the last act, when the scales *metaphorically* fall from his eyes, and he is forced to admit his own folly" (*Shakespeare the Director*, Sussex, 1982, p. 191). See also Robert Grams Hunter, *Shakespeare and the Comedy of Forgiveness*, p. 128; and J. Dennis Huston, "'Some Stain of Soldier': The Functions of Parolles in *All's Well That Ends Well*," *Shakespeare Quarterly*, 21 (1970), 434.

17. For a treatment of "Both, both; O pardon!" as "nothing less than the climax of the play," see Michael Shapiro, "'The Web of Our Life': Human Frailty and Mutual Redemption in *All's Well That Ends Well*," *Journal of English and Germanic Philology*, 71 (1972), 522–23.

18. In addition to the disposition of Bertram's patch and of various on-stage figures to echo IV.iii, there is also the possibility (admittedly, quite hypothetical) of an on-stage figure in V.iii carrying a hooded falcon (and therefore heightening the blindfold-seeing motif). For such a suggestion, based upon the Folio's "*enter a gentle Astringer*" at V.i.6 (a stage direction almost invariably emended by modern editors) and the reappearance of this same figure in V.iii, see Alan C. Dessen, *Elizabethan Stage Conventions and Modern Interpreters* (Cambridge, 1984), pp. 132–34.

19. *Mannerism* (Middlesex, 1967), p. 136.

Chapter 7

1. "Dramatic Allegory; or, Exploring the Moral Play," *Comparative Drama*, 7 (1973), 71–73. See also Kantrowitz's *Dramatic Allegory: Lindsay's "Ane Satyre of the Thrie Estaitis"* (Lincoln, Neb., 1975), pp. 134–35.

2. *Meaning in Comedy: Studies in Elizabethan Romantic Comedy* (Albany, 1975), pp. 22–24. Weld's first three chapters on the "dramatic tradition" contain many astute comments on form, technique, and meaning in the moral plays.

3. *Shakespeare and the Allegory of Evil* (New York and London, 1958), p. 252.

4. "The English Moral Play Before 1500," *Annuale Mediaevale*, 4 (1963), 18.

5. *Two Centuries of Epigrammes* (London, 1610), E3v.

6. For an argument linking this passage to *Volpone*, *The Alchemist*, and *Bartholomew Fair*, see Alan C. Dessen, *Jonson's Moral Comedy* (Evanston, 1971).

7. For a very useful account of late moral play dramaturgy, with an emphasis upon the techniques necessitated by the limited personnel and facilities, see David Bevington, *From "Mankind" to Marlowe* (Cambridge, Mass., 1962). See also T. W. Craik, *The Tudor Interlude: Stage, Costume, and Acting* (Leicester, 1962).

8. E. N. S. Thompson, "The English Moral Plays," *Transactions of the Connecticut Academy of Arts and Sciences*, 14 (1910), 315.

9. *Shakespearean Tragedy* (London, 1904), p. 264.

10. *The Dramatist and the Received Idea* (Cambridge, 1968), p. 217.

11. For a fuller discussion of the stage psychomachia, see chapter six of my *Elizabethan Drama and the Viewer's Eye* (Chapel Hill, 1977).

12. *Dynamics of Drama* (New York, 1970), p. 26.

Chapter 8

1. The continuing debate about how Isabella should respond to the Duke's offer of marriage at the climax of *Measure for Measure* provides an excellent example of the gap between "Jacobean" and "modern" interpretations of a Shakespearean problem (as do the widely varying views about the Ghost and Revenge in *Hamlet*).

2. Boston, 1924.

3. See R. A. Foakes and R. T. Rickert, eds., *Henslowe's Diary* (Cambridge, 1961), p. 164.

4. Prologue to Book 3 of Virgidemiarum, ll. 11–12, in *The Collected Poems of Joseph Hall*, ed. A. Davenport (Liverpool, 1949), p. 33.

5. For example, at the end of *Love's Labor's Lost* Berowne observes: "Our wooing doth not end like an old play; / Jack hath not Jill" (V.ii.864–65). Similarly, at the end of Marston's *Antonio and Mellida* Piero states that "we should have shut up night with an old comedy," an ending he associates with couples being united (V.ii.49–51).

6. For the familiar distinction between "old" and "new" comedy, see various passages included in G. Gregory Smith, ed., *Elizabethan Critical Essays*, 2 vols. (London, 1904). Thus, according to William Webbe (1:295): "the old manner of Comedies decayed by reason of slandering which therein they used against many"; similarly, Puttenham notes that "this bitter poem, called the old *Comedy* being disused and taken away, the new *Comedy* came in place, more civil and pleasant a great deal, and not touching any man by name, but in a certain generality glancing at every abuse" (2:34).

7. *Return of Pasquill*, in *The Works of Thomas Nashe*, ed. Ronald B. McKerrow, 5 vols (Oxford, 1905), 1:92.

8. See, for example, ibid., 1:100; and Dekker, *The Gull's Hornbook*, ed. R. B. McKerrow (London, 1904), p. 21.

9. *Shakespeare and the Comedy of Forgiveness* (New York, 1965), p. 21.

Plays and Editions

Included in the list below are the plays quoted in my text or dealt with in any detail, especially those likely to be unfamiliar to the general reader (as opposed to commonly anthologized plays like *Everyman* and *Cambises*). I have used the following abbreviations: *MSR* for the Malone Society Reprints, published by Oxford University Press; *TFT* for the Tudor Facsimile Texts, edited by John S. Farmer; *Dodsley* for *A Select Collection of Old English Plays Originally Published by Robert Dodsley in the Year 1744*, edited by W. Carew Hazlitt, 4th edition, 15 volumes (London, 1874–77); *Revels* for the Revels Plays, published by Manchester University Press; and *RRD* for the Regents Renaissance Drama Series, published by the University of Nebraska Press.

Alphonsus Emperor of Germany. Ed. Herbert F. Schwarz. New York and London, 1913.

Apius and Virginia. Ed. Ronald B. McKerrow and W. W. Greg. MSR, 1911.

Chapman, George. *The Widow's Tears*. Ed. Akihiro Yamada. Revels, 1975.

Chapman, George; Ben Jonson; and John Marston. *Eastward Ho*. Ed. R. W. Van Fossen. Revels, 1979.

The Contention between Liberality and Prodigality. Ed. W. W. Greg. MSR, 1913.

Fulwell, Ulpian. *Like Will to Like*. Dodsley, 3:303–59.

Garter, Thomas. *The Most Virtuous and Godly Susanna*. Ed. B. Ifor Evans and W. W. Greg. MSR, 1937.

Greene, Robert. *Friar Bacon and Friar Bungay*. Ed. W. W. Greg. MSR, 1926.

Histriomastix. TFT, 1912.

Jonson, Ben. *Ben Jonson*. Ed. C. H. Herford and Percy and Evelyn Simpson. 11 vols. Oxford, 1925–52.

King Darius. In *Anonymous Plays*, 3d ser., ed. John S. Farmer. London, 1906. Pp. 41–92.

A Knack to Know a Knave. Ed. G. R. Proudfoot. MSR, 1964.

The Life and Death of Jack Straw. Ed. Kenneth Muir and F. P. Wilson. MSR, 1957.

Lodge, Thomas. *The Wounds of Civil War*. Ed. J. Dover Wilson. MSR, 1910.

Lodge, Thomas, and Robert Greene. *A Looking Glass for London and England*. Ed. W. W. Greg. MSR, 1932.

Lupton, Thomas. *All for Money*. Ed. Ernst Vogel. *Shakespeare Jahrbuch*, 40 (1904), 129–86.

Marlowe, Christopher. *Marlowe's "Doctor Faustus," 1604–1616*. Ed. W. W. Greg. Oxford, 1950.

Marston, John. *Antonio and Mellida*. Ed. G. K. Hunter. RRD, 1965.

———. *The Malcontent*. Ed. George K. Hunter. Revels, 1975.

———. *What You Will*. In *The Plays of John Marston*. Ed. H. Harvey Wood. 3 vols. Edinburgh and London, 1938. 2:227–95.

Nashe, Thomas. *Summer's Last Will and Testament*. In *The Works of Thomas Nashe*. Ed. Ronald B. McKerrow. 5 vols. Oxford, 1905. 3:227–95.

Nice Wanton. TFT, 1908.

Peele, George. *The Battle of Alcazar*. Ed. W. W. Greg. MSR, 1907.

Pickering, John. *Horestes (The Interlude of Vice)*. Ed. Daniel Seltzer. MSR, 1962.

Shakespeare, William. *The Complete Pelican Shakespeare*. Gen. ed. Alfred Harbage. Baltimore, 1969.

———. *The Norton Facsimile: The First Folio of Shakespeare*. Ed. Charlton Hinman. New York, 1968.

———. *Shakespeare's Plays in Quarto*. Ed. Michael J. B. Allen and Kenneth Muir. University of California Press, 1982.

Sir Thomas More. Ed. W. W. Greg. MSR, 1911.

The Trial of Treasure. Dodsley, 3:257–301.

The True Tragedy of Richard III. Ed. W. W. Greg. MSR, 1929.

Two Wise Men and All the Rest Fools. TFT, 1913.

Wager, W. *The Longer Thou Livest* and *Enough Is as Good as a Feast*. Ed. R. Mark Benbow. RRD, 1967.

Wapull, George. *The Tide Tarrieth No Man*. Ed. Ernst Ruhl. *Shakespeare Jahrbuch*, 43 (1907), 1–52.

A Warning for Fair Women. TFT, 1912.

Wealth and Health. Ed. W. W. Greg. MSR, 1907.

Wilson, Robert. *The Cobbler's Prophecy*. Ed. A. C. Wood and W. W. Greg. MSR, 1914.

———. *The Three Ladies of London*. Dodsley, 6:245–370.

———. *The Three Lords and Three Ladies of London*. Dodsley, 6:371–502.

Index

sport," 22, 24–28, 45; and Falstaff, 55, 78–80, 88–89, 93–94,
106–7, 111–12; and Parolles,
119–20, 132–33; and Richard
III, 39–54; as entertainer, 18, 22,
28, 33–34, 36–37; as tempter,
33–34, 36–37; as threat, 18–19,
22; linked to dagger of lath, 19–
20, 22, 24, 29, 31, 37, 41–43,
54, 78–79, 84–85; linked to distinctive exit, 20–21, 22, 24, 29,
35, 37, 53, 87–89; role in two
phased structure, 24–32, 36–37,
47, 93–94, 111–12, 132–33;
used to isolate public issues, 23–
24, 36, 111–12, 132–33. See also
Late moral plays

Wager, Lewis: The Life and Repen-
tance of Mary Magdalene, 142
Wager, W.: Enough Is as Good as a
Feast, 4, 20, 60, 78, 85, 87, 89–

90, 142; The Longer Thou Livest,
20, 57
Wapull, George: The Tide Tarrieth No
Man, 33, 34, 57, 59–60, 136,
142, 143, 163; two phased struc-
ture in, 29–31, 50, 94, 100
Warning for Fair Women, A, 137,
142–43
Wealth and Health, 23–24, 28, 143
Webbe, William, 188
Webster, John, 13–14
Whetstone, George, 6, 11
Williams, Raymond, 5–6
Wilson, Robert: The Cobbler's Proph-
ecy, 31–32, 181; The Three Ladies
of London, 7, 12, 94, 135, 143,
162, 170; The Three Lords and
Three Ladies of London, 7, 12, 14
Woodstock, 63

Yarington, Robert: Two Lamentable
Tragedies, 137